SHADOWMAN

SHADOWMAN

An Elusive Psycho Killer and
the Birth of FBI Profiling

RON FRANSCELL

BERKLEY
NEW YORK

BERKLEY
An imprint of Penguin Random House LLC
penguinrandomhouse.com

Copyright © 2022 by Ron Franscell
Penguin Random House supports copyright. Copyright fuels creativity, encourages diverse
voices, promotes free speech, and creates a vibrant culture. Thank you for buying an
authorized edition of this book and for complying with copyright laws by not reproducing,
scanning, or distributing any part of it in any form without permission. You are supporting
writers and allowing Penguin Random House to continue to publish books for every reader.

BERKLEY and the BERKLEY & B colophon are registered trademarks of
Penguin Random House LLC.

Library of Congress Cataloging-in-Publication Data

Names: Franscell, Ron, 1957- author.
Title: ShadowMan : an elusive psycho killer and the birth of FBI profiling / Ron Franscell.
Description: New York : Berkley, [2022] | Includes bibliographical references.
Identifiers: LCCN 2021021990 (print) | LCCN 2021021991 (ebook) |
ISBN 9780593199275 (hardcover) | ISBN 9780593199282 (ebook)
Subjects: LCSH: Meirhofer, David, 1949-1974. | Serial murder
investigation--Montana--Case studies. | Serial murderers--Montana--Case studies. |
Criminal behavior, Prediction of--Montana--Case studies. |
Criminal psychology--Montana--Case studies. |
United States. Federal Bureau of Investigation.
Classification: LCC HV6533.M9 F73 2022 (print) | LCC HV6533.M9 (ebook) |
DDC 362.88/29309786--dc23
LC record available at https://lccn.loc.gov/2021021990
LC ebook record available at https://lccn.loc.gov/2021021991

Printed in the United States of America
1 3 5 7 9 10 8 6 4 2

Book design by Daniel Brount
Interior art: Wool string © Picsfive/Shutterstock.com;
tack pin © Robyn Mackenzie / Shutterstock.com

CONTENTS

THE SHADOWS: SOME HIDE, OTHERS REVEAL.
—POET ANTONIO PORCHIA

THIS WAS A NORMAL TOWN ONCE,
AND WE WERE NORMAL PEOPLE.
—R. L. STINE

SHADOWMAN

SHADOWS COME

MONDAY, OCTOBER 10, 2005
MANHATTAN, MONTANA

A hired man discovered the stuff in the hidden space behind an old wall. He'd boast years later that he always knew these things—these ghosts—were hidden there, but really he was as surprised as anybody.

Manhattan's got a past. It is one of those places where winter and shadows come early, but it isn't the town it was before everybody died.

It is just one of those things that nobody wants to talk about. You can ask, but the memories are always fuzzy when it comes to *him*. They'll pick out a few, switch around a couple of facts, and point to some old pictures on the bank wall.

But those photos are like the memories: They'll never tell the whole truth, because the photographer decides what he wants you to see. They recall something that isn't there anymore.

Except *him*. He's still there, hanging over everything.

The hired man called the boss, who called the sheriff. A deputy came out to look at the stuff and take it away. His boss, the sheriff, saw nothing of value in the old bad memories, and took them to a mother who'd grieved for thirty painful years.

Why does this damn thing keep coming up? he thought.

There are no degrees of separation here. Everybody knows everybody, they tell you. That whatever you did, they always knew you would. That they know who's driving past their houses by the sound of the engine—although they don't know where the car's going. That they know about the skeleton of the old wrecked car beneath the Lover's Leap—although they don't know how it got there. That they know everybody by first name—although they don't know their secrets.

What goes on behind those doors goes on, they say.

Asking about *him* is like picking a day-old scab and waiting for blood. There's an uncrossable line that outsiders can't see.

All these years later, some of them say they knew all along he was evil. But nobody said anything then.

He's still got family here, they say. *You'll be stepping on toes,* they say. *Let sleeping dogs lie,* they say.

But what about the secret the hired man found hidden in the wall?

Aw, hell, they say, *there are secrets hidden behind all the walls.*

CHAPTER I

PRELUDE TO NIGHT

MANHATTAN, MONTANA

One expects more from a place called Manhattan, but it's just a southwestern Montana village (pop. 900) more than two thousand miles from that other Manhattan. While that one screams for attention, this one keeps to itself. Not impenetrable, but not very approachable.

Except for a forlorn old grain elevator, the Conoco sign out near the frontage road, and a church steeple that's slightly closer to Heaven than the trees around it, the town mostly hides itself from passersby on the interstate. Not that there's much to see. Get off the highway and you'll find, way back, an aimless congregation of buildings divided smack down the middle by the "NP"—the old main line tracks of the Northern Pacific Railway.

If you happened to be here at noon, you'd hear the firehouse whistle that goes off every midday, as it has since it got a whistle.

Manhattan calls itself the Potato Capital of the World, but that might be more chamber-of-commerce hype than a genuine agricultural fact. Nevertheless, the town sponsors the Manhattan Potato Festival every year, highlighted by a grand parade and the volunteer firefighters' breakfast. Spuds are a big deal.

A town has existed here since before Custer was slaughtered at the Little Bighorn. The town has had a few different names, but in 1891 when beer-brewing executives of New York City's Manhattan Malting Company moved operations closer to the Dutch barley fields out West, they simply renamed the whole town Manhattan out of pure puffery.

Since then, nothing much out of the ordinary has happened here. Manhattan's history is static and unexciting, the way its subdued, devout Dutch settlers intended. Farmers and ranchers passed their land to their kids, not Hollywood stars and rich guys wearing cowboy boots from Fifth Avenue. No traffic jams (except parades), so no traffic lights. More keggers than baptisms, more paperboys than parking spots, more steeples than stop signs.

Oh, they still talk about the time the whole town was in a national TV commercial for beef (which is definitely true), and some folks are proud that Manhattan, Montana, has raised up more military generals per capita than any other municipality in America (which might not be true, but nobody can say otherwise).

Probably Manhattan's biggest celebrity wasn't really a celebrity in the traditional sense. William Frankena was born in 1908 to Dutch-immigrant farmers in Amsterdam, an unincorporated hamlet near Manhattan. He moved away as a youngster, and in adulthood he became one of America's most celebrated postwar philosophers. Almost nobody in Manhattan in the 1960s recognized his name, but if they had, Frankena would have been thrown a parade of his own. He earned his doctorate from Harvard University in 1937 with a dissertation entitled "Recent Intuitionism in British Ethics." His strengths were in metaethics and moral psychology, subjects that curiously weren't in Manhattan High School's curriculum. He said high-handed stuff like, "We should not see the relationship between action-based and virtue-based ethical theories as disjunctive, but as conjunctive." He also was an enthusiastic bird-watcher, which might have impressed folks back home if they had known who he was.

So Manhattan's past, like that of a thousand other little towns that nobody had made famous, was ordinary.

Even its depravity was ordinary. Kids didn't get away with much because everybody was watching and everybody knew every kid. They recognized the girls with reputations. The local druggist usually called the parents of teenage boys who bought condoms at the Rexall.

As such, transgressions were always minor. There was a "night cop," who usually had some innocuous day job. His role was mainly to spotlight horny teenagers at Lover's Leap, bust up parties, and call kids' parents if they were out after curfew. Delinquent behavior involved drinking beer in the graveyard and skinny-dipping in the rainwater that collected in potholes left by railroaders quarrying ballast.

Some naughtiness was funny. Folks fondly recalled the time when some local kids tunneled under the local liquor store in hopes of popping out in the basement to steal booze. That one was always worth a laugh.

But there was that time back in '64 or '65 when some unidentified late-night hoodlums were nailing stray cats and puppies—alive—to power poles and trees around town. Damn kids. When the night cop stopped caring, and folks no longer gossiped about it down at Cookie's Café, the anonymous cruelty stopped. Nobody ever knew who among them would be so cruel to animals, or why.

And back in '67, a thirteen-year-old kid named Bernie Poelman was doing what Manhattan kids did on warm days: He and his buddy Ricky were climbing the steel girders of the Nixon Bridge, a nineteenth-century truss bridge out north of town, and cannon-balling into the Gallatin River below. The cold springtime water ran fast enough to make it a medium-powerful rite of passage, slow enough for a kid to dog-paddle to a riverbank not too far down-stream.

On that March Sunday, the short and skinny Bernie sat atop the bridge's highest beam and prepared to leap. Down below, Ricky dared him to make a big show of it. Suddenly, Bernie grabbed his chest and hollered something—possibly "I'm shot," but Ricky couldn't be sure. Bernie plunged twenty feet onto a shallow sandbar under the bridge, then appeared to be swimming before he disap-peared below the surface. The current carried him away.

Ricky ran a half mile to the nearest farmhouse, where they called the sheriff. A posse quickly searched the river downstream from the bridge. They found Bernie's horn-rimmed glasses in knee-deep water, but no Bernie.

Searchers slung a wire net across the river about five miles downstream to catch anything—or anyone—that might float past. They set up searchlights on the shore and sat up all night . . . but no Bernie.

Although the kid's body hadn't been found, he was presumed dead. The local parish priest conducted a memorial requiem mass a few days later. Even in the 1960s, Catholics were still viewed with some suspicion in mostly Protestant Gallatin County, and there was only one small Catholic church, up in Three Forks, twelve miles away. Nevertheless, a good number of non-Catholic Manhattan folks filled up the modest Holy Family Church.

Bernie's sad father walked miles of riverbank every night, looking for his boy. Men in boats dragged the channel with no luck. Nearly every boy at Manhattan High School, a couple of dozen in all, walked and canoed all the way to Logan, almost five miles downstream. No Bernie.

The mystery of young Bernie Poelman dominated the chatter in the hallways at his junior high, where his eyewitness friend told and retold the story breathlessly and with great drama. Even for these kids who lived around the harsh realities of farms and ranches, human death was a curious concept, especially when it came randomly and without warning. Of course, this wasn't murder, but even terrible accidents were hard for kids to grasp.

Three weeks later, deputies found Bernie's waterlogged body tangled in the wire net downstream. His wristwatch had stopped precisely at three twenty p.m. An autopsy showed he had, indeed, been shot through the heart with a small-caliber gun, probably a .22. The bullet was sent for ballistics testing in Washington, DC, but it revealed nothing of value.

Even as Bernie was buried in the Three Forks cemetery, the closest consecrated Catholic graveyard in these parts, the mystery remained unsolved. Informal juries convened down at Cookie's Café, Keen's Hardware, and the Stockman's Bar. Since murders never happened in Manhattan and it wasn't hunting season, folks concluded that Bernie must have been killed by an errant bullet from a crappy marksman's shooting range or a distant shot that missed a prairie dog. The aimless shooter—literally—probably never even knew he killed a kid. Dumb, but accidental. It wasn't a satisfying explanation, but freak accidents, by definition, defied explanation.

So Manhattan's most notable 1960s homicide—the official word for a death caused by another person, not always murder—was an accident.

The only other unnatural local death for the rest of the decade wasn't even in Manhattan, but in Three Forks, which was close enough to be Manhattan's principal rival in high school sports, far enough to be thought of as completely different. But truth be told, Three Forks and Manhattan were more alike than anyone in either town would have admitted. High school boys from one town always thought the girls in the other were prettier.

So naturally, a Boy Scout's unexpected death near Three Forks in 1968 was felt by Manhattan, too, even if it wasn't "local." That it was clearly not accidental made it especially rumor-worthy.

In early May 1968, Bozeman sixth grader Michael Raney was one of two hundred Scouts at a camporee at Missouri Headwaters State Park, just outside Three Forks—where Lewis and Clark discovered that the Jefferson, Madison, and Gallatin rivers merged to become the mighty Missouri River. The Scouts' two-man pup tents were arrayed in close ranks across a two-acre grassy area, each not more than three feet from the next.

Troop leaders finally got their juiced-up eleven- and twelve-year-olds to bed by midnight that Saturday night. Michael Raney, a well-liked kid, shared his tent with his eleven-year-old friend Kenny Summers. Their tent was only thirty feet from their adult scoutmaster, so they weren't inclined to any hijinks, unlike some of the other kids, who jacked around all night. When the troop leader ordered all his Scouts to their tents, they went.

That was fine with Michael and Kenny. They'd played together all day, riding horses and tussling like young boys everywhere. They were exhausted. They crawled into their sleeping bags laid out on rubber air mattresses, their heads toward the back of the tent, and quickly fell asleep. It sprinkled a little that night, but Kenny and Michael never heard the rain dappling their tent. Nor did they hear a passing train. They were dead to the world.

Kenny awoke at five thirty the next morning, as dawn broke

and the sky tiptoed toward daylight. As he rubbed the sleep from his eyes, he was startled to see Michael's face covered in blood. His first thought was that Michael had suffered a bloody nose in the night. Kenny couldn't rouse his friend, so he hollered for his adult troop leaders nearby.

They couldn't wake up Michael, either, so they dragged him out of his tent feetfirst. They peeled his sleeping bag away and found his sweatshirt bloody. Michael was breathing heavily and had vomited on himself. The startled men found a lump above his right ear and dirt in his hair. Had he been roughhousing during the night or fallen down in the dark?

Michael mumbled something incoherent as a couple troop leaders drove him to the nearest phone in Three Forks, then to the hospital in Bozeman, the county seat, a half hour away.

There, doctors found a small stab wound just under Michael's right armpit. The lump on his head indicated somebody had clubbed him with something small but hard.

Back at camp, deputies discovered that the back of Kenny and Michael's tent had been sliced open, and someone had reached in and stabbed him through his sleeping bag. But nobody had seen anybody moving around the night before, other than a few Scouts goofing off.

However, now deputies knew there'd been a knife. None was found in the immediate area, but before the troops decamped that Sunday morning, all their knives—hundreds among the "always prepared" Boy Scouts—were collected. Over the next few weeks, the Gallatin County Sheriff's Office administered a lie detector test to every single kid and troop leader in camp that night. They all passed.

Somebody mentioned that Michael's troop had wrested a victory trophy from another troop in a contest, so maybe some of the losing

Scouts had sought revenge. But such wins and losses were common among troops, and nobody reckoned it'd end in foul play. Ever.

Somebody else reported hearing a little boy yell, "Help! Help!" in the middle of the night, but maybe it was "Dale! Dale!" He couldn't be sure.

Suspicion fell squarely on Michael's tentmate, poor Kenny Summers. The kid had had a weapon and opportunity, but what would have caused an eleven-year-old to stab his friend? What kind of wicked genius would it require for a fifth grader to brutally assault his tentmate in the night, lie beside him until dawn, pretend to find his victim's body, and yell for help? Those were impossible dots to connect.

Michael Raney died a few days later. At his autopsy, the coroner found the single knife wound hadn't punctured the boy's lung. It was a slit only an inch wide and an inch deep. The wound might have been inflicted with a pocketknife or by a tentative poke with a larger camp knife.

Bottom line, it hadn't been enough to kill Michael Raney.

What, then? The coroner found extensive brain damage. Whatever had caused the quarter-sized wound on the side of the boy's skull, the blow hadn't fractured the skull but had caused a concussion so violent that it literally killed a fist-sized chunk of Michael's cerebrum, turning it to necrotic mush.

Cause of death? The smashed brain, said the coroner, not the stab wound.

When the news hit the weekly papers in Manhattan and Three Forks, tipsters came out of the woodwork. One witness saw a green Studebaker, another a 1959 Ford, yet another an old Jeep . . . a guy and a girl drinking beer, a guy with a knife, a boyfriend who hated kids, a peculiar troop leader . . . None panned out. Apparently, nobody saw anything that anybody else saw.

With that, the second strange death in Manhattan's little universe became as much a mystery as Bernie Poelman's shooting. Folks concluded quite naturally that Michael had died in horseplay gone too far, made worse by the inept, good-ol'-boy deputies who fouled up another investigation by unintentionally obscuring or misinterpreting evidence. That's just the way it was. Ruining a grade-school kid's life for a horrible accident served no purpose.

The diligent (and ultimately unsuccessful) searches for answers reflected the town's best beliefs in loyalty and justice. That would have to be enough. They'd tried.

In a nutshell, that was wickedness 'round Manhattan, Montana. If anything worse than those two unfortunate deaths had happened, folks would have assumed it was done by outsiders, because nobody they knew would sin like that . . . and they knew everybody.

Life goes on. Life and death aren't always neatly explained. Eventually, those two unrelated mysteries stopped being lunchtime gossip. The kids still graduated and went off to Vietnam, college, the big city, family farms, or menial jobs in gas stations and shops.

The parades still happened every year. The trains still ran through town every day. The whistle still blew every noon. Stray cats still died mostly natural deaths. Nobody got murdered. And Manhattanites could say, once more with feeling, that nothing out of the ordinary ever happens here.

The Dutch spirits were pleased.

Then this.

CHAPTER 2

MONDAY . . . AND EVERYTHING AFTER

JUNE 25, 1973
HEADWATERS STATE PARK, MONTANA

The breeze. It wasn't right.

Heidi Jaeger was only twelve years old but she knew the wind didn't blow *inside* a tent. Maybe she'd left the tent flap open when she stumbled back in around midnight. She hadn't taken more than a few steps toward the outhouse when she felt suddenly afraid of the dark, as if something wicked watched her. She darted back inside and burrowed deep in her sleeping bag. She said Susie's name out loud a few times, but her little sister was fast asleep. So Heidi lay back, comforted by the mere presence of her brothers' and sister's warm bodies, and fell back to sleep.

But this peculiar draft was coming from the opposite end of the tent. That didn't make sense.

Morning hadn't yet broken. The sun would rise in a half hour, maybe less. The air was cool and close, made humid by the rivers on every side of the campground. The birds weren't yet stirring in the old cottonwoods.

Heidi propped herself up in the semidarkness to see if a canvas seam had ripped or one end of the tent had collapsed. After all, they'd been camping in it since Bill and Marietta Jaeger left Michigan with their van and five kids on their big summer vacation out West. They had driven past the Dakota Badlands, the ultimate roadside attraction Wall Drug, Mount Rushmore, Wyoming's endless grasslands, and the Little Bighorn. Here in western Montana, they had met up with Marietta's retired parents, who had traveled up from Arizona and staked out a camping space on a grassy spot at Headwaters State Park.

Four of the Jaegers' five kids—Heidi, fourteen-year-old Frank, nine-year-old Joe, and seven-year-old Susie, the baby of the family—slept every night in the family tent. Their oldest brother, Danny, sixteen, holed up alone in the family van, while Bill and Marietta bunked under a camper shell in the back of Marietta's parents' pickup.

It was their happiest time. All of them had shed their ordinary monotonies. Back home in Michigan, the boisterous Susie shared a bedroom with Heidi, and the first grader mostly annoyed her older sister. But on this trip across the West, they played I Spy endlessly and talked like sisters, and the long road seemed shorter. Heidi finally thought Susie wasn't so bad, actually fun to be around. Maybe it was this landscape, or maybe Susie's exuberance belonged out here in these endless spaces. Didn't matter. It finally felt right.

And the night before, the younger kids had all nuzzled down side by side in their sleeping bags, their heads toward the back of the tent, keeping one another warm. After dark, Bill and Marietta crawled inside to kiss each one of them good night. Susie was the farthest, in her red sleeping bag, just beyond Marietta's reach. Her kiss barely touched Susie's cheek.

"Oh, no, Mama," she said, "not like that!"

Susie clambered out of her sleeping bag and over her siblings and planted an exuberant kiss right on Marietta's mouth.

"There!" Susie said proudly as she crawled back and snuggled deeper into her sleeping bag. "That's the way it should be!"

But this breeze now . . . that was *not* the way it should have been.

Heidi was, again, suddenly uneasy. She stretched her hand toward the tent wall behind her, just to feel if one of the poles had foundered. But instead of a crumpled pile of canvas, she felt . . . wet grass.

Heidi sprang upright. Through a peculiar half-moon-shaped gap, she saw one of Susie's beloved stuffed animals on the lawn outside. None of it made sense.

Wide-awake now in the semidarkness before dawn, she glanced around her. Her two brothers slept snugly in their bags.

But Susie's bag was empty.

Time wobbled. Heidi sprinted from the tent, shrieking bloody murder for everyone to wake up. She pounded on the camper shell.

"Susie's gone!" she screamed. "There's a big hole in the tent and I can't find Susie!"

Bill Jaeger leapt out and rushed to the tent with Heidi. He saw the half circle cleanly cut in the canvas above the spot where Susie had slept inside. He saw Susie's stuffed toy horse in the wet grass.

But no Susie.

Bill bolted back to the camper. He yanked Marietta out and grabbed a flashlight.

"It's true," he said urgently. "Susie's gone."

Suddenly, everybody was up and running around with flashlights. Had she wandered alone to the outhouse in the dark and not been able to find her way back? Sleepwalked to another camp? Gone down to the river and fallen in?

They needed help, fast. Other campers joined the frenzied search. People ran in every direction, knowing only that they were looking for a little girl. Marietta's father roared off in his pickup to alert somebody in the town of Three Forks, a mile and a half away, to call the sheriff.

Back at the Jaegers' campsite, an overwrought and confused Heidi crawled into the van where her older brother Danny had spent the night, and she fell back to sleep. When she woke five hours later, nothing seemed in focus. Nothing slowed down enough to register in her twelve-year-old mind, and nothing seemed to have changed. Strangers—more of them now—were still running around. They still hollered from every corner of the park. Her parents were still part benumbed, part panicked.

It felt to her as if she'd suspended time in her dreams. But it wasn't a dream.

Susie was still gone.

It was as if darkness itself had stolen her away.

GALLATIN COUNTY DEPUTY DON Houghton was working alone on the graveyard shift, nearing the predawn end of his tour when he got the call: A tourist family camping at Headwaters State Park was reporting their little girl missing.

It had been a long night and he was looking forward to some rack time, so it pissed him off that he had to drive out to Headwaters to take a report and look around for a big-city kid who had probably just wandered off to pee and gotten lost.

Houghton was just twenty-four. In Gallatin County, if you were a police officer, you were either the sheriff or a deputy. He was the son of a Montana Highway Patrolman who had bounced around small towns all over the western half of the state. He had never intended to follow his dad into law enforcement, so after high school he had joined the Marine Corps, gone to Vietnam, and come home to major in engineering at Montana State University in Bozeman. The GI Bill helped, but money was tight. So to help pay for college, he applied for an opening at the Gallatin County Sheriff's Office and got it. Suddenly he was one of only eight uniforms (including the old-time country sheriff, L. D. W. "Andy" Anderson) at the podunk GCSO.

Anderson was the son of Depression-displaced farmers and a former shore patrolman in World War II Okinawa. He'd started as a lowly jailer in Bozeman twenty-five years before. Once upon a time, he was known as a dogged, if old-school, cop. Now he was almost a caricature, butt-sprung and burly, more politician than peace officer.

So Anderson sent rookie Deputy Don Houghton forth with almost no training to protect and serve the mostly good citizens of Gallatin County.

The sky was lightening up when Houghton arrived at Headwaters. The Jaegers were flipped out. Their little camp was just a van, a pickup, a couple trailers—and a tent with a peculiar, cleanly sliced hole in the back. *Never seen a thing like that,* he thought.

But he saw something else: an unexplained path heading northward. Not footprints, but a kind of wake where somebody had walked and disturbed the morning dew. The climate was dry and it hadn't rained in more than a month, yet the nearby rivers humidified the air enough that dew formed on cool mornings.

Questions flew faster than answers.

The little girl's tracks? One of the searchers'? Somebody else's? A lost child's, or something more sinister? Who'd snatch a girl on vacation seventeen hundred miles away from her home? How could the many campers surrounding them—more than a dozen—have seen nothing?

He didn't know.

But the dew path and the clean cut in the tent bothered him.

Just looking around wasn't enough, though. He wanted to be methodical, but the Jaegers begged him to go searching for Susie. They wanted him doing more and doing faster . . . just *doing*.

Houghton had never worked a case like this. He relied more on instinct than on training. He knew people, and he allowed his human side to take over. He couldn't calm them down if he was ruffled. But the more composed he got, the more agitated the Jaegers became.

He knew these western Montana towns. He wasn't gonna be the goat. He called for backup and told the dispatcher to alert Sheriff Anderson.

As soon as the morning shift started, other deputies arrived. They closed roads into and out of the park. They looked among the willows along the river and in the barrow pits, the surrounding hills, and the shallows for any sign of Susie Jaeger.

As the first officer on the scene, Deputy Houghton managed the operation until Sheriff Anderson finally came out. Andy wasn't really a take-charge guy, so he was all too happy to hand this one off.

The sheriff called for his own backup and waited under the park's cottonwoods until the two local FBI guys in Bozeman, Special Agents Byron Dunbar and Bill Terry, showed up.

Ghosts hung in those cottonwoods.

The unsolved 1968 murder of Michael Raney—the twelve-year-old Boy Scout stabbed and bludgeoned by a brazen intruder who'd sliced into his pup tent while campers slept all around him right here in Headwaters State Park, no more than fifty yards from Susie's tent—still spooked Sheriff Anderson. His incompetent cronies, who were more drinking buddies than detectives, had bungled the investigation. Folks were pissed, and the department's reputation was still in the toilet five years later.

To repair his department's image, Andy had hired a few college kids like Houghton and called it "reform." And the cop work improved slightly, especially on the rookies' scut shifts. The sheriff's buddies still kicked back, as loose as ever. Houghton wasn't one of them, and he liked it that way.

But even a dumbass night cop could see haunting similarities between Michael Raney's murder and Susie Jaeger's abduction. True, the Boy Scout's death had been attributed to little boys' tragic horseplay, and it had been a stabbing, not an abduction, but the locals would hear only "little kids . . . sliced tents . . . Headwaters . . . middle of the night . . . no suspects."

Around here, elections were won and lost on back-fence gossip.

AFTER DAYBREAK, BUT BEFORE breakfast, FBI Special Agent Dunbar wheeled his unmarked, un-FBI-like Chevy Biscayne into the blacktop parking area at Headwaters State Park. He hated getting up this early, mostly because he stayed up too late most nights, but Sheriff Anderson had awakened him with urgent news about a kidnapping or some such.

Agent Dunbar unfolded himself from the driver's seat. He was a tall man, near six two. Dark haired and sturdy, without the usual cowboy belly. Squared away. Quiet, not brash. He loved John Wayne and Louis L'Amour, fat black stogies, and a good argument.

He wore a bolo tie, a snap-button Western shirt, a vest, a tooled leather belt, boot-cut jeans, and roper boots. His style matched his old Biscayne more than the late J. Edgar Hoover's strict dress code: a dark business suit, white shirt, conservative tie, black shoes, and black socks. (Maybe dark blue socks in a pinch, but colored socks were otherwise forbidden.)

Local cops knew him as "Pete," a nickname bestowed by his patrician maternal grandfather back East who didn't think young Byron was dignified enough. He called his grandson "Pete" as a sort of blue-blooded diminutive for the son of the cowboy who married his little girl. Whether it was intended as a playful moniker or a sly epithet didn't matter. It stuck (although starting in grade school, Dunbar always signed his secondhand name with a lowercase "p").

Dunbar was a local guy.

His great-grandfather homesteaded a sheep ranch here in 1862 and built a fine house in old Three Forks, where Pete grew up. They sold some of their land to pay taxes in the Depression, and when their sheepherders all enlisted to fight in World War II, the Dunbars switched to cattle.

Pete's mother was a purebred Catholic girl from Minnesota, so proper that she sent little Byron to his first day of school in dapper big-city knickers and a suit coat, which he threw out when the other ranch kids teased him.

As a kid, Pete probably had a little more fun than he should have, but he stayed focused. He played football and basketball, had lots of friends, and worked on his dad's ranch when he wasn't in town. In fact, he usually missed the first week of every school year because it was harvesttime.

When he was seventeen, toward the end of World War II, the US Navy rejected him because he was color-blind. So Pete walked across the hall and joined the Merchant Marine instead. Three years later, he went to the University of Montana in Missoula, where he eventually earned a law degree in 1952.

But Pete Dunbar didn't want to be a small-town lawyer. He had a bigger plan.

Fresh out of law school, he joined the FBI. He liked Hoover and Hoover liked him. Dunbar was posted to a half dozen high-crime cities, from Washington, DC, to New York City. But when his parents grew frail, he requested a transfer to Montana, where he could take care of them. It wouldn't be a promotion, but that wasn't important to him.

In 1970, it happened. His home base was the Butte field office—long considered "Siberia" for wayward out-of-favor agents. But Pete was posted eighty-five miles away, in Bozeman. Home at last.

In the 1960s, when Pete was off fighting crime and his family could hardly keep up with the ranch any longer, they sold off or gave away most of its land. One of their big donations was a historic parcel at the sandbar that would become Montana's Missouri Headwaters State Park—where Agent Pete Dunbar now strode across the dewy lawn toward a clutch of anxious campers and cops.

To the nervous Deputy Houghton and desperate mother Marietta Jaeger, he looked like John Wayne come to save the day.

Sheriff Anderson might have asked for his help this morning, but Dunbar and the FBI would have been involved by the next day anyway, with or without an invitation.

On the night of March 1, 1932, a bold kidnapper had climbed into the second-floor nursery of heroic aviator Charles Lindbergh's twenty-month-old son and snatched him—not unlike Susie Jaeger's audacious kidnapping in the middle of the night forty years later. Given that Lindbergh was arguably America's most gloried hero at the time, every local crime-fighting resource was mobilized to find the child and capture his abductor.

The toddler's decomposing corpse was found on May 12, and it would be thirty long months before the kidnapper was arrested. The delay was caused, in part, by inexpert local cops with limited reach.

Federal agents were dispatched by President Hoover himself, but it was too little too late.

The press went wild. Lindbergh's celebrity made the kidnapping national news, not a hometown scoop. Headlines drove politics, so Capitol Hill didn't wait for an arrest. Five weeks after searchers found Charles Jr.'s crushed little body, Congress enacted the Federal Kidnapping Act—which everybody called the Little Lindbergh Law—to bring the full power and capital of the FBI and other federal agencies into play immediately after an abduction. The new law said that if a child is not released unharmed within twenty-four hours of being kidnapped, it is presumed the child has been transported across state lines and federal agents must take control of the investigation.

Special Agent Bill Terry, Dunbar's partner, supervised the collection of physical evidence, such as it was, while Dunbar interviewed the Jaegers.

Terry picked up Susie's sleeping bag, mostly red with a single blue stripe and a white lining. Her stuffed animals—a red horse and a brown dog—some cigarette butts, soda can pop-tops, and some bits of yarn. A swatch of the tent's blue canvas where the abductor had cleanly sliced his hole. Susie's hairbrush, which only she used (except when she brushed the family dog, Otto). And an odd rock covered in reddish brown stains, found by one of the searchers at a campsite more than four miles away.

That was all they could find, and it wasn't much.

Marietta and Bill Jaeger sat with SA Dunbar at a picnic table nearby. Getting an immediate description of Susie to local and national law enforcement was a priority.

Marietta fetched her purse and pulled out Susie's latest school picture, almost a year old now. She was six years old in the picture, and her two front teeth were missing. Like any mother familiar with every contour of her child's skin, Marietta thought it mightn't look enough like her little girl to really help, but it was all she had.

"Full name?" he asked.

"Susan Marie Jaeger," Marietta said, "but we call her Susie."

As she rattled off her daughter's description, Dunbar scribbled it all in his notebook.

Female. White.
Three foot eight to four feet tall.
Fifty-five pounds.
DOB 4/19/66 in Detroit, Michigan.
Light complexion.
Brown hair, shoulder length.
Hazel blue eyes.
Last seen wearing blue jeans, a reddish orange shirt with a
zipper in front, yellow socks, and a silver ring with a small
Navajo-style turquoise stone.

And, Marietta added, her two front teeth had grown in.

Dunbar ripped the page out of his notebook and handed it to a nearby deputy, with instructions to speed back to Bozeman to put out an all-points bulletin.

He also noted that Marietta did most of the talking, and Bill didn't engage much. It struck Dunbar as odd that the father of a suddenly missing child would be so detached.

Before the sun set on the day of Susie Jaeger's disappearance, the FBI guys had ruled out a wandering child—and that was what made the pursuit of Susie Jaeger's kidnapper SA Pete Dunbar's baby.

THE LOCAL SEARCH FOR Susie Jaeger took flight almost as quickly as the rumors flew.

The Gallatin County Sheriff's Office, with only twenty-five or so employees—including the sheriff—was woefully unprepared for such an operation. Before breakfast, burly Sheriff Anderson, the goodest of the good ol' boys, dispatched Gallatin County's small but earnest search-and-rescue team, but the search area was far too big. By lunch, the bigger sheriff's posse—a motley batch of deer hunters, cop wannabes, retired game wardens and deputies, old cowboys and their horses, even the two night cops from Manhattan and Three Forks—joined the hunt. Still not enough.

Agent Dunbar ordered that a command post be set up at the park in a Gallatin deputy's unused camp trailer. A phone was installed for rapid communications and teletype machines, but also for the Jaegers to make any necessary calls.

Sheriff Anderson ordered meals for everybody—a lot of them—with pop for the cops and beer for the civilians. The sheriff forbade anybody in uniform from drinking, so the hot and dusty sworn officers often just changed into old jeans and covered their badges so they could drink free beer.

The civilian underground started buzzing early. Before dinner, eager citizen volunteers were arriving by the truckload. The search coordinators sent them out into the hills, sage flats, quarries, outhouses, abandoned mine shafts, line shacks, hobo and hippie camps, gullies, river willows, pastures . . . anyplace they might find any trace of a scared little girl or the little girl herself.

They hauled ice, fetched groceries, cooked meals, and looked for Susie. While sworn officers searched the spaces where evidence might be harder to spot, the volunteers linked themselves arm in arm and slowly traipsed across fields, staring at the ground.

As luck would have it, twelve thousand Airstream trailer enthusiasts had gathered for their big summer convention on the campus of Montana State University in nearby Bozeman. Rather than just polish their shiny camper trailers and drink beer all day, dozens came out to find Susie. (And simultaneously those thousands of nomadic out-of-towners became instant persons of interest for the FBI, which requested a list of all the caravanners' names and addresses.)

The governor ordered five Montana National Guard helicopters to help. Montana Highway Department workers scoured every barrow pit. The Civil Air Patrol dispatched its pilots to fly low over all rivers and watersheds. Professional divers waded into every lake and river in southwestern Montana. And the rivers were soon crowded with all manner of motorized boats full of searchers dragging the river bottom and scanning the banks.

It didn't help that early-spring thunderstorms and snowmelt had swelled the Missouri River to a swift-moving flood stage. A fifty-pound child who stumbled into the dark river at night might have been swept twenty miles downstream before dawn, so dam keepers all the way to Great Falls—a couple hours north of Three Forks—were alerted.

Odd-shot reports came in. One distressed fisherman called to say he'd been boating in a water-filled pothole that locals called the "Gravel Pit" when he saw a huge fish rise to the surface, then disappear. On second thought, it might have been an arm, he said. Divers found nothing.

Headwaters State Park's outhouses were all pumped. Freight trains that had passed that night were checked. The credit and arrest records of every employee of every major business within a fifty-mile radius were inspected. Every camper in the park that night was screened. Every frame of Marietta's parents' Kodachrome home movies and every vacation photo shot by the Jaegers since they left Michigan were magnified by FBI technicians looking for strange people or cars in the background.

Teams were dispatched all night and all day. They ranged to every corner of Gallatin County and beyond. Suddenly there were more people within the borders of Gallatin County than at any other time since statehood.

More feet trod on more square inches of the county than in all of human history.

Nobody found anything.

When the reins of the investigation had been safely turned over to the FBI, Deputy Don Houghton joined the searchers. At one point, he was wading through river mud and hacking through thick willows with a machete. For two days, he searched in ever-widening circles from the park, and caught catnaps over his steering wheel. Finally, after two full days on the ground, he was sent home to sleep.

When he got home, he took his shotgun down and put it on the kitchen table.

"Don't let anybody in the house," he told his wife, Donna, "and if anybody tries to get in, shoot him."

Half of him wanted to sleep; the other half wanted to search. He couldn't talk, even to Donna, about anything he knew (which wasn't much). Finally, he just went to bed and fell into a deep but troubled sleep. The next day, he went back out.

Among the more uncomfortable moments of the investigation, the whole Jaeger family submitted to lie detector tests. Even country-boy deputies knew a victim's closest associates—too often immediate family members—might be involved. They were taking no chances that the Jaegers themselves—whether grandparents, parents, or siblings—had played a pernicious role in Susie's disappearance.

Young Heidi was petrified about her impending polygraph test. Not because she'd caused Susie's vanishing but because she felt guilty about the way she treated Susie at home and about her petty preteen resentments of her annoying little sister. Could the machine tell the difference between kinds of guilt? She also worried that her subconscious mind knew something that her conscious memory couldn't summon. *What if I know something that I can't remember?*

But the machine sensed no guilt in Heidi or any of the other Jaegers. They all passed polygraph examinations. Lie detectors were the best investigative technology Gallatin County had to offer. Lawmen had used the machines since 1923, and they had undergone constant scientific and technological improvements over the next fifty years. Although Gallatin's exams were administered by a deputy with only modest training in questioning and operation, the polygraph was generally considered a far better gauge of honesty than a cop's gut.

SA Pete Dunbar, who never truly had doubts about the Jaegers, assigned Deputy Houghton and a Salt Lake City FBI agent to search door-to-door in the piddling village of Logan, not far from the park. They knocked on doors, belly-wriggled into crawl spaces, poked their heads into outhouses and well houses, and clambered into cobwebby attics.

They found nothing.

Two-man teams of deputies and FBI agents were also dispatched in every direction from the park. Their assignment was to drive all night and stop at every place that'd be open late—convenience stores, gas stations, saloons, motels, etc.—and ask about suspicious people who might have passed through around the time Susie disappeared. One team went all the way to Salt Lake City, more than six hours away.

One night, Dunbar and Houghton walked into a place Houghton genuinely never knew existed. Everybody else knew the old Western Hotel in Three Forks was the local whorehouse, even if nobody talked about it. The two lawmen gathered the girls together and asked about any "clients" who stood out. Not the repeat customers or ranch hands who came in every Tuesday night for a drunken poke, but any out-of-character johns, odd ducks, weirdos, or outlanders with requests that were more depraved than usual. *Anybody like that?*

They got nothing.

By week's end, the volunteer searchers were exhausted. Their workaday lives beckoned and they knew they were chasing shadows. By the weekend, most had gone home.

That was exactly when the investigation's most tantalizing clue fell in Dunbar's lap.

A Bozeman cop had driven deep into the barrens, where he stumbled upon a collapsed mica mine up Little Bear Creek Canyon. There he found a ramshackle shanty that appeared to have been recently occupied.

Inside, he found a child's drawings and an old dinosaur picture book. In one corner were a little girl's stretch pants, a small sock, a leather belt with a silver buckle, three pieces of yarn—unfaded blue, lavender, and rust—and a small, broken toy car. Three stinking deerskins hung on the walls. Remnants of potatoes and other food lay around. There was a woman's suitcase filled with plant specimens, all wrapped in wax paper. And there were dozens of little footprints made by a child no older than eight or nine.

The excited cop radioed the sheriff, who, in turn, called Agent Dunbar.

Finally they had something, even if none of it looked familiar to the Jaegers.

AT THE SAME TIME hundreds of searchers were beating Montana's bushes, Detroit FBI agents were flooding the Jaegers' Farmington Hills neighborhood in Michigan in case Susie's kidnapper was a local with an ax to grind.

They knocked on all doors within a three-block circle of the Jaegers' modest white single-story house. It had been recently renovated, but like most of the older homes in this predominantly white Motor City suburb, it was valued at no more than twenty-five thousand dollars, while new houses were being built nearby in the thirty-thousand range. In short, the Jaegers didn't live a conspicuously affluent lifestyle that might afford a big ransom.

The neighborhood was tight-knit. Most of the kids were involved in a variety of extracurriculars like peewee football, scouting, and ballet, so their parents necessarily became car pool and bleacher friends. But some neighbors told agents that Bill Jaeger allowed his kids to play Little League and other extracurriculars only grudgingly, preferring that they participate in private family activities.

They knew Bill had worked for a few engineering firms in Detroit and that Marietta had taken brief odd jobs over the past few years but mostly stayed home with her five kids.

Bill was a Korean War combat vet, the neighbors told agents, but he didn't talk much about it. In fact, he didn't talk much about anything. He was quiet and generally awkward around other people. Maybe he'd seen things in the war that had darkened his heart.

Nevertheless, the Jaegers were well-liked. Everybody knew them. They attended the local Roman Catholic church; their kids often came around to collect money for local charities and played with all the kids up and down the street. And everybody especially loved Marietta.

FBI agents asked all the neighbors if any strangers had recently asked about the Jaegers. *No.* Had any unfamiliar vehicles been prowling around? *No.* Had they seen any activity at the house since the Jaegers left on vacation? *No.*

Bill and Marietta's mail had piled up since they left, but it was only bills and junk mail. Agents made arrangements for the next-door neighbor to collect it every day and look for anything odd.

None of the Jaegers' neighbors stood out as suspicious to FBI agents. Nobody had been gone during the last week of June. Nobody had seen Susie since the news broke in the local weekly. It wasn't yet out of the question, but the feds found no evidence whatsoever that the kidnapper was in the Jaegers' neighborhood.

SAFELY CLOISTERED IN MONTANA'S outback, Manhattan always struggled to keep the rest of the world at arm's length. *Manhattan is what America was,* they said. And what America had become scared the hell out of them.

Even now, a couple years on, Manson and his butcher whores remained a pustulant gash. A bunch of dirty hippie cutthroats with swastikas carved in their heads doing to humans what nobody around here would do to a dead coyote. Every hitchhiking longhair might be—probably was—a distant killer cousin of the Family. *Damn hippies.*

Then soldiers shot up some college kids in Ohio. *Wouldn't happen at Montana State. Good school, good kids.*

Then a mass-murdering Mexican named Juan Corona raped

twenty-five migrant field workers in California and buried their hacked-up bodies in shallow graves in an orchard, where fruit trees might suck up their blood. *You might wanna stay away from the peaches down at L&F Market for a while.*

Then the Supreme Court made it illegal to execute killers. *Fergawdsakes, they could kill all of us in the middle of the night and get a slap on the wrist.*

Then the Arab terrorists killed all them Israeli athletes at the Olympics over in Germany. *How long before they come over here and start killing Christian folks?*

Then that black kid shot up a New Orleans hotel and killed nine people, including five cops, because he didn't like white folks. He set the whole place on fire before the cops killed him with a helicopter and a couple hundred bullets. The "race war" wasn't new, but for black folks like this Essex kid and the Black Panthers to shoot back, that was a frightening wrinkle. *Thank the Lord, Black Power is a big-city thing.*

Then some radical Indians invaded a shithole called Wounded Knee over in South Dakota, a little too close for comfort for white folks who'd settled in Montana, where some of the biggest fights in the Indian Wars went down. *What if they seized the Little Bighorn next, or, God forbid, the Big Hole? Table Mountain wasn't gonna keep 'em out of Manhattan.*

Then the Supreme Court made it legal for women to kill their babies like they were tossing a burlap sack full of unwanted kittens in the river. *You can't kill killers but babies are fair game. That ain't right. Not right at all.*

Then some sex pervert down in Houston named Dean Corll tortured and killed at least twenty-eight young men, almost all teenagers, in a sick, sadistic series of horrors in his nice little suburban house. For three years, the former candy seller buried them in mass graves on the beach and under storage sheds. Then a couple of his henchmen killed him and led cops to the dead kids' rotting corpses. They stopped digging when Corll's body count set the new American record for mass murder. *But Texas is a long ways, and down there, they got an express train to Death Row, yessiree.*

Then that whole miserable Watergate mess. Damn Democrats and some reporters trying to sell some papers were going after Nixon in some kinda modern witch hunt over, what, a little political sneakery? *They all do it back East. Those hypocrite liberals give their boys Kennedy and Johnson a pass, but no Republican is gonna get away with it, no, sir.*

Then this Kemper kid out in California decapitated his mom and had sex with her head. *Lord Almighty.*

And that didn't even count Vietnam, Kennedy and King and Wallace, Apollo 13, sit-ins, folks talking out loud about deep throats and the joys of sex, and a bunch of doped-up rock 'n' rollers dropping like freaked-out flies.

Out *there*, the whole wicked world was falling apart, but Manhattan remained a good place to raise kids, they said. No way, they said, would the circus of depravity out there ever come to a town way out *here*.

Well, here it was.

BEFORE THE SUN SET on that first day, Manhattan and Three Forks buzzed with a thousand rumors, hundreds of hunches, and dozens of "prime suspects." Every unfamiliar face belonged to a potential sex deviant who'd steal a little girl for only one perverse reason.

As the days and weeks passed without progress, the sheriff's phone rang off the hook and well-meaning citizens buttonholed deputies on Main Street. Every lawman in the county chased leads down every dark alley. SA Dunbar sent out alerts to every field office in America. Nothing.

At one point, FBI agents and local cops compiled a lengthy list of known sex criminals in western Montana since 1958—more than one hundred names on eleven teletype sheets. They ranged from peepers and flashers to rapists and child molesters. One was an elderly former Episcopal minister who descended from a Boston Tea Party revolutionary. Another was a World War II Purple Heart recipient who followed young girls around. Another was a dirty-talking twelve-year-old boy who made obscene phone calls to his neighbor ladies. And there was the guy who'd been busted for fondling women's clothes at a local department store. No lead panned out.

Everybody saw phantoms. Everywhere. Every day. Imaginations leapt around like jackrabbits. Shadows came to life. Folks locked their doors—some for the first time ever—and kept loaded handguns under their pillows. Kids couldn't go outside after dinner or sleep out in their backyards. And some old scores were settled.

One landlord suspected the peculiar mother and son who'd left their rented apartment in shambles . . . fifteen years earlier. Someone ratted on a neighbor who wrote poetry about sex. A suspicious rancher told the FBI the new owner of the next ranch over didn't know anything about cows (a sure sign that he was hiding something). Another rancher reported his neighbor purely because he had junked cars all over his place. One circus worker snitched on the carny who had filched his concession stand at a Great Wallendas high-wire act in New Orleans and had traveled through Montana this summer. A woman recalled that her cheating ex-boyfriend had once told his hooker-slut mistress that he fantasized about sex with little girls. A mother red-flagged her itinerant son, a reformatory alum, even though she hadn't seen him in years. A seventy-six-year-old spinster reported that her foster brother had molested her in

Michigan in 1906. She'd lost track of him twenty years ago, she said, but the cops should check out his two sons, wherever they were, because they might be molesters, too. A hitchhiker told agents he'd thumbed a ride with a guy who bragged about his meat-cutting skill, his bent toward bestiality, and how a well-honed boning knife could slice a camp tent like it was lace. Twenty-six workers on a railroad section crew were interviewed in Chicago.

College kids, fishermen, carpenters, cowhands, ex-husbands, current and former asylum patients, artists, traveling salesmen . . . everybody had a sneaking suspicion about them.

For some, being odd was the surest sign of guilt.

There was Dr. Malin Shaw, a retired professor in a Pontiac and a proper black suit who stopped for a female bicyclist and offered to take her as far as she wanted to go. Turned out Dr. Shaw was eighty years old and a desperately lonely widower who liked to pick up hitchhikers just so he had someone to talk to.

And there was Buel Reed, who at seventy-two was earning a princely seventeen dollars a day as the caretaker of Headwaters State Park. A couple of campers reported Ranger Reed was a little too "familiar" with their children, not in a sexual way, but in a playful way. Creepy. Reed subsequently submitted to a lie detector test and passed. (Although he failed to satisfy his state bosses about why he allowed a homeless, disabled war veteran to camp in the park beyond the ten-day limit. He was fired.)

And there was David Meirhofer, a quiet kid who came home to Manhattan from Vietnam to work odd jobs at local ranches for pocket money. He was friendly enough, but he didn't talk much about the war or anything else. 'Round here, everybody had something to say, even if it was nothing. But David was a hard worker who knew how things worked, the rancher said. He was just . . . odd.

Joe Hunsinger, a seventy-something trailer dweller over in Winston, Montana, lived an hour away—not far by the standards of drivers in the wide-open West and surely close enough for a midnight child snatching in Gallatin County. Hunsinger was mostly blind from cataracts in both eyes, but he'd done hard time up at the state prison in Deer Lodge for trying to rape a little girl he bought in Mexico to be his wife.

Then there was the family who locked their mentally handicapped child in his room, purportedly to shield him from the cruel world, as if imprisoning him in his own home wasn't cruel.

Agent Dunbar's team determined these hapless oddballs—and others—had played no part in Susie's disappearance. But more tantalizing were some real bad guys and sexual predators who popped up on Dunbar's radar.

One was Bert Sturgeon, a drifter also known as Paul David Burkett, Jimmy Jackson, and Gordon Greentree. He'd been busted in Huntington Beach, California, where he was awaiting trial for kidnapping and raping two little girls, four and seven years old. When agents questioned Sturgeon, he was vague about almost everything: birth date (New Year's Eve in 1910 or 1912), birthplace (Tonawanda, New York, or Hollywood, Florida), his most recent address (an Indianapolis suburb or Benton Harbor, Michigan), and his whereabouts during Susie's disappearance. He thought maybe he was working on a chain gang clearing roadside weeds, but maybe not.

The Los Angeles FBI agent who interviewed Sturgeon was suspicious enough to send Dunbar a teletype that said Sturgeon shouldn't be eliminated as a suspect.

Then there were two punks in Casper, Wyoming—Ron Kennedy and Jerry Jenkins—who'd kidnapped two sisters, eleven and eighteen, from a grocery store parking lot one night in September 1973. They terrorized them through the night, then drove them to a high bridge over a deep canyon in the middle of nowhere. There they dumped the eleven-year-old over the bridge railing, and she drowned in the river twelve stories below. Then they gang-raped her older sister before dumping her off the bridge, too. But the older sister survived and identified the two hoods, who now awaited murder trials. Might these perverts have taken Susie as their plaything three months earlier?

An angry biker chick fingered her whole gang, the Bandidos. The outlaw bikers had taken Susie and two other girls, she swore, and sacrificed them in a cult bonfire down in Texas. When the Butte FBI field office looked into it, they learned that no Bandidos had been anywhere near Montana in June 1973 and that their confidential source had a long history of paranoid schizophrenia.

An abandoned Michigan wife called the FBI to say her unemployed husband, Donald Watson (who had a degree from Michigan State, had dropped out of Syracuse twice, and had served three tours in the US Air Force), had lit out to find himself in Montana just before Susie vanished. She said Donald was a decent guy, but a "sex pervert" who suffered blackouts after which he didn't remember what he'd done. He owned a shotgun and two big Bowie knives, and he camped in his beaten-up 1964 Ford. He'd called collect from the road a couple times, but she had no idea where he was now. Neither did the FBI.

Franklin Gray was an AWOL Marine who'd traveled through Montana on a cross-country bus ride. When his money ran out, he hooked up with a hitchhiker with whom he shared drugs and a penchant for little girls. Together, they kidnapped and raped a thirteen-year-old girl in the Washington State park where they camped out. In the afterglow of their depravity, Gray boasted to his cohort that he'd once kidnapped a little girl who had escaped, and he'd chased her down and stabbed her to death. When his accomplice was later arrested on other charges, he snitched on Gray. Problem was, the Marines had no record of him. He'd disappeared forever—or maybe never existed at all.

A shadow.

FBI agents questioned some self-described witches and warlocks at a trailer-park coven in Bozeman, but they proved to be harmless kooks.

And the hippies. Oh, God. Every longhair and love child who crossed Montana that summer was guilty of something. Nobody had known Manson before he was Manson, and the supposedly ghastly crime against Susie Jaeger was no less horrifying in the imaginations of locals. Obviously hippies weren't all about love and peace. Manson had proved that.

Hardly a day passed that summer when somebody didn't report seeing hippies at every gas pump, diner, market, park bench, rest stop, motel, bus stop, on-ramp, underpass, campground, sidewalk, and cemetery within a hundred miles of Bozeman. They all wore their hair long, Afro style, braided, ponytailed, frizzy, shaggy, or untamed (like Manson). They always wore jeans, beads, headbands, wild shirts, go-go boots, or sandals—or went barefoot. Usually, they escorted little girls who looked like Susie, who acted weird and said strange things like "Yes, Daddy" as if maybe she wasn't theirs.

And they all drove Volkswagens. Everybody knew that hippies drove only Volkswagens. Vans or Beetles, didn't matter. Most were old and dirty. Yellow, blue, black. Oregon plates, or California, New York, Washington . . . you know, hippie places. In the dust on one Bug's window, somebody had scrawled, *Hurry up!* Oddly, nobody ever got any plate numbers.

Several folks reported seeing a man in a blue Volkswagen with a small blond girl, and a BOLO went out. As a result, the Bug was stopped six times traveling across Montana—and each time, the cop, patrolman, or deputy realized the little girl was, in fact, an adult dwarf.

The Montana Highway Patrol grew tired of pulling over every Volkswagen on I-90. But Dunbar knew if he polled the citizens of Gallatin County that summer, most would have said hippies had taken Susie, maybe to live as their own in one of their free-love communes with their gurus and whatnot, unschooled by the Man and raised on pot. That poor child.

Some tipsters believed they had actually seen Susie—almost always living with a sketchy family or riding in the back of a filthy car—but none of those sightings ever panned out.

Agents spent substantial time reinterviewing all the suspects and key witnesses in the Michael Raney cold case. No obvious link emerged, just a dreadful coincidence.

Hoaxers and scammers came out of the woodwork, too. A month after Susie disappeared, a hand-printed letter postmarked in Detroit arrived at the *Detroit News*.

Tell the Jaegers to come back [to Detroit] as soon as possible as they can have Susie back July 27, 1973. Your Girl is okay. Follow instructions. Put money in small bills in brown shopping bags with your telephone number on it. There is a state park on Utica Road east of Van Dyke Road. Cross the bridge and take first path. Turn left. Put money on right-hand side, Friday, July 27, 1973, at 8:00 pm will call you at 9:00 pm to come get Susie.

The letter had been lost in the *News*'s mail room until several days after the ransom demand expired. But there was nothing to identify Susie, and no real evidence the writer had her. The FBI labeled it a hoax.

One night a few days after the kidnapping, an anonymous call came into the FBI's Denver field office. The male caller claimed to be Susie's kidnapper and said, "Tell someone the ransom is twenty-five thousand dollars." Then he hung up. Not the first crank caller, they knew, and not the last.

A few other swindlers contrived various wild stories in an attempt to grab some of the ransom/reward money that was accumulating in a Detroit bank, but none succeeded.

In November—five months after the kidnapping—Agent Dunbar had an idea: Might Susie's abductor want to follow the Jaegers more closely than local papers were able to? What if he subscribed by mail to the Jaegers' hometown paper, the *Detroit News*? He called the paper's circulation department, which reported five new Montana subscriptions (before Susie's abduction they'd had only one Montana subscriber). Alas, none of those readers were likely kidnappers.

Tipsters and tricksters piled up, but not a single good suspect emerged. Utterly stymied, Dunbar grew disheartened. Susie's mystery was no closer to being solved than it had been that June morning when she vanished. But where there's a mystery, there are psychics. Susie Jaeger was national news, and clairvoyance knows no borders.

Some visions were extraordinarily detailed, some frustratingly vague, allowing the psychics to claim that their visions weren't wrong, merely misinterpreted by the cops. Some believed their visions to be genuine, while others were pure hucksters.

One claimed a town that was exactly 134 miles south of Headwaters State Park—its name started with an "L"—was significant. There was a pool within a half block of a church, and if one stood looking at the pool from the normal direction (presumably south), the sun would set to the right. The two abductors were both blond, one tall and one with fat legs and glasses, one Greek and one Indian. The older one wore a yellow shirt and had B-positive blood. He also had a two-color tattoo on the inside of his right forearm, although he'd never been in the Navy. The younger one worked in a bakery, and his mother had a scar on her left breast. They drove an off-white car with green upholstery, and there was a Nazi helmet in the backseat. After the abduction, they stopped at a farmhouse for water, which they received from the farmer's son, who was missing his little finger and was mentally retarded. Susie was alive and near water in a $2.50-a-night motel room.

Another believed Susie had been stolen from her tent by a bear. She had four visions: a bear prowling around the campsite, Susie's head (or part of it) in a see-through box, a Canadian family with five kids who had a clue, and a 1918 Ford belonging to a spinster school teacher who lived in a very old house with dusty curtains where some evidence was hidden. She heard the word "raven" and talked to an ethereal couple who gave her some keys to the front door.

Still another "saw" a two-story house with two little girls leaning out of a north window, and an old mine shaft running east and west at the foot of a great mountain. Dunbar just needed to find a dog named Boots that tracked by smell but refused to work for anybody but a twelve-year-old boy . . . "and he is death on dope and hippies."

Then there was the water witcher who guaranteed he'd lead agents to Susie if they'd give him only a lock of her hair. They didn't.

One mentalist claimed to have used "radiesthesia"—a combination of thought control and a pendulum—to locate hijacker D. B. Cooper. He was certain he and his magic pendulum could find Susie, too, if agents gave him a chance. They didn't.

Another revealed that the word "carpenter" was associated with Susie's abductor. She didn't know if it referred to the Wyoming town of Carpenter or his occupation, but it was important.

Different visions for different mystics. Susie was in Montana's

Custer National Forest, faceup, near a stream, alive but immobile. Or Susie was pierced with a steel something-or-other during a child's game and she now lay dead in a cavern. Or her abductor was a traveling handyman who probably killed the Boy Scout in the same park five years ago. Or Susie was taken by two human traffickers who followed her family from Michigan. Or Susie walked away with a fake priest and now moldered in a shallow grave. Or Susie was living with an Indian couple in Thermopolis, Wyoming. Or search planes were missing the exact spot where Susie's body lay (this particular clairvoyant had also predicted the assassination of Richard Nixon). Or Susie had been buried under a large tree ten miles from the campsite by "a man with perverted sexual desires and much frustration."

Various FBI field offices, street cops, and sheriffs' posses pursued every vision the best they could. They found no shallow graves, no haunted houses, no bloody steel, no illusory children, no fat-legged Greek blonds, no suspicious ravens, no D. B. Cooper.

And no Susie, alive or dead.

Hundreds of leads went nowhere. A hundred professional lawmen found nothing solid. The hardest evidence they had was a sliced tent and an indistinct footpath through dewy grass . . . and that wasn't hard evidence at all.

Everybody knew everything, but they really knew nothing. Everybody saw something, but nobody really saw anything.

FBI Special Agent Pete Dunbar—who'd solved big-time cases in New York City and Washington, DC, who had grown up here, and who didn't get pissed off easily—was now pissed off.

ONE MIDSUMMER MONDAY AFTERNOON, after the ground search broke up, Gallatin Deputy Ron Brown took the day shift in the operation's command center—in fact, just his personal camp trailer parked at Headwaters. Back at home in Three Forks, his two young daughters were out playing in the neighborhood.

His wife, Jane, was home alone cooking supper when the phone rang.

"Hello?"

There were no pleasantries. A man said he was calling for "Sheriff Brown."

"The FBI must think I'm a crank," the man said. "I'm raising the ransom to fifty thousand dollars. Put it in a suitcase in small bills in the end stall of the men's bathroom at the Denver bus stop. Get rid of the Negro shoeshine boy."

He wasn't done.

"I've got the Jaeger girl. To prove it, her first fingernails are humpy."

Jane asked the caller to repeat himself so she could take a message like she usually did when somebody called for Deputy Brown. Calmly, he said it all again.

Then he hung up.

Jane radioed her husband. He immediately reported the call to Agent Dunbar, who fired off an urgent teletype to the Denver office. The special agent in charge ("SAC" in FBI parlance) promised to review all recent calls that might have come in about the Jaeger case, and to immediately post surveillance in the main bus terminal. Since the Jaegers didn't have fifty thousand bucks to pay, the Denver office began assembling a suitcase full of dummy bills for the drop. Daughter Heidi Jaeger even contributed to the ruse by precisely cutting up blank paper in the shape of dollar bills. On the assumption that the kidnapper was watching, the plan was for Bill to leave the campground in a rush, as if he were collecting the ransom money at a bank and going to Denver to make the drop.

But the caller hadn't left any further details, such as the time and date of the exchange, or whether there'd be an exchange at all. So they installed a tap on Ron Brown's phone line in case another call came. The rest was up to Pete Dunbar.

"What's this about 'humpy fingernails'?" he asked Marietta and Bill back at the camp.

Marietta gasped. She had described Susie's every scar, birthmark, and bump on that first awful day—but she'd forgotten to mention those "humpy" fingernails.

When nurses handed the newborn Susie to Marietta in the delivery room, she immediately noticed a strange deformity: the infant's index fingers both ended in sharply pointed, oddly clubbed fingernails, almost like a dog's claws. The obstetrician wasn't worried, although he said little Susie would probably have them for the rest of her life.

As she grew, her fingernails didn't, except to expand with her fingers. At first they were prominent but eventually the family stopped noticing. Nobody really saw them anymore. Susie's spirit was a great distraction from such an inconspicuous deformity.

So inconspicuous that Marietta, Bill, and all the kids forgot to mention it. Thus it had never been mentioned in any of the BOLOs or press releases that went out.

Only the kidnapper would have known.

Dunbar asked the Detroit office to collect the arrest and background information on all of Susie's teachers, doctors, and other adult acquaintances who might have known about her fingernail deformity.

How odd it would be, Marietta thought, if Susie's one tiny defect was the thing that saved her life.

ONE DAY, AGENT DUNBAR brought his parish priest from Bozeman to Headwaters State Park to minister to the Jaegers.

Father Joseph Mavsar was a Slovenian immigrant who knew about violent personal loss. His whole family, except for him and his eleven-year-old brother, had been arrested, tortured, and burned to death in a horrifying Communist purge. They'd been fingered as subversives by a desperately sick shoemaker they'd taken into their own home. In return for his useful treachery, the commissar gifted the shoemaker with the Mavsars' family farm.

On that hot, sad July day in Headwaters State Park, Father Joseph had just returned from Slovenia. He'd traveled to his father's old farm, specifically to forgive the shoemaker who had collaborated with the Communists to murder his family and other townspeople that day. *To reconcile with the enemy,* he said. Alas, the shoemaker had died, but Father Joseph shared a glass of wine and a prayer with the informer's grown daughter. "After that, I pretty much let things go," he said.

Whether it was the way he told it, the harmony of their pain, or the slant of light, Marietta couldn't know. But when she heard Father Joseph's story about loss and forgiveness, the ground shifted under her feet. This priest was magically transfigured into a beacon of hope. If he could forgive someone who'd caused his family to be murdered, she could forgive, too. She made a promise to God that day that she would forgive Susie's captor—no matter how this turned out. It wasn't an easy promise, because she'd spent so much time wanting to tear the man limb from limb with her bare hands, and she truly didn't know if she had such forgiveness in her heart.

As much as her world had suddenly turned upside down, other things happened to realign it a little.

Dunbar checked on the Jaegers almost every day, not just updating them, but also holding their hands. And every morning, noon, and night in those weeks after Susie evaporated into the thin air of Montana's summer, the women of Gallatin County brought food to the Jaegers' sad little camp. Some brought games and toys for the kids. Some would linger at the picnic table under the trees for a while, grasping at something, anything, that might offer comfort.

But there was no comfort.

And no news.

Bill Jaeger's uneasiness with people, his flat affect, and his nervous habit of covering his mouth when he spoke continued to cause Dunbar to go to Marietta when he needed unambiguous answers. When reporters started to swarm around, Marietta spoke from her heart—a pretty young mother made for better photos anyway. She quickly became the public face of their private torment.

But this campground wasn't home, and it wasn't forever. As close as it might have been to the unknowable shadows out there, the Jaegers couldn't simply press a button that made the rest of the world stop just for them. The excruciating questions persisted— *Where's Susie? What's become of her? Is she suffering?*—but school would start soon for the other four kids, jobs couldn't be abandoned much longer, and bills must be paid. They couldn't just take up permanent residence in the archive of alternate endings.

So after six weeks of waiting in vain for any word about Susie, they packed up the trailer and made the long journey back to their dark, quiet house in Farmington Hills, Michigan.

They settled reluctantly into an unfamiliar routine of loss. Life moved on . . . except when it didn't. Bill dealt with the damage in his stoic way. Marietta wept in secret. They insulated the kids from their heartbreak. The children never talked much among themselves about what little they knew. Marietta and Bill did what they could, but when they were distracted, the usual rules relaxed.

"We're not complete without Susie," Marietta told one of the newspaper reporters who came around regularly. "Normally, if you lose someone you love, you grieve and that's a healing process. But we can't grieve."

A kind of magical anguish suffused Marietta. Her heart performed this clever trick by which a fearsome reality was transformed into a hope that it wasn't real at all.

Marietta often told those reporters that her "mother's intuition" let her know that Susie was still alive, and she always talked about her daughter in the present tense, as if Susie was still out there someplace. But at night, in the dark, she wasn't so sure.

By mid-August 1973, with all the national press coverage, the *Detroit News*'s ransom fund had swelled to fifty thousand dollars, which drew only more hoaxers, trolls, and scammers like corpse flies.

The FBI advised the Jaegers to buy a tape recorder at RadioShack, with a little suction cup that held a microphone to the phone receiver, just in case one of the calls was genuine. The whole Jaeger family knew to push the "Record" button whenever they answered the phone. All they got were several cassette tapes' worth of "Is Heidi there?" and "Can you come over on Saturday?"

One day, Marietta Jaeger answered a collect phone call. Whoever it was hung up without saying anything. The call was traced by the FBI to a trailer in Rock Springs, Wyoming, but the owners swore that nobody there had made such a call. A few months later, the Wyoming family's youngest son confessed that he'd telephoned out of curiosity after he saw the Jaegers' number in the local paper.

Another day, a psychic called to say that Susie was lying on her back in a dry wash somewhere in southeastern Montana, alive but unable to move. A flash flood was coming. The self-described clairvoyant's vision was detailed and frightening. The sheriff organized a massive hunt, and it got a lot of publicity in Montana, but they didn't find Susie.

In fact, none of the daily collect calls ever did anything but balloon the Jaegers' phone bills.

Nevertheless, for more than a month after they came home, Marietta never left her house. She didn't want to miss a legitimate call that offered genuine information. None came, and her hope flagged.

After school one evening—September 24—Marietta picked up a call from one of her kids. Joey had been stuck in a drenching downpour and missed his usual ride, so he called his mother to fetch him. His school was close, and weeks of waiting by the phone had yielded nothing, so Marietta put Danny in charge and left her house for the first time.

Ten minutes later she came back through the front door, sopping wet, Joey in tow. Danny was hanging up the phone, and she could tell by the stricken look on his face that something wasn't right.

The collect caller had been taunting and urgent. The whole call hadn't lasted more than two minutes, but sixteen-year-old Danny had captured it on the Jaegers' little RadioShack tape recorder.

"Now, you're Susie's brother, huh?" the man asked. He was an adult, but not old. His accent was Western.

"Yeah."

"You like to know where she's at?"

"Yeah, I would."

"Well, you're gonna have to wait awhile."

"Why?"

"You've had too much police and FBI activity. You may think I'm a hoax, but I know something about Susie that nobody knows."

"Oh? Why don't you tell us?"

"OK. Fingernails of her first fingers are humped."

"I know that. I meant, why don't you tell us where she is?" Danny persisted.

"Because I can't hardly do that. . . . It's a pretty dangerous situation, you know."

"Well, can't you just drop her somewhere and let us pick her up?"

"You want to come west quite a ways?"

"Yeah, no problem there."

"Well, we'll make arrangements one of these days, but for right now, you're gonna have to wait awhile."

"Why do we have to wait?"

"'Cause that's the way things have to be."

"Why?"

"Well, 'cause a person does things like this, he can't get caught. He's got to figure out ways not to get caught."

Danny didn't think long about his next response.

"Just drop her somewhere a day ahead of time and just leave that place."

"Yeah, sure," the caller said dismissively. "I don't want to drop her just for nothing. Anyway, I just want to tell you to wait awhile. You will be contacted. It may be another week. It may be a month or two months or so. But you'll get contacted."

Click.

The voice had slipped away into the electronic shadows.

A month later, Mountain Bell found a toll ticket for the call and reported it to the FBI, which had red-flagged the Jaegers' number for phone companies and operators all over America. They were to report any such calls to the feds, although it was never instantaneous.

This particular number belonged to a puny three-pump truck stop and greasy spoon outside Cheyenne, Wyoming. Woody's sat across the road from an oil refinery and had three pay phones. Two were outside its front door and the other was on the pump island a few steps away. Whoever called the Jaegers had used the phone between the pumps, but by the time FBI technicians got there weeks later, a hundred fingers had touched the weather-beaten receiver. No useful prints could be lifted.

However, the caller's reference to "humpy nails" made him real. Dunbar didn't know why he'd picked this particular day to call, but he was Susie's kidnapper, without a doubt. Dunbar didn't know who he was, but he knew he was the right guy. He was the "unknown subject," or UnSub in Bureau speak.

And there was something else SA Pete Dunbar didn't know as fall slipped into a fruitless, discontented winter with no more answers.

That the UnSub wasn't done.

By a long shot.

GIRL . . . GONE

FEBRUARY 5, 1974
MISSOULA, MONTANA

Even at five years old, Siobhan McGuinness was a free-range kid.

The North Side was her playground. The working-class neighbor-hood sat literally on the other side of the tracks from the better parts of town. Its ranks of dog-eared cottages had been thrown up cheaply and quickly at the turn of the century for a flash flood of railroaders who were all long dead by the mid-1970s. Yards were scabby in sum-mer, worse in winter. The winter bones of Norway maples lined the narrow streets, which had been dirt roads not so long ago.

A few North Siders inherited their two-bedroom shotgun bun-galows from their railroading grandparents—some could afford only that much house—and many rented.

Like Siobhan's mom. She was a divorced young bohemian, an artist who let itinerant freaks and free spirits crash at her place. Some shared drugs, booze, and more, then moved on, while Sio-bhan often slept on a mattress on the floor. Whether because of all the coming and going or the idea that kids shouldn't be tethered, Siobhan wandered free.

The streets weren't heavily traveled, so a vagabond kindergartner needn't dodge a lot of cars. Travelers who took the I-90 off-ramp into the North Side, just a couple blocks from Siobhan's house, tended to grab gas and road food on Orange Street before hitting the highway again, or found sit-down meals farther into town. Unless they were lost or passing through on the main street, they never ventured into Siobhan's neighborhood.

By afternoon on this day, a north wind had picked up so the subfreezing air felt even colder. Siobhan wore a little purple coat and boots, but she stayed warm by being in almost constant motion in every direction.

Siobhan was outgoing and fearless, unfazed by seeing a strange car. She might even have started up a conversation with the driver.

After school, she went home with her bestie, where she stayed until her mom called around five o'clock. Supper was on. She left her friend's house, heading toward home until she crossed paths with a little boy in her class. He'd been sent by his mom on an errand to a convenience store a block or so away, and she went with him. On the way back, they bumped into another friend. Siobhan wanted to play, but it was cold, and the little girl encouraged Siobhan to head home for dinner.

They parted, but Siobhan never got home.

She vanished into thin, cold air.

TWO DAYS LATER, AFTER an all-out manhunt by two hundred city cops, county deputies, and volunteers, a snowplow driver spotted a flash of purple off the side of the highway. It was down in a low spot, just outside of an I-90 off-ramp culvert about fifteen miles east of

Missoula, beside the frontage road to Turah. In the general direction of Bozeman.

It was Siobhan's frozen corpse, in her purple coat.

Cops soon swarmed all over the crime scene. They had invested a lot of time and emotion in finding this little girl, and now they had found her. However well-meaning and heartsick, they unwittingly obliterated any tire tracks or footprints the killer might have left. They found no knife, no cast-off evidence, nothing.

Her head had been split open with a blunt object and she'd been stabbed three times with a big knife. The bludgeon—a club or a stick, maybe—left a Y-shaped mark, with a long tail. Semen was smeared on her belly and red T-shirt.

It appeared that her lightly clothed body had been stuffed, not yet dead but unconscious, inside the culvert. When she revived, she tried to crawl out, but when her shock, the snow, and the frigid air were too much, she turned around. Before the snow blew in that night, she died of hypothermia—not her wounds—while crawling back to the pitiful shelter of her culvert.

An autopsy confirmed her cause of death: exposure. No rape test was done but she'd clearly been sexually assaulted in some way. And she was cremated soon after the coroner released her remains to her mother. Her ashes were scattered on a mountaintop looking down on Missoula and in a river running through it.

Later, a couple of witnesses reported seeing a big green Cadillac with New York plates at the off-ramp. A BOLO went out and they found a big green Cadillac with bloodstains in the trunk.

After some initial excitement, forensics said it wasn't what it seemed.

And the Montana lawmen would always talk about the New Yorker in a Cadillac who once hauled a bleeding deer in his trunk.

CHAPTER 3

BADLANDS

SATURDAY, FEBRUARY 9, 1974
MANHATTAN, MONTANA

Manhattan High School's varsity basketball team was literally un-beatable this season—and last. The Tigers were Montana's defend-ing Class B champions and hadn't lost a game in two years. Tonight was their last regular season game before the state playoffs, so damn near the whole town of Manhattan caravanned ten miles down to Belgrade to watch their boys whip the Panthers.

Among them were Sandy Smallegan and her parents, John and Betty Dykman, big fans of the undefeated Tigers.

Sandra Mae Smallegan was Sandy Dykman when she gradu-ated from Manhattan High a few years earlier. School had been easy for her, and she'd had a lot of friends. Her long dark hair was always fixed perfectly. She cheered on the pom-pom squad and she always dressed a cut above the other girls. In fact, despite her austere Dutch upbringing, she dreamed of a career in fashion design.

And Sandy openly loved her family at a time when teenagers

never admitted it. She was especially close with her mother, a gentle presence for the only girl among four brothers. She never missed Sunday dinner at her parents' house and usually joined their nightly prayer hour.

Sandy had her flaws. She couldn't drive worth cow flop. She wrecked Manhattan High School's only driver ed car by plunging it into a canal. Then she backed her dainty white Ford Cortina—a two-door, British-made coupe her dad gave her when she turned sixteen—into a neighbor's tree.

She loved her exotically cute Cortina. She seldom ventured farther than nearby Amsterdam, but when she drove it around among Manhattan's farm trucks, she felt so cultured, so . . . European.

When she was still a senior, she met a young carpenter named Jack Smallegan on a blind date. He was a few years older, but after that first night talking by the fireplace in the bunkhouse where he lived, he was smitten. One night they parked out at Lover's Leap above the Gallatin River, and he asked her to marry him. She said yes, and as soon as school let out she married Jack, on her eighteenth birthday—June 15, 1972—in a simple ceremony at the Three Forks Baptist Church, wearing her mother's wedding dress.

After honeymooning in Jackson Hole, they moved into a two-room walk-up apartment over the Manhattan Machinery Company, the local farm-implement dealer and the biggest employer on Main Street. It was only $150 a month, previously rented mainly to the bachelor mechanics who worked in the shop below. Sandy's dad was the shop foreman at his close friend Clifford Meirhofer's implement store, and together they made sure she had a safe place to start her new life.

Sandy fixed the place up and made it feel warmer than it was. Life was good in those first months. She and Jack played in a little gospel-folk band together. Jack built houses and Sandy waitressed at the cozy café inside Manhattan's bowling alley. Folks loved her because she was always sunny, and she made them feel so sunny that they never would have guessed she'd secretly miscarried Jack's baby.

Jack loved her, too, even after he had an affair with his mixed-league bowling partner. The marriage busted up in less than a year. When Jack broke the sad news to Sandy's parents, her father socked Jack in the nose.

Sandy and Jack didn't actually divorce but merely separated because neither one could pull the trigger. No matter. They were still done, maybe for good. Jack moved out, but kept a key. Hell, he knew he'd made a big mistake and he wished desperately he could win back Sandy's trust. Maybe it'd happen someday. But neither Sandy nor her parents were having any of that right now.

She was depressed for a while. She confided a lot in her mother. Her friends urged her to forget about Jack and start dating somebody else, but it was hard to forget about Jack because she still saw him around town. She kept working down at the bowling alley, where he'd come some nights for dinner. Occasionally, she and her Cortina escaped Manhattan—never very far—to sell some Mary Kay cosmetics to country women and slip away from her blues.

After a while, Sandy started going out again, but nothing was ever serious, even when Bob Harrison asked her out. He was a family friend who was about five years older, muscular, handsome, blond, and a hot-rodder. A basically good guy who knew how to have fun. He'd just returned to Montana after a few years in California, which immediately made him worldly in Manhattan folks' eyes. His reputation as a playboy was tolerated because, well, playing around was just what worldly California guys did.

His and Sandy's relationship never ran especially hot; she casually dated other guys pretty much the whole time they were together. But she kept all of them at arm's length. Friendly, not romantic.

A few other guys had eyes for Sandy and they took their shot at her. Some were more successful than others, but none really clicked.

Then there was David Meirhofer, her landlord's son, a nice enough guy who'd been a few years ahead of Sandy in high school. He'd asked her out a few days before Christmas and she went, but it wasn't a good fit. For one, he was five years older and knew Bob Harrison. For another, the deep black pools of his eyes unsettled her a little. But he was her dad's boss's son, and he sent Sandy roses and chocolates for a couple weeks—actually, he was sorta shy-cute and conventional about courting, which was old-fashioned in those revolutionary days. He repeatedly asked her out again, but Sandy always invented something else to do. Finally, after the first of the year, she told him in the kindest way possible that they probably shouldn't go out again. He stopped calling.

However, as popular as she was, Sandy didn't have a date for the basketball game between the Tigers and the Panthers. In fact, she sat with her parents. Bob Harrison was in the gym but sat with some high school girls elsewhere in the bleachers. At halftime, Sandy sauntered over and chatted briefly with him. One of the girls overheard their conversation: "You know where the key is," she told Bob. "Come on up to the apartment after the game."

That night, Sandy and her parents cheered as their Tigers walloped Belgrade 66-46 and officially became Montana's winningest basketball team, big or small, in 1974. Manhattan would talk about it for years.

When the cheering finally died down, it was after ten p.m. Sandy headed back up to Manhattan with her parents, and they dropped her off at her little apartment over the implement store. It was after eleven, but Sandy was still pumped up and wanted to be around people. One or two drinks, she'd promised her dad, then home. She changed her clothes—a white sweater and dark slacks under a long red cashmere coat—and walked in her fashionably heeled snow boots a half block over to the American Legion bar, the rowdiest place on a Manhattan Saturday night.

As usual, the bar was jumping. All the regulars were there, and a few unfamiliar faces. She chatted with some old friends who came up to her. Flirted with some guys. A fat, greasy-haired hippie dude wearing a headband checked out all the girls the way a coyote watched sage hens. And leaning against the bar was Jack Smallegan.

Sandy and Jack made small talk. He was coaching Little League; she was still down at the bowling alley. They hugged politely and said good night.

A few minutes past midnight, Sandy walked out of the bar. She waved to a friend who was also leaving, then stepped off the curb, into the shadows, toward her apartment.

And just like that, she was gone.

Nobody ever saw her again.

MONDAY AFTERNOON, DEPUTY BILL Slaughter, one of the college kids the Gallatin County sheriff had hired, caught a call from John Dykman. His daughter, Sandy, hadn't answered her door or picked up her phone since he dropped her off in Manhattan Saturday night. Her little Ford was missing. He'd phoned some of her friends, too. They hadn't seen her, either.

Sandy probably took off somewhere, he told Slaughter, and hadn't told her parents. But they were a little concerned because she just didn't do stuff like that. Maybe she ran away for some unfathomable reason. Maybe she was with her boyfriend Bob Harrison or one of several other suitors. Maybe her estranged husband, Jack Smallegan, knew something, he said.

Dykman suggested that local deputies discreetly look around for Sandy, maybe put out a quiet bulletin to patrol cars, but he didn't want any press releases. Not yet.

The next morning was different. When the Dykmans still hadn't heard from Sandy, they were seriously worried. They used a spare key to get into her apartment, where they couldn't find two blue suitcases—an overnight bag and one slightly bigger—and one of Sandy's favorite white suits. The visit was quick. Nothing else seemed to be obviously missing. Except Sandy.

John asked the sheriff's department to pull out the stops: Call all the local radio stations and newspapers, and teletype all cops everywhere to be on the lookout for his missing daughter. He described her in the only way cops cared about, not the way a worried father might: white female, age nineteen, about five foot two, one hundred and ten pounds, hazel eyes, and brown hair.

The sheriff sent Deputies Slaughter and Jim Jordan, and a Bozeman detective, to interview the Dykmans a little more, to buttonhole Harrison, Jack Smallegan, and about sixty other potential witnesses, but only after they searched Sandy's apartment with cops' eyes.

They examined the spot at the bottom of the alley stairs behind the stick-built two-story implement store, the spot where she typically parked her car. No signs of a scuffle, blood, or a hasty getaway. The door at the top of the stairs showed no signs of a forced entry, although they knew the family had already been there.

Sandy's studio apartment had a little kitchenette, a cheap dining table, and a sitting area separated from a "bedroom" by a knee wall. Apart from her unmade double bed, it was neat and clean, a "girl place," Slaughter thought.

Unopened mail was stacked neatly on her plastic tablecloth. Slaughter pawed through it. Just some bills and junk with no discernible investigatory value.

A jacket was draped on the back of her kitchen chair, the same one Slaughter had seen her wear at the café, where he ate dinner or lunch about four times a week. A few other familiar outfits hung in the closet with her shoes.

Sandy led a small-town girl's small life in a small room that held no explicit clues to her whereabouts or whether there had been foul play.

Well, it did strike Slaughter as odd when he spotted a half-empty glass of beer on Sandy's headboard, because he knew she didn't like beer. Maybe she'd brought somebody home from the bar or had a last-call visitor. Could be nothing, but he raised a little stink about it back at the GCSO. Nobody took him seriously. He was just a wet-eared college boy who didn't know shit. The beer glass was never even collected as evidence.

Deputies questioned her boyfriend, her ex-husband, the fat hippie, various admirers, first dates, friends, local perverts, and other townspeople. Of course, current flame Bob Harrison commanded their attention, but a popular and pretty waitress was more than an invisible servant in a small-town bowling alley. Hundreds of Manhattanites knew her.

In fact, everybody checked out. If there had been foul play—a big "if"—none of these guys was likely involved.

Truth be told, Sandy's disappearance was merely a missing-person case, workaday stuff for the Gallatin County Sheriff's Office. It wasn't a low priority, nor was it all-hands-on-deck. Sheriff Anderson drafted a couple city cops to help chase leads, but the FBI was busy with the missing Jaeger girl—although that case had gone cold after almost eight months—and other federal work. Special Agents

Dunbar and Terry, sensitive to reports of young gone girls, kept an eye on the Smallegan investigation, but a missing nineteen-year-old wasn't usually the FBI's kind of case.

Six days after Sandy was last seen—February 15—it became Manhattan's kind of case, though. Everybody in town knew her and her parents, and they weren't going to sit around to wait for the sheriff and his good ol' boys to crack the case. They pressured Sheriff Anderson to mount a full-scale search, and he did. There were votes to consider. And when batting oh for one, who wouldn't want to rescue at least one missing girl?

Anderson set up a command center in Manhattan's fire hall. County deputies, city cops, and several trusted volunteers—even Sandy's brothers Ron and Doug—fanned out across town. Her estranged husband, Jack, searched, too, but he stopped hunting when he considered how fishy it'd look if he actually found her.

A bloodhound loped from barn to garage to outhouse. Lawmen and volunteers searched the dump, parked cars, gravel pits, and culverts. At the end of the day, they'd found nothing, not even a strange scent.

With every passing day, with no shred of evidence, foul play seemed more unlikely.

THE OLD LOCKHART RANCH was an abandoned homestead just this side of nowhere.

Here at the numb bottom of winter, the terrain was half dead, half alive. It was all dirt and sagebrush, with just enough grass to keep a small herd of cows alive. The winter sun cut low across the sky, throwing longer shadows earlier in the cold days. Down in the coulee, the cottonwoods were cadaverous. The nameless creek, such as it was, ran only during the spring runoff, so in winter the coyotes and other predators ate snow and rabbit blood when they were parched.

Nobody had lived on the place since old man Lockhart died a long time back. A retired Navy guy in Helena ran some tough old cows out there and used a few tin sheds to park some corroded implements, but he left the hardscrabble one-room shanty and barn to decompose. *Rust to dust.*

The search for Sandy Smallegan was rippling outward in ever-widening circles. Every lawman in Gallatin County had been mobilized. Satisfied she was no longer in Manhattan, they fanned out into the peripheral clusters of folks who'd gathered into what passed for villages, like the Dutch farmers out in Amsterdam and the railroaders of Logan, where the posse knocked on every door and peeked in every attic and outhouse.

A week after Sandy vanished—February 17—Sheriff Anderson dispatched tired searchers even farther from Manhattan to explore the draws, bottomlands, barns, and farmsteads.

Deputy Don Houghton and Manhattan town marshal Ron Skinner drew the short straw. The godforsaken Horseshoe Hills were way northwest of town. It was open range borrowed from the desolate outer edge of Hell. Out there, the dirt was bad; roads were worse. Humans didn't truly live out there; they just hung on for dear life to miserable outposts like the Lockhart Ranch. Then they died, like old man Lockhart. But, hey, in the dead of winter at least the rattlesnakes would be hibernating.

The sheriff's only four-wheel-drive vehicle was deployed elsewhere, so Houghton and Skinner hopped in Skinner's four-wheel-drive babyshit green Chevy pickup. Where they were headed was maybe only thirty miles from Bozeman on the map, but at least a bone-rattling hour overland. Skinner had hunted in the Hills and it was his truck, so he drove and Houghton rode shotgun.

Closer parts of the Hills had already been searched. In the past few days, deputies had poked their heads into every line shack and old well. The search leader told Houghton and Skinner to plunge deeper into the badlands and kick every stone.

A dirt road can be complicated. First, it's sometimes not really a road. In the Hills, the county's gravel access quickly disintegrated into a two-track, which eventually frittered into a couple frozen ruts. The so-called Horseshoe Cottonwood Road was used infrequently by ranchers who lived in town and occasionally checked on their free-ranging cattle in the Hills. Now it was mostly reclaimed by the prairie.

Skinner took it slow. He was a lawman only in the technical sense. As Manhattan's town marshal, he was tasked primarily with the surveillance of the school crosswalk every afternoon to keep Manhattan safe from villainous speeders. And he was still a rookie, not yet experienced enough to be promoted to night cop. Skinner himself had been busted in high school for brawling with an out-of-town boy who was poaching the local girls. His punishment? The town's only judge—a retired housebuilder who held court in his basement—sentenced him to paint the firehouse doors on a Sunday, when all the churchgoers would pass . . . and know.

Patches of snow dappled the ruts. The dirt underneath was frozen solid, downright slippery in spots. The day was clear but frosty, and it was noon, the warmest it'd get all day. Wind made it colder. Skinner knew if they got stuck out there, nobody would likely happen by before dark. And they couldn't just call for a tow: Skinner's family truck had no police radio, and they carried only a piddling Handie-Talkie with limited range. They were on their own.

At some point, the ruts diverged. One set sidetracked toward the Damuth ranch, which Skinner knew was a good distance out of the way. The other set would lead them right past the Lockhart homestead just ahead. None of this was on a map. Folks just knew. So Houghton and Skinner chose the rutted path of least resistance: Lockhart first, Damuth later.

The Lockhart homestead sat at the end of a nearly invisible truck path, across a dry creek and through some cottonwoods. It was surrounded by a rusty fence that once kept cows and strangers out of the yard, but the rickety barbed-wire gate was open, lying in a tangle to one side. It no longer kept anything or anybody out.

It wasn't—and probably never had been—a proper "yard." Now cow paths and deer trails crisscrossed the property, none straight. Now nobody cut weeds. Now dried-out prairie grass poked up from the bare ground like stray, stubborn hairs on top of a bald man's head.

The buildings were old and had obviously been unoccupied for a long while. Time and weather had stripped most of the red paint off the barn. A steel Quonset hut bore spots of rust. A granary off in the sagebrush had collapsed in on itself. A rusty grain auger lay abandoned in a dead pasture.

A cracker-box house sat to one side, forlorn. Maybe old man Lockhart had died in there, but nobody knew for sure what ever became of him. Its white siding wasn't white anymore. The tar-papered privy out back looked sturdier than the house.

The front door was unlocked, so Houghton and Skinner went inside.

The place was colder than outside, and dark. Everything about it was in disrepair. Dead lights, dead air, just dead.

A tiny kitchen area adjoined the living room, and in the rear were two small bedrooms. The whole place was barely bigger than a two-car garage. It was thoroughly vacant but still felt claustrophobic. Hermit ranchers didn't live in mansions. The only surviving furniture was an old table, covered by an oilcloth, and one chair in the kitchen area, where it looked like somebody had recently sat. *Probably a cowboy eating his lunch or getting out of the weather,* they thought. *Nothing more.*

Just outside the broken kitchen window, Houghton saw a blackened burn barrel, encircled by an uncommonly wide, sooty ring of burned grass and charred dirt from flying cinders. It was a typical farmhouse feature; it was easier for ranchers to burn their garbage than haul it to town. Sometimes an ignored trash fire just got away from a guy. *Nothing more.*

Inside, Skinner climbed some stairs for a quick look-see at the attic while Houghton poked his head in the empty bedrooms. *Nothing.*

Outside, they decided to search the big weathered barn next. It'd been a long time since it saw paint. No tire tracks, no disturbed earth, no evidence of any recent human activity. They opened the big doors and stepped into the main space. It was cold, dark, and musty. Its high ceiling reminded Houghton of a dairy barn. It was connected by a two-by-three-foot "hatch" to a smaller, garage-sized room to one side, probably used for hay storage. The hatch would allow a bale to be shoved into the barn without lugging it outside and all the way around to the front door.

But the hatch was jammed tight, so Houghton and Skinner went outside to the smaller barn's double doors. They were nailed shut and maybe hadn't been open since the old man died. They left them sealed.

Houghton had another idea. He went back inside—to the hatch—and bent down to his hands and knees to peek through a crack in the ramshackle barnwood. Through his peephole he could see some hay, old cardboard boxes, dented fifty-five-gallon drums, and other garbage. Nothing unusual for an abandoned homestead in the boonies.

There weren't many other places to search here. The winter sun would set early and they had a couple of other stops before dark, so they headed back across the yard to Skinner's truck. Next stop, the Damuth place.

Something caught Houghton's eye as they walked. Something out of place in this worn-out landscape. Something white, snagged in the sagebrush. A tissue, maybe? A shiny beer can? He went over and picked it up.

Panties.

White panties with little blue flowers. They were clean, unweathered. Not ragged, still elastic. And they'd been worn. Recently.

Skinner rummaged in his truck and found a reasonably sanitary plastic sandwich bag from a recent hunting trip. They bagged the panties as possible evidence.

They hustled back to the barn, partly because it was the closest structure . . . and partly because that unsearched garage now haunted them.

Inside the main barn, Houghton kicked the hay hatch off its corroded hinges and crawled in.

The hair prickled on the back of his neck.

There, surrounded by a phalanx of oil drums and boxes, partially covered by an oiled canvas tarp and camouflaged with loose straw, was a small white car. It had no plates, but he knew what he'd found.

It was Sandy Smallegan's little white Cortina.

Houghton quickly scrambled out through the shattered trapdoor and told Skinner what he'd found. His heart raced. He ran back to Skinner's truck to grab the plastic Handie-Talkie and clicked the button. Dead air.

So Houghton jumped into the driver's seat and headed for a nearby hill, where he'd get a clearer signal to the sheriff's distant radio tower.

Skinner was left guarding the barn. He grew suddenly paranoid that there was a body inside . . . or a killer outside, watching and waiting to pick off a straggler. *What if whoever hid the car is still out there?* When one of the barn doors caught the wind and screeched on its arthritic hinges, Skinner damn near emptied his Smith & Wesson .357 into it.

"Gallatin County Sheriff, six-five-two," Houghton said, clearly speaking his badge number into Skinner's little gray radio. He wasn't nervous, just adrenalized. "We found the car."

Now it was real. This was a big break in the case. Just like that, they weren't searchers anymore; they were detectives on a crime scene. Other deputies had been dispatched, but it would be an hour before they arrived.

Getting inside the hay shed was the only way they'd know if somebody was in the Cortina, alive or dead. Houghton and Skinner pried open the shed's nailed doors with a tire iron from the truck.

Inside, the cramped space was dark and unnerving. They had to sidestep around the crap.

They stripped off the tarp and loose hay without leaving any new fingerprints on it. They couldn't see through the car's side windows. Houghton stood back and cautiously peered through the windshield, half expecting to see a corpse peering back. To his relief, he saw only some scattered clothing in the front seat, no bodies.

Maybe we're being watched, they both thought. They wanted to believe it was unlikely, though. Too cold, too isolated, too open. Out there, who'd sit around waiting? Nobody. Probably.

They now had one job: to secure the scene and protect the evidence. Help was on the way.

AS EXPECTED, IT TOOK a good hour for backup to arrive. They were already losing the light.

A dozen uniforms spread out and searched everything again. Sandy Smallegan's hidden car meant her abductor, whoever he was, had been here within the past week. While some of the searchers examined the Cortina more closely, others crawled all over the house and outbuildings. They even poked around in the burn barrel's ashes. Just before sunset, a deputy found a bedroom closet door that had been nailed shut. He pried the one-by-fours off and squinted inside, but the room was dark, the closet darker. *Nothing.*

Nobody found a damn thing. Night was falling fast. They needed a new day's light.

Somebody was assigned to spend the night in a camp trailer that did double duty as a mobile command post—the same one they'd used during the Susie Jaeger search. *Chain of custody.* Everybody else went back to town planning to caravan out to the Lockhart place before sunrise the next morning.

It was still predawn dark when nearly every sworn officer in Gallatin County rolled up on Sunday morning. Anderson assigned them to different parts of the search area—the barn, house, implement sheds, well house, yard, the coulee, and the hills behind the homestead, anyplace that might have more clues about what befell Sandy Smallegan.

After sleeping on it, lots of cops were wondering how somebody might hide Sandy's car in the shed and, in the middle of a frigid February night, get back to Manhattan or Three Forks. Were they looking for more than one kidnapper? Her car was here, but might Sandy be stashed alive in some hideaway?

Suddenly, SA Pete Dunbar and the FBI were intensely interested.

After the sun came up, the lawmen scattered to their assigned sectors. Early on, somebody found the Cortina's license plates—Montana 6-16097—wrapped in a rag and stashed under some straw in the hay shed. But it didn't matter much. There'd been no shred of doubt about whose car it was.

Inside the car, deputies found some clothes and an overnight bag that contained two stockings, some hats, some foreign black debris, and some strands of hair. Two other suitcases in the Cortina contained a mishmash of clothes, including a plaid suit that Sandra had worn to the basketball game the night she disappeared.

The car itself yielded other evidence of unknown forensic value, but it was collected for the FBI's scientists. They dusted for fingerprints, inside and out. They chipped out a blue scuff on the white paint of the Cortina's fender. Floor mats and the trunk liner were removed. They swept the floorboards and trunk, where they found a blue shag rug, some brown paper, and a burlap sack. Under the hood, a perceptive cop noticed stains that looked like dried, dirty blood. A crime-scene tech scraped that up.

On the shed's dirt floor lay two small pieces of yarn—maybe hair ties? A deputy bagged them.

The barn search took a more sinister turn when they discovered a handsaw, a bloodied leather whip, and a knotted rope. The saw appeared clean to the naked eye, but who knew what microscopic traces might be hidden there? The whip might be just an old ranch whip, or it might be an artifact of sadism. Dunbar ordered them not to untie the rope, since the nature of the knot might give FBI examiners a valuable clue about the UnSub.

Somebody pried loose the two-by-fours that had been nailed over the shed door. The hammerhead's dents contained traces of blue paint, and the highest of them was about seven feet from the ground. The sheriff imagined the FBI technicians might be able to discern from the hammer marks whether the UnSub was right- or left-handed.

At the same time, the dinky farmhouse was yielding clues that Houghton and Skinner had missed.

Searchers collected the oilcloth that covered the table, as well as a large knife, some bloodlike scrapings from the cupboards, and the cap from a liquid soap bottle that bore some strange red fibers. They also took a candle and wax drippings from the top of the kitchen stove.

In one of the stale back bedrooms, a deputy saw a scrap of burned cloth and a water glass clabbered with dribbled wax drippings, not much else.

Then he opened the closet door.

With as much daylight as could seep into the cramped little room, he could see some black slippers in one corner, and a blob of . . . *Oh, Christ, it's a pile of shit!*

Upon closer inspection, the closet door looked like it had once been nailed shut, like the shed door. The trim bore irregular nail holes that had no other reason to be there.

But the bleakest evidence came from outside, from the burn pile and the pump house.

Somebody picked up a used tissue, clearly not a remnant of old man Lockhart's time. Pieces of burned cloth were scattered behind the house. A single filament of long hair was found near the door. A hammer was stashed in the well house. A stick burned at both ends lay in the dirt near the scorched circle around the burn pile, where there were globs of something nobody could identify, and even veteran lawmen secretly dreaded to learn what it was.

The ashes around the burn barrel—speckled with tiny bone shards—were bagged and tagged. Some other, larger bone fragments trapped in the unidentified congealed gunk were scooped up, too, gunk and all, for an expert to separate.

Although she was estranged from her husband, Sandy Smallegan still wore her gold wedding band because they weren't properly divorced. So, while sifting the burn pit's ashes, deputies kept an eye out for the ring or its melted remnants. They found nothing, but they just bagged it all up for the lab techs.

Before nightfall, one of the many deputies dispatched to search the surrounding wildlands returned to the homestead with a black scarf he found about a mile away in the sagebrush.

Uneasiness seeped through the posse. Some of these things—charred bones, a whip, a saw, tiny shotgun pellets, several photographer's flashbulbs, a pile of crap, trickles of candle wax, brownish stains—might not be what a cop wanted them to be.

Or they might.

Except for the Cortina, none of them were out of place on an abandoned homestead . . . but *because* of the Cortina, they were all artifacts of possible foul play.

Over the next few days, the intense search continued. A grid was laid out in three-by-three-foot squares all over the yard and a hill behind the house. A whole cadre of cops was on its knees, noses to the ground, picking a three-inch chunk of jawbone, four teeth, and tiny fragments of burned and shattered bones—most smaller than a fingernail—from the dirt, which was then sifted with big screens. Some of the cops had dressed out big game and knew the telltale scoring that a saw leaves on bone. They collected more than twelve hundred bits, some bigger than others but all small. Maybe human, maybe not.

At one point, Deputy Houghton proposed sending one of the

sheriff's posse, a weekend diver named Charlie Papke, down into the ranch cistern to look for more remains or weapons. But the cistern was narrow and old, and the frigid, stagnant water wasn't exactly pure, so diving into it was risky. Nobody went down.

The sheriff showed some of his evidence to Sandra's grieving parents, who confirmed the clothing was hers, but the disorganized contents of the suitcases suggested to them that their fastidious daughter had not packed them. They gave deputies Sandy's hairbrush and the bolt of fabric from which she made the nightgown they surmised she'd worn to bed the night she vanished.

Less than ten days after Sandra Smallegan disappeared, SA Pete Dunbar had seen enough to fear the worst. The evidence whispered to him that she had been murdered, then cremated in the trash barrel. From a thousand nights sitting around campfires, he knew the relatively low heat of a trash fire made it unlikely unless the UnSub used a highly flammable accelerant—a lot of it. And unless the corpse had been chopped into small pieces, her flesh and bone couldn't have been completely consumed. Either way, it would have taken most of a day and night.

Then the bones must have been crushed somehow and scattered across the homestead, where they could be hidden in plain sight.

Dunbar shuddered to think what might have happened at the Lockhart place, where a killer could build a huge, hot fire that burned for hours, maybe days, and nobody would notice. Where Sandra Smallegan's abductor could drive a car across open range and never be seen, night or day. Where a young woman might scream in a dark closet—or worse—and never be heard.

Soon, word spread through town like a grass fire. Everybody was either whispering about it, volunteering to help, or just gawking. A number of Manhattan's menfolk stepped up every day to help, but were tactfully turned away. Civilians simply couldn't be allowed into an active crime scene like the Lockhart place. Never-theless, some of them couldn't resist rubbernecking.

One day, deputies spied a pickup truck on a nearby hill. *Another looky-loo.* Before they could go shoo the driver away, the truck trun-dled down to the homestead.

It was just a local guy, an overeager cop wannabe everybody knew. Anytime David Meirhofer popped into Jessie's Café, he'd make a beeline for any deputies who might be grabbing lunch. A former Boy Scout and Marine, he was in his early twenties, friendly, squared away, reasonably bright . . . and he loved to talk cop. Like a lot of people's, his name had come up in the Susie Jaeger investiga-tion months before, but after Dunbar interviewed him, David was quickly cleared. Now he wanted to help, bad.

A budding amateur sleuth stomping on evidence was the last thing they needed right now.

David hopped out of his green and white Jeep pickup, a big smile on his face, confident he was gonna break Sandy's case for them.

"I found this up there," he said. "Maybe it'll help."

He handed a woman's red blouse to one of the cops. They thanked him, but David stuck around, asking questions and shoot-ing the breeze, until the sheriff politely asked him to leave.

This was, after all, an active crime scene, and David Meirhofer didn't belong here.

THE DAY AFTER THE Lockhart search wrapped up, Special Agent Pete Dunbar had an unexpected visitor in his Bozeman office.

The man introduced himself but Dunbar already knew him. He was there about Sandy Smallegan's disappearance, he said. He'd heard through the grapevine about the macabre discoveries out at the Lockhart place. And he wanted Dunbar to swear that he'd remain anonymous. Dunbar agreed.

The man told Dunbar that he had a gut feeling his son was involved somehow. The son, a young man, had had a brief relationship with Sandy, who had a little apartment on the same block as his boy. The "circumstantial evidence" was no more than a hunch, but he believed Dunbar should do the heavy lifting of proving his hunch wrong. *But you didn't hear it from me, OK?*

The secret conversation took less than fifteen minutes. The father slipped out of the federal building, hoping nobody would see him. But if somebody did, maybe they'd just figure that the guy was paying his taxes or some such. He was, after all, a big-time businessman in Manhattan and made a lot of money.

MOST OF THE GRIM evidence, including the bigger chunks of bone, the teeth, and the possible bloodstains, had been shipped off to the FBI labs in Quantico, Virginia. From there, the crime lab shuttled all of the suspected biological material to the forensic anthropologists at the Smithsonian Institution for more expert evaluation.

At the same time, a Gallatin deputy personally drove more than twelve hundred smaller bits of bone and other possible human remains to Columbus Hospital in Great Falls, where Montana's only forensic pathologist, Dr. John Pfaff, worked.

It didn't take long.

Without a doubt, some of the remains were Sandra Smallegan's. The teeth and the piece of lower jawbone matched her dentist's recent X-rays. No cause of death could be determined from the mess, but clearly something unnatural had happened. Sandy had been murdered.

After that, things got murky.

Separately, Pfaff and the Smithsonian concluded some of the bone fragments came from animals, but most belonged to a human female . . . or two. The goopy material found in the burn pile was congealed melted fat and human entrails.

The bloodstains were human, blood type AB. Sandy's blood type wasn't known for sure, but the combination of her father's and mother's types made it very possible hers was AB.

The bone shards came from every part of a skeleton: the skull, spine, pelvis, ribs, arms, legs, toes, clavicles . . . everything except the hands and the pubic bone. Maybe those were in the pile of unidentifiable pieces, but it seemed so odd to Dunbar that a Smithsonian anthropologist specifically mentioned them in his notes as missing.

Part of the girl's left leg suggested she had been five feet to five foot four. The development of teeth and other bones indicated she had been eighteen to twenty-two years old. Both were a match for Sandy.

The condition of the burned bones suggested that the fire had burned below 1,000 degrees Fahrenheit, far cooler than a crematorium's minimum 1,800 degrees. Still, it was hot enough to incinerate most of the soft flesh, which must have been carved into chunks that probably no bigger than a rump roast. Some kind of accelerant, maybe gasoline, had been used.

"The fire must have been tended," the author of the Smithsonian's two-page report surmised, "and could hardly have been accidental."

The estimated time of death was between a few months and a year previous, long before Sandy disappeared.

So some of these bones belonged to somebody else. And close examination suggested they came from a girl between five and eight years old.

The experts' verdict was shocking: The collected bones came from at least two different females, one a young woman and the other a child. One killed recently, and one killed within the past year. They couldn't prove it beyond a reasonable doubt, but every little ghastly scrap pointed to one obvious conclusion.

"These remains may represent other missing persons," Dr. Pfaff wrote in his direct report to FBI Director Clarence M. Kelley. "One of these might be Susie Jaeger, reported missing on June 25, 1973, from a nearby area."

THIS WAS NO LONGER a simple missing-persons case.

Deputies were dispatched far and wide to chase down every lead . . . and there were more than they could count.

Folks freely called the sheriff's department with their "funny feelings" . . . the trailer park bachelor who skipped town mysteriously; the runaway tenant who left a lot of women's clothes behind; the teenager who was looking at Sandra kinda funny at the basketball game; a guy who borrowed an extension ladder from a friend that night; another guy who rented a floor scrubber from the hardware store the next morning; a onetime flasher who lived flamboyantly but had no job; a one-eyed, "very weird" short-order cook named Willie Pickle who abandoned his newlywed bride after four days and lit out for Missoula. The list of forebodings was long.

Somebody called anonymously about a strange-bird college kid in Bozeman who was failing all of his courses except photography and who was obsessed with police-scanner traffic. She'd heard from a friend of a friend that the cops found flashbulbs in the debris at the Lockhart Ranch, and that hammer marks on the barn were made by a lefty (which had been confirmed by crime-scene techs). This kid was left-handed, she said, and he took many pictures of old barns and country roads. Bozeman cops paid a visit, and although the young man was "a little queer," they found nothing to suggest he was a child molester or sex deviant—just an oddball shutterbug.

Somebody else reported seeing a strapping local fella named Steve Ronning spraying out the cab of his pickup and changing all its tires. Maybe not especially suspicious behavior—except that this guy's ex-wife now lived with Sandy's estranged husband, Jack Smallegan. Ronning swore to deputies that he didn't own a pickup, hadn't borrowed one recently, and hadn't even been in the area at the time. His story sounded vaguely truthful, but they made a note to check it out anyway.

Then there was the suspect for all seasons, David Meirhofer. Again, because he was a little odd, he inspired a lot of misgivings in a town where uniformity was prized. Characters were acceptable; oddballs were fishy. Meirhofer was socially awkward, had no real friends, never drank or smoked. In groups, he made himself invisible. This kid was hexed by his quirkiness. In a weird way, SA Dunbar felt both wary about and sorry for him. Either way, Dunbar's gut told him David wasn't a serious player in this tragedy.

As if the Smallegan case wasn't taxing enough, the cops were dragged in wild directions by unrelated misdeeds and calamities that demanded immediate attention. Burglars busted into the Cartwheel Supper Club. Vandals—probably kids—stole the mailbox from Pete Dyke's place up on Reese Creek. First-time skydiver Jim Ferguson's parachute malfunctioned, and he plunged three thousand feet to a messy death. And somebody—probably a power company lineman—knocked over a fence in the Kimms' yard.

Nevertheless, SA Dunbar and the Gallatin County Sheriff's Department compiled a list of their seven "top suspects" and started making arrangements to polygraph each of them in-house, just to cover all the bases.

At the top of their list, of course, was boyfriend Bob Harrison. His uneasiness and evasiveness in their initial interviews didn't sit right. And intriguing questions swirled around him. Detectives found his palm print on Sandy's front door; might it have been left when he forced his way in? His fingerprints were all over her vacuum cleaner—not especially implausible for a boyfriend who spent a lot of time there, but what if the vacuum had been used to clean up a crime scene? Harrison had also married a different girlfriend two months after Sandy disappeared; what if he needed to get rid of one to get the other? They wanted to know.

Jack Smallegan, Sandy's estranged husband, was up there, too. Philandering husbands, even estranged ones, were always going to catch a homicide detective's eye.

They tossed in a couple of suitors whose stories didn't quite add up, some known "sex deviants," and the operator of an industrial kiln out toward the Lockhart Ranch where a human body might have been cremated easily.

None of these "top suspects" were obviously guilty, but none of them were obviously innocent, either.

They focused first on Harrison. One of his uncles told deputies that Bob could have killed Sandy if he was high. Then he tanked his first polygraph exam by coming in drunk. The next day, the lie detector results were inconclusive; the sheriff's examiner—really, just a deputy with a couple weeks of training on a polygraph—determined he had lied on several questions. The examiner suggested Harrison should take a truth serum test at the state mental hospital in Warm Springs. Harrison agreed.

Five days later, Harrison called Dunbar to say he wouldn't do the sodium amytal in Warm Springs, after all. His wife and his buddies down at the bar didn't think it was a good idea. *I didn't do it*, he said, *and that's that*.

Dunbar told him that if he didn't submit to the test, nobody could be absolutely certain he hadn't hurt Sandy. If he was really innocent, the truth serum would remove all doubt (actually, the reliability of such questioning wasn't fully embraced by the medical, legal, or law enforcement worlds, which didn't trust truth serum tests as much as they did polygraphs).

Harrison never showed up in Warm Springs. The FBI could be as skeptical as it liked, but Harrison wasn't under arrest, and he didn't have to volunteer a damn thing.

JACK SMALLEGAN PASSED HIS polygraph test and was ruled out. So were most of the other "top suspects." The list was dwindling. Only two remained, and Dunbar's teletypes referred to both as "excellent suspects" because they weren't garden-variety freaks. They were much more.

One was a tough-guy railroader in Gallatin County who'd raped a woman several years back and was now on parole from a stretch in Deer Lodge. Back then, when cops came to his trailer to arrest him, he'd shot at them with a hunting rifle. While they were pinned down, waiting for backup, he threw his wife on the floor and raped her while firing indiscriminately (and gymnastically) out his window. When cops stormed the place and arrested him, they found several five-gallon cans of gasoline strategically stowed around the trailer. Later, he told them he intended to light it up, incinerating himself, his wife, and their kids if the cops got to him.

The other was a paroled child molester, also in Gallatin County, who'd raped a little girl. He kept hundreds of dolls in his house, most of them naked.

But SA Dunbar added one more, almost as an afterthought.

David Meirhofer wasn't one of those seven "top suspects," but his name kept popping up like a bad penny. A couple sources casually mentioned David Meirhofer to lawmen, for no better reason than his "oddness." Dunbar knew David's mother from high school, and he thought it unlikely her son was a killer. But part of his job was to rule out suspects.

David had no criminal record and had been candid, even helpful by suggesting new leads, every time he was questioned. There was no evidence against him in either the Jaeger or the Smallegan case. He'd refused to sit for a polygraph after Susie's disappearance last summer, but he'd said it was on principle.

Dunbar had done his homework. David never had many friends, but he worked hard and did good work. A childhood accident left a small scar on his chin, which made him self-conscious. He was a beloved son and brother, although he'd once plugged his younger brother, Alan, in the head with a BB gun. As a kid, he set fire to the family garage while playing with matches. In first grade, six-year-old David made a construction-paper Mother's Day card for Eleanor in which he hand-printed somebody else's sentiment: *Who ran to help me when I fell and would some pretty story tell or would kiss the place to make it well[?] My Mother.*

David's favorite movie was *The Sound of Music.* He loved to sing, even had a decent voice. For the forty-seventh birthday of his mother, Eleanor, in December 1973, he recorded himself singing the Broadway show tune "Mama, a Rainbow" and some of her favorite songs on a cassette tape. She called it the best gift anybody ever gave her.

He was also a Marine sergeant who had served in Vietnam. That counted for something in Dunbar's book. A doting son even in a combat zone, he wrote home regularly about camp life and homesickness. Once, on R & R, he ordered some fine china to be delivered to his mother, who prized it so much that she immediately declared it would be used only on special occasions.

78

Yeah, he was a quiet loner—albeit a bright, articulate, and well-groomed loner. Yeah, it had made some deputies leery when he showed up at the Lockhart Ranch at precisely the wrong moment. Yeah, he had had a brief fling with Sandy Smallegan that fizzled.

But none of those things was hard to explain in a small town, much less hard evidence of murder.

Dunbar wanted . . . something. Either a solid empirical reason to rule David Meirhofer out, once and for all, or a reason to keep digging.

So, a few days after Houghton and Skinner found Sandy's Cortina hidden at the Lockhart Ranch, Dunbar and his partner, SA Bill Terry, paid a visit to Meirhofer's carpentry workshop in Manhattan. It was a Saturday, but David didn't keep regular hours. He worked for himself, did anything that paid the bills, and stayed busy.

No introductions were necessary. Neither was small talk. David knew Pete. In fact, Pete had dated David's mother in high school. Small town. It was no secret.

David gladly led them on a tour of his spacious Main Street warehouse, which covered most of one block. He had bought it when he came home from the Marines to become a self-employed carpenter and sometime ranch hand. He needed a place to store his construction stuff. He renovated old houses and took occasional contracting work from the town council when he wasn't delivering farm machinery throughout the Mountain West for his father.

He kept the place tidy and well organized. The agents peeked in the back of his two-tone 1972 Jeep Gladiator and saw nothing. Assorted cuts of lumber were stacked along the walls, with various shop tools around. A friend rented one corner for his car-repair business; another rented a stall to store some personal junk. David had walled off the back end, where he rattled a padlocked door. He apologized profusely that he didn't have the key right now, but he'd bring it to the federal building later so they could see for themselves that it was a mostly empty room where he stowed some hand tools and building materials.

Dunbar and Terry examined it all closely, but David didn't mind. He didn't have anything to hide.

Dunbar spoke like an old friend. He told David that he was not under arrest and that he didn't have to answer any questions. David shrugged it off. He had nothing to hide. Dunbar asked him to sign the FBI's standard release anyway and David obliged. *Just a formality.*

Dunbar reminded David that he'd been questioned about Susie Jaeger last summer, and he wondered if David had learned anything more in the eight months since.

David was offended that Dunbar would even ask. His word was his bond, he said, and he said he resented being "constantly harassed" by the cops about Susie Jaeger.

Dunbar reminded David that he'd refused to take a polygraph examination back then, leaving things murky. If he'd take one now, it might prove he was telling the truth.

David shook his head.

Then Dunbar asked about Sandy Smallegan. Again, David admitted he'd dated her one time—before Christmas, a few months back—and the would-be relationship never got off the ground. And again, David denied knowing anything about Sandy's disappearance . . . or any other crime, for that matter. He hated what had happened to Sandy, but he and she had truly been two ships passing in the night. He hadn't talked to her in more than a month, although he'd frequently seen her down at the bowling alley.

SA Terry noted that David showed no sign of anxiety or evasiveness on the subject. He wasn't hesitant or reluctant to talk about

Sandy at all. If he knew *anything*, no hint showed on his face or in his voice.

So take the polygraph, Terry suggested. *Let us take you off the list.*

Exasperated, David finally agreed. He wanted these feds to stop coming around, and taking their damn test was the only way to get them to stop. He brusquely signed all their bullshit federal forms, acknowledging that he knew he could end the interview and walk around at any time, and permitting the polygraph . . . everything they wanted. He had nothing to hide, he repeated.

Now the agents were in a pickle. With a couple of strong, intriguing possibilities in a dwindling pool of suspects, Dunbar wanted someone more skillful than the sheriff's part-time polygrapher, but there was no FBI examiner in Montana, Utah, or Idaho. The nearest was in Denver, and there was no guarantee that the Bureau would send him seven hundred miles on what was essentially a fishing expedition.

That night, Dunbar sent an urgent teletype to Quantico, laying out his case and asking—begging, really—for an FBI polygrapher to be sent as soon as possible. The cases of Susie Jaeger and Sandy Smallegan now seemed related and were getting a lot of media attention, he said, knowing that might be his most effective argument to the beleaguered Bureau, which was mired in Watergate and needed some good news.

Director Clarence M. Kelley himself approved Dunbar's request. Three days later—February 20, 1974—an FBI polygrapher from Denver was setting up his machines in a conference room at the Bozeman federal building. Dunbar sat in, just to ask questions before and after the examiner questioned his three best suspects, although none was especially good.

First came the Doll Collector. He was timid and panicky, even childlike. After being read his rights, he immediately said he was so distraught about losing his job that he had been awake all night.

His agitation was so profound that the polygrapher stopped the exam after just a few questions. Unless there was some pernicious psychopathy, the examiner believed the Doll Collector had no personal knowledge of either crime. The examiner suggested to Dunbar that the guy be sent home and not questioned further unless the investigation found new evidence against him. It probably wasn't him.

Then came the Would-be Incinerator. He was a different kind of mess. He denied being ill (except for chronic ulcers) or on any medication, but he trembled so badly that an agent got him a cup of hot cocoa. He had also slept fitfully the night before, he said, because he was anxious about missing his seven thirty appointment.

The Would-be Incinerator admitted he was an alcoholic who had loved his whiskey until the ulcers started. Sometimes he lost track of time, he said. After the police standoff, his wife took the kids and moved away, and he hadn't worked much since his parole. He said he had trouble remembering things, although his responses seemed to be graphing normally.

The test began. *Yes,* he liked the great outdoors. *Yes,* his wife's reports of his bizarre sexual habits were true. *Yes,* he liked to inflict pain on women while fucking them. *No,* he didn't date but he "gets taken care of." *No,* he'd probably never get married again, because women were nags. *No,* he didn't know how those girls were killed. *No,* he wouldn't talk about tying women up with ropes.

He expressed sympathy for any children who might have been killed, but when asked about Sandy Smallegan, he had a strange answer: "She should be able to take care of herself, right?"

Then the polygrapher asked how Sandy's corpse might have been burned so thoroughly. He responded that he'd already thought about that and he couldn't imagine how any normal trash fire could burn hot enough to consume a whole human body—even though he'd planned to use gasoline to incinerate his entire family.

Several times he seemed to want to confide in Dunbar, but he stopped just short. He was hiding *something*, Dunbar thought, but none of his answers suggested guilt. It probably wasn't him, either.

David Meirhofer came last.

Dunbar read him his rights, which by now he'd heard a half dozen times. David read them back to Dunbar out loud—*You're not under arrest and you don't have to answer any questions . . . etc.*—then signed the waiver. He just wanted to clear his good name.

Early on, most of the questions centered on Sandy Smallegan. A few of his responses caused the polygraph needle to jump a little, but not enough to alarm the examiner.

Did you have anything to do with the death of Sandra Smallegan? "I've been thinking that maybe she isn't really dead."

Do you have any idea how she died? "I'm thinking her husband was with her until the night she was missed. He might have done this. He's the type who could do it, but that's just me. He coulda been with her at the ranch."

Where were you on the night of February 9, 1974? "I was home alone. Well, I own two houses, but I only live in one."

How old are you? "Twenty-five. No, wait, twenty-four."

Have you ever been in trouble with the law? "When I was a kid, I tried to beat up a boy who was younger than me. It was just kid stuff. But I don't really remember what it was about."

Have you knowingly broken any laws? "No."

Have you ever tried to hurt anybody? "No. But maybe I slapped my mother a couple times."

Do you have a driver's license? "Yes. No, wait. It's a chauffeur's license."

David glossed over several critical questions. Maybe he just didn't know the answers or was confused; the machine didn't detect any agitation or lies. He didn't sweat, squirm, or avert his eyes. *Nonchalant,* Dunbar thought.

Have you answered all of these questions truthfully? "Yes. Except the one about breaking laws. I'm wearing socks I took from the Marine Corps when I was in the service. Maybe it's illegal for me to wear them. I dunno. But that's all."

When the polygrapher was done, Dunbar followed up with a few questions of his own. David answered calmly.

"I know certain people around town think I'm an 'oddball' because I want to wait until after I'm married to have sex," he said. "And I like little kids but I'm no pervert."

That was it. Dunbar thanked David for coming, then showed him out.

Back in the conference room, the FBI polygrapher reported that David's alibis were solid: According to the lie detector, he'd truthfully accounted for his whereabouts during and after both disappearances.

"None of the questions caused him any real difficulty," he told Dunbar. "Unless he's got some kind of pathological condition that would affect his reactions, I think he has no personal knowledge of either Susie's or Sandra's case. He showed no evidence whatsoever of guilt."

Three strikes. David Meirhofer probably wasn't the UnSub, either. Twice he'd popped up on Dunbar's radar, and twice he'd been dismissed as a harmless casualty of uncharitable neighbors.

And just like that, Dunbar was back to square one. Literally dozens of potential suspects had been ruled out, and his bucket was empty. Sandra Smallegan's and Susie Jaeger's fates now seemed entangled, but all Dunbar had were charred and pulverized bones, a stolen car, and a hellish nightmare scenario. Nine months after Susie vanished, he'd hit a brick wall.

No suspects.

No good leads.

No murder weapons.

No confessions.

No witnesses.

No frigging idea who had killed two girls and had so far gotten away with two of the grisliest murders of his career.

THE REVEREND ROGER HILL, the Three Forks Baptist preacher who'd married Sandy Dykman to Jack Smallegan less than two years earlier, officiated at the bride's memorial service on March 4, two weeks after her shattered bones were found at the Lockhart Ranch.

Reverend Hill's own church was too small for the expected crowd of mourners, so the service was moved to the big white Christian Reformed church in Amsterdam, the Dutch farming community where Sandy's ancestors had settled long ago. Every Saturday night and Sunday morning, a sexton rang a big bell to remind distant farmers that the Sabbath was at hand, when the church's massive pipe organ could be heard a mile away. But more important, it could seat six hundred congregants, and every pew was filled.

No part of Sandy was present at her memorial. Those bits were still being cataloged as evidence of a hideous crime. There'd be no burial for now. Maybe ever.

But Sandy's spirit filled the sanctuary. Her family and friends were there, of course, and many grieving, frightened townspeople. Her estranged husband, Jack Smallegan, sat in the balcony, apart from Sandy's family, a simple man's act of grace. When it was over, he blended into the crowd of mourners leaving the church, trying hard to be invisible.

A few of Sandy's recent beaus were scattered in the crowd, like Bob Harrison and David Meirhofer, who quietly took a seat in the back. Meirhofer seemed to have been especially shaken by the news of Sandy's murder. A few days after the cops confirmed she'd been minced and cremated, he commiserated with Jack Smallegan over breakfast at the diner. "Who could have done such a thing?" he asked Jack, sounding faintly more accusatory than curious.

At the front of the church sat many of the weary cops who'd been chasing ghosts nearly all day and all night for weeks. Despite their exhaustion, they had asked if they could attend the memorial, so Reverend Hill reserved one pew especially for Agent Pete Dunbar, Sheriff Andy Anderson, and several local lawmen, including Deputy Don Houghton, who struggled to stay composed.

Reverend Hill was a close friend of the Dykmans. He'd visited every day since Sandy's disappearance had become more than a case of a runaway teenager. Other family and friends had sat with them night and day, too. They were never alone.

When Sandy's dentist confirmed the remains were hers, Sheriff Anderson called Reverend Hill to ask if he would be there when Andy delivered the sad news to John and Betty. Reverend Hill met Andy outside the Dykmans' little house, and the sheriff bluntly described what they'd found. The pastor went back inside and led Sandy's parents into the front yard, where they heard what they could never unhear. Then they all went back inside to tell the friends and family who'd gathered that day.

Now he stood before all of them, trying to find the right words.

He began with Psalm 46. *"God is our refuge and strength, an ever-present help in trouble. Therefore we will not fear, though the earth give way and the mountains fall into the heart of the sea. . . ."*

Then, after a hymn and a brief reading of Sandy's obituary, Reverend Hill spoke from his own heart.

"When one is asked to go down into the depths of sorrow, where do we find the strength?" he asked the silent mourners before him. Not in whys and what-ifs, he said. Unbearable burdens and unacceptable answers required faith and friends. The Dykmans had them both.

"There have been difficult days and there will be difficult days ahead for John and Betty and their family," he said. However, he hoped none would be as difficult as the day they knew, for sure, that Sandy was dead.

The entire memorial wasn't long. Nobody truly knew what to say to take away the sorrow, not even the preacher.

Reverend Hill closed with Isaiah: *"When thou passeth through the waters, I will be with thee. . . ."*

But in his typed notes, he crossed out the rest of the passage, and left it unsaid: *". . . when thou walkest through the fire, thou shalt not be burned."*

OTHER CASES SPRANG UP for Pete Dunbar. Local cops went back to their usual beats. Tips slowed to a trickle. The Jaegers still desperately awaited a phone call with good news, but no such calls ever came, and they had to resume their fractured lives, too. Sandy's and Susie's cases hadn't gone cold, but their fat folders were moved to a different corner of his desk. And the habitual petty frictions between local law enforcement and the FBI, which had been set aside early in the Jaeger case, now resumed.

After working pretty much around the clock since the previous summer, Dunbar needed a break. He'd ducked some overdue FBI refresher courses in Quantico during the height of the search for Susie, but now that the hunt was simmering down, he couldn't stiff-arm his SAC in Butte any longer.

And maybe a breather back East would help him get his head straight.

CHAPTER 4

WOUNDED MINDS

APRIL 1974

QUANTICO, VIRGINIA

The thaw came early that year.

The new FBI Training Academy, a relatively recent idea of the Bureau's brass, was in a single small building nestled in a few hundred acres of woodland inside the US Marine Corps' massive and historic base in Quantico.

A pet project of J. Edgar Hoover himself, it trained cops from all over the world—oddly, training actual FBI agents was a lower priority. Its faculty was a small cadre of seasoned agents with special talents—urban policing, criminal behavior, firearms, sociology, management, psychology. . . . One guy even imagined that computers might someday help fight crime. They recruited the best and brightest among the Bureau's far-flung agents and charged them with teaching what they knew.

Among those teachers were Patrick Mullany, a former New York field agent with degrees in psychology and human behavior, and

Howard Teten, a cerebral ex–beat cop who'd joined the FBI and was fascinated with why certain criminals committed certain crimes. They shared a cubby at the Academy and something else: Neither of them had been homicide detectives.

Mullany had become a Christian Brothers monk straight out of high school. Eventually, he taught in Catholic schools during the academic year and spent summers tutoring juvenile delinquents in the order's Lincoln Hall Reformatory and La Salle Reformatory in upstate New York. What should have been very different institutions were disturbingly similar for the young Mullany, who was pursuing a master's degree in psychology at the time. In both, he saw the same kind of throwaway kids. Some would be tomorrow's criminals, he knew. A new theory had just popped up in forensic psychology, that psychotic killers tended to share a "triad" of childhood markers: bed-wetting, playing with fire, and cruelty to animals. That description fit many of his kids perfectly.

He left the order in 1965, unsure whether the monastic life was right—or enough—for him. He toyed with the idea of teaching in secular schools but instead took a path that veered radically from the ascetic, an abrupt transition he described as "monk to madness." He joined the Federal Bureau of Investigation.

Hoover's men sent him to Florida, Los Angeles, and New York City, where he saw psychology made flesh.

At the height of the Vietnam War and the sometimes violent protests against it, newly minted Special Agent Pat Mullany monitored every significant demonstration across America, dissecting the mindsets of both the agitators and their militant throngs. In 1970, Mullany crashed through the locked rectory door of a Catholic church in Manhattan (the *other* Manhattan) and arrested the fugitive anti-war priest Philip Berrigan, who'd appeared on both the cover of *Time* magazine and the FBI's Most Wanted list. Because he was still a devout Catholic himself, it disturbed Mullany to hand-cuff a priest, but he had a job to do.

In 1972, Mullany was transferred to the FBI's training academy—which existed not as a facility but only as an idea at the time—in Quantico, Virginia. When it finally opened, Mullany and Teten were both assigned to the first faculty of the new training division.

Teten was a Nebraska kid, a former Marine whose street smarts and crime-scene expertise would make him one of the Bureau's shrewdest criminologists. Some agents retched at brutal murder scenes, but Teten was inured to them. Being buried in crime scenes eight hours a day had made him less sensitive to the gore, more attuned to the evidence.

He'd joined the FBI in 1962. After bouncing around between field offices in Oklahoma and Ohio, he landed in Memphis, where he earned a master's degree in social psychology. In 1968, he was the first FBI agent on the bloody balcony of the Lorraine Motel where Martin Luther King Jr.'s body lay.

Before the new academy opened, Teten's day job was teaching management at the FBI's Washington headquarters. It wasn't his strength, so off the clock, he immersed himself in research about criminals' minds and their methods.

Separately, Mullany lectured on criminal psychology, and Teten taught a three-hour seminar about the relationships between crime scenes and offender characteristics. Even then, Teten genuinely believed a good, observant detective could know exactly the kind of perpetrator he was hunting by what he could see at the crime scene.

After class, Teten's agent-students often came to him with their most vexing unsolved cases, and he'd spend hours poring over their autopsies and crime-scene photos. But he paid special attention to the initial police interviews, which contained the best human observations. Sometimes he walked down the hall and asked what his new friend Pat Mullany thought.

They shared a keen interest in criminal behavior—they both asked not just "Whodunit?" but "Why?" But they were two very different guys.

Mullany saw crime scenes from a higher altitude, and he tended to be more absorbed in human motives. Teten wanted to be up close, where he could see the tiniest, most telling details. Mullany believed abnormal behavior was rooted in unresolved sexual issues; Teten saw clues in body types. Mullany was philosophical; Teten was more cynical. Mullany knew heads; Teten knew hearts.

They agreed on one overarching idea: Certain patterns of behavior appeared to be related to certain types of crimes.

People kill the way they live . . . and they live the way they kill. Behavior reflects personality.

Teten had a brainstorm: What if they teamed up and taught a course in which Teten would present the physical characteristics of both the crime scene and the criminal, and then Mullany would explore what psychological disorders were most likely indicated? They believed it was possible to pry into the mind of an unknown criminal through often inconspicuous clues he left at the crime scene.

In short, Teten and Mullany—or, as they became affectionately known inside the Academy, "Frick" and "Frack"—believed it was possible to work "backward" from a messy crime scene.

Their ultimate team-teaching goal was to help investigators develop a portrait of an unknown offender by sorting through the clues gathered from crime scenes, witness interviews, and victims. This portrait would be painted with psychological peculiarities like personality markers, behavioral habits, and psychopathologies. But it would also include demographic traits like race, location, age, and occupation. All told, investigators could use this "profile" to narrow their pool of suspects or inform the best way to interrogate suspects.

After class, Teten and Mullany continued to hear individual investigators' most vexing cases, which constantly expanded their understanding of what was going through perpetrators' minds. The agents often went back to their posts with new hints about whom they were hunting.

Nobody had ever methodically studied the entanglement of psychology and crime, but both Mullany and Teten believed that knowing what motivated an UnSub could be useful for boots-on-the-ground detectives. *Imagine a reverse engineering of crime,* they said, *in which physical evidence could give a cop insight into a criminal's psychology.*

In the earliest days, it was more art than science, to be sure. A general gesture in the right direction, not a precise road map. It involved some educated guesswork and a little low-hanging fruit. There were no rules. The field was wide open.

Very soon, Mullany and Teten's seminar became one of the Academy's most popular courses and a new name was attached: Psychological Profiling.

The fancy label might have been new, but the roots of criminal profiling were a hundred years deep, although not exceedingly wide.

In the 1880s, two London doctors, George Phillips and Thomas Bond, analyzed Jack the Ripper's bloody work for traces of his personality, believing doing so would eventually lead to his unmasking. It didn't.

Over the next sixty years, various psychology experts occasionally weighed in on criminal minds with limited success.

In 1932, Dr. Dudley Schoenfeld, chief psychiatrist at New York's Mount Sinai Hospital, analyzed ransom notes in the famous Lindbergh baby abduction. He told police the kidnapper was an antisocial loner who was disgruntled by his station in life. When Bruno Richard Hauptmann was eventually arrested, the Bronx carpenter proved to be a happily married family man with many friends. Ultimately, Schoenfeld's psychological portrait played no significant role in solving the crime.

In 1943, a Boston psychoanalyst named Dr. Walter Langer pored over reports about Adolf Hitler and Hitler's own writings. Using techniques he learned from Sigmund Freud himself, Langer prepared a dossier for American intelligence officers, sketching the murderous Nazi dictator as "a neurotic psychopath bordering on schizophrenia." He delved into the Fuehrer's troubled childhood, his depression, and his fascination with pornography, masochism, and sexual perversions. He summarized Hitler as a weakling pretending to be a superman.

There were two Hitlers "that inhabit the same body," Langer wrote. "One is a very soft, sentimental and indecisive individual who has very little drive and wants nothing quite so much as to be amused, liked and looked after. The other is just the opposite—a hard, cruel and decisive person with considerable energy—who seems to know what he wants and is ready to go after it and get it regardless of cost."

Langer also forecast how Hitler would respond to various developments, including a rout of his Third Reich.

"As Germany suffers successive defeats," Langer predicted, "Hitler will become more and more neurotic." Rather than accept his defeat, the psychiatrist said, he would commit suicide—which he did on April 30, 1945, as the Soviets advanced on Berlin.

He was right, but his was a profile in reverse: The perpetrator was known and his crimes were the mystery.

In 1940, a serial bomber began terrorizing New York City by planting pipe bombs in crowded spots like Radio City Music Hall,

Penn Station, the New York Public Library, and the subway. For sixteen years, "the Mad Bomber" eluded police while detonating twenty-two of his crude devices (another eleven never exploded) in unpredictable places at unexpected moments. Fifteen people were injured but, against the odds, none were killed.

Cops were flummoxed. Old-fashioned street-beating investigation wasn't working. So in 1956 they turned in desperation to an unlikely resource: a psychiatrist named James Brussel, who worked in New York City's Department of Mental Hygiene.

To assemble a psychological portrait of the Mad Bomber, Brussel analyzed the taunting notes the bomber sent to the New York Police Department—mostly railing against the city's electric company, Consolidated Edison, and always signed "F.P."—crime-scene photos, and details of the explosions.

These clues led Brussel to conclude the bomber was unmarried, foreign, clean-shaven and tidy, prompt and polite. He'd wear no jewelry. He was probably a virgin, probably Catholic, self-educated, in his fifties, resentful of authority, a resident of Connecticut, unhealthily sexually fixated on his mother, and contemptuous of his father. He likely had heart problems and was unemployed or held colossal workplace grudges, with a twisted sense of right and wrong. Brussel expected him to live with an older female relative and be a wound collector with a vendetta against Con Edison.

Oh, and one more thing, Brussel told the cops: When you finally find him, he'll be wearing a double-breasted suit, perfectly buttoned.

What the hell? How could he know all that from looking at some pictures and reading some notes? The detectives were dubious, to say the least.

Dr. Brussel explained.

The Mad Bomber was clearly a classic paranoid schizophrenic

who couldn't simply move on from any slight. As such, he obsessed about every discourtesy, wrong, and snub.

Studies had found most paranoiacs' symptoms peaked in their mid-thirties. So, if the first bombing was in 1940, he'd be at least in his mid-forties, probably older.

Studies also found that paranoid schizophrenics tended to be athletically built with proportional body frames. Brussel was merely going with the odds.

The bomb maker's letters to police were impeccably written in perfect block letters, featuring excellent spelling, some uncommon words such as "treachery" and "injustice," no slang, no smudging, and no erasures—as if conceived in one language, then translated carefully into English. Judging by the subtle idiosyncrasies of his handwriting, his first language was probably Germanic. This all suggested he was a tidy and precise man, Brussel surmised, who was fastidious in his grooming, dress, and habits until he was triggered by something that caused him to lash out. And the source of his anger seemed to be Con Edison, which might even be his employer.

Because his exceedingly beloved mother (as Brussel surmised) was already taken by his father, he hated his dad. He projected his hatred in ever-widening concentric circles: father, boss, company, politicians, and finally, massive corporations that held power over his daily life—like the electric company.

His perverse affection for his mother made him a loner, without friends, and certainly without a girlfriend or spouse. He mightn't even like women in general, because they weren't his mother. Brussel mused that the bomber might never have even kissed a girl. And he probably lived with an older woman—likely a relative in the close-knit Slavic community—who reminded him of his mother.

The bomber often used sharp knives to cut into the places where he hid his bombs. Separately, bombs and knives were most preferred in central European cultures. The use of both at the same time indicated he was likely Slavic.

If Slavic, then likely Roman Catholic, which was the predominant faith in central Europe. His compulsions to right what was wrong with the world probably made him a religious zealot, too, Brussel said. His relationship with God elevated him (in his own mind) to the status of an avenging angel who punished lesser beings. So he wouldn't get along with coworkers or work with an accomplice. To him, they were all untrustworthy, conniving idiots.

Most of his letters were mailed from White Plains, New York, just north of the city. Brussel deduced that the bomber, to disguise his true location, would have chosen a convenient place between his home and Manhattan. That pointed to Connecticut, where a thriving community of Slavic immigrants had settled.

In one early letter written to a local newspaper, the bomber referred to having an illness. Brussel said it was unlikely to be cancer or tuberculosis, which would have probably killed him by now; a heart condition was more likely.

With these points in mind, the cops started a new investigation at Con Edison, where a search of its "troublesome employee" files turned up one that contained the word "injustice." It was on a former laborer who'd been laid off in 1934 after being "gassed" by a boiler explosion, injuring his lungs. His name was George Metesky, and after his appeal was denied, he wrote several letters to his old boss, promising to "take justice into my own hands."

The investigation ramped up quickly.

Metesky, son of a Lithuanian immigrant, lived in a poor neighborhood in Waterbury, Connecticut, in his shabby childhood home with his unmarried sisters. Even at fifty-three years old, he had no criminal record at all, not even a parking ticket. Neighbors described him as a seriously ill loner, a little crazy. Neighbor kids avoided the "crazy house," where a wild-eyed Metesky had once angrily confronted some of them as "spies."

They reported that they often heard Metesky banging loudly in his closed garage, like he was building something, but they never saw any of his projects.

One former coworker told detectives that Metesky was an irritable, odd guy who wrote nasty letters about him to the boss.

And Metesky had been rejected from service during World War II when an X-ray revealed chronic lung problems, probably from the Con Edison explosion. He went ballistic and wrote more angry letters, to President Roosevelt among others.

Metesky fit Brussel's "profile" perfectly.

The cops moved in. At midnight on a January night in 1957, they knocked at the ramshackle door of the Waterbury house.

George Metesky, a slightly thickened middle-aged fellow, answered. He let them into the house, which looked to be neatly kept, certainly not like the outside. A painting of Jesus hung in the hall. They looked around while Metesky excused himself to change out of his pajamas in his room. They found some notebooks with familiar block lettering.

When Metesky emerged, he was wearing brown Oxfords, a necktie, a cardigan that matched his shoes, and a blue double-breasted suit, properly buttoned. He surrendered meekly.

When asked what the initials "F.P." stood for, Metesky answered, "Fair Play."

Dr. Brussel had called it almost perfectly. George Metesky was arrested as New York City's Mad Bomber. He was committed to an insane asylum until he was seventy, when he moved back into his drab Waterbury house, where he died twenty years later.

Brussel had plowed new ground. His methods offered clues and insights, although they seldom, if ever, actually slapped the cuffs on a perp after the Mad Bomber. Despite the success of that case, the police never fully embraced Dr. Brussel's voodoo. They occasionally called upon psychiatrists and other experts on the criminal mind when they needed special help with a baffling case—such as the Boston Strangler case in 1964—but there was always pushback from old-school, tough-guy investigators who believed Sherlockian deduction, forceful tactics, and shoe leather solved crimes, not psychological hocus-pocus.

So profiling died shortly after its birth.

IN 1974, JUST TWO years after the FBI Academy opened, Mullany and Teten were up to their elbows in bizarre cases. They were wading around in the blood let by freakish psychopaths like Ed Kemper, a family-killing necrophiliac who screwed the severed heads of his victims and slept with their bodies. Each case added to their understanding of criminal minds, but more and more research and interviewing criminals meant less and less time for helping fellow agents and local cops.

The two agents had started to see a direct link between specific mental disorders and certain crimes: A true psychopath could commit any crime at any time and possessed a bottomless appetite for violence; a paranoiac tended to act alone and had an assassin's bent; manic-depressives gravitated toward murder-suicides; and simple schizophrenics were inclined to linger with their corpses, sometimes literally and figuratively burrowing into them. Nothing was set in stone, but the penchants were real.

Truth be told, Mullany and Teten had very little scientific data about criminal minds. Most of their assumptions were based on their own cop work, gut feelings, and educated guesswork. Some

FBI higher-ups backed their research, but Director J. Edgar Hoover thought what they were doing was hokum, so they were kept on a short leash, operating quietly. They'd occasionally drop in at San Quentin or Sing Sing to chat with killers and rapists, never really seeking official approval that might never come. It was better to ask forgiveness than permission.

While they had offered a lot of good advice to cops about what their UnSubs might be like, they'd never actually constructed a profile that helped investigators arrest a killer. First of all, it wasn't the purpose of their work to magically identify murderers by name. Second, while their research was leading them to compile more information about forensic psychology than anyone else, they weren't seeing a direct correlation between their work and solving crimes. They wanted more of a system, and profiling wasn't lending itself to a system. A certain proportion of agents was resistant to this new "headshrinker" approach, so Teten and Mullany knew they risked banjaxing the whole enterprise if they crashed and burned.

Yet the torrent of exasperated detectives never stopped. In April 1974, yet another one walked through Pat Mullany's door, wearing cowboy boots.

FBI Special Agent Pete Dunbar, a field agent on the frayed edge of civilization—otherwise known as Montana—had fidgeted through a daylong criminal psychology seminar, constantly superimposing what he was hearing on the cases of Susie Jaeger and Sandra Smallegan.

When the class ended, he didn't wait for an invitation. He followed Mullany to his puny office and soon spilled his grim story all over the profiler's neat little desk. He hadn't brought his case file to Quantico, but enough filled Dunbar's head to arouse Mullany's interest.

One problem: Dunbar's case, in reality, involved only two

kidnappings, and they weren't clearly related. They involved dissimilar victims abducted in very different ways. Smallegan was certainly dead; Susie was likely dead, too. The trails had gone cold, and the investigations stalled. No autopsies, no suspects, no leads—only the forensic presumption that the bones at the Lockhart Ranch belonged to both Susie Jaeger and Sandra Smallegan, and their intermingling suggested the same kidnapper, who was probably a killer, too.

The presence of Sandy's car at the ranch could have been just a coincidence.

Or not.

Mullany didn't believe in coincidence. He believed Dunbar was on the right track. He had a gut feeling both girls were dead. But gut feelings were crap. He had to be able to connect real dots. He had to see hard evidence.

When Mullany shared Dunbar's perplexing case with Teten later that night, Teten was more skeptical. It wasn't a particularly unusual case, and with dozens of more pressing and solvable mass murders—they had tossed around a potential new term, "serial killings"—he was lukewarm.

That changed when Dunbar went home to Bozeman, collected his entire case file in a box, and sent it to Quantico. Photographs, interviews, forensic reports from the Lockhart place, long lists of evidence, even the transcript of the ransom call—it was there in all its violent colors.

Sorting through all the paperwork, Mullany and Teten were disappointed by the unprofessional reports from untrained or poorly trained deputies. Photos were of questionable quality. And Dunbar had no conspicuous suspects, no existing leads, not even hunches. It was obvious to them why the agent was disheartened.

But there was something intriguing about these crimes, something they hadn't seen before: a kidnapper who had taken both a seven-year-old girl and a nineteen-year-old woman, one victim chosen seemingly at random, the other specifically targeted. What if he had killed them both, cremated and pulverized them, then scattered their bones to the wind? How had he eluded attention in such a sparsely populated place, especially with cops crawling all over the county?

Could this man—and he was most certainly a man—add to what they already knew about criminal psychology?

Moreover, could this be the first active FBI case to test whether criminal profiling was useful, maybe even valuable?

Yeah, it was.

Just like that, SA Pete Dunbar's case became the top priority for the only two guys in the Bureau who might know more about Susie and Sandy's killer than any cop on the ground two thousand miles west of Quantico, Virginia.

EVEN BEFORE THEY'D BURROWED to the bottom of Dunbar's box, Mullany and Teten had a broad-brush picture of the UnSub, based on the circumstances of the abductions and the victimology. They focused mostly on Susie's abduction. It had the most crime-scene information, and it was no ordinary kidnapping.

They were handicapped by a lack of hard evidence. All they had was a slit tent in a campground with plenty of other campers close by, and a faint trail in the dewy grass. No body, no weapon, no witnesses, no blood.

They started with a central, if imperfect, premise: An adult male boldly snatched a child without inflicting any serious injury and took her to a secret location, and she couldn't be found.

Most crime scenes yielded a lot of information about the perpetrators. But not this one. Every element of their profile must be based on those scant facts, and maybe a little intuition.

As a starting point, Teten and Mullany presumed the UnSub to be a subtle combination of simple schizophrenia and sadistic psychopathy, probably with some kind of sexual component, almost certainly a mother or father issue. Their profile unfolded from there, starting on a disheartening note:

Susie was probably dead within two days. After the "golden hour"—one hour after a disappearance—the likelihood of death becomes exponentially higher. Considering the likelihood that Susie's bone shards had been found at the Lockhart Ranch last February, it was not a question of *whether* she'd been murdered, but *when*.

The UnSub was probably a white male in his mid- to late twenties. His race was a low-risk deduction: Gallatin County was almost exclusively white. And the psychotic killers Teten and Mullany studied—murderous shoe fetishist Jerry Brudos, homosexual sadist Dean Corll, psychotic visionary Herb Mullin, and cannibal necrophile Ed Kemper, among others—had mostly started their killings in their twenties and early thirties.

He was at least modestly intelligent. Susie's kidnapping showed a highly organized thinker who anticipated every investigative move. There was a remarkable level of planning and organization. The UnSub took her to another location, instead of dumping her, which would have been easier. He had a stronger, more developed fantasy. He brought a knife and was able to move around in the dark. He drove an inconspicuous vehicle and knew exactly where to park—far enough to be unsuspected but close enough for a quick getaway. Even worse for Dunbar and other investigators, the UnSub had already picked a place to take her with almost no chance of discovery.

He was a loner, unmarried, and probably had little experience with women—and when he did, it didn't last. In fact, his whole history of heterosexual relationships would be defective. They presumed he was such a sophisticated psychopath that he'd never trust anyone long enough to have a long-term or married relationship. Sure, married perps have twists and kinks, too, but it was a good chance this UnSub wouldn't be interested in a real marriage. But Teten and Mullany didn't have enough evidence to know for sure; it was just an educated guess.

He had military experience. There were three other children in Susie Jaeger's tent. Her parents were in a trailer a few feet away. Other tourists camped nearby. This abduction had required extraordinary stealth, patient reconnaissance, and boldness under cover of darkness. He had to be fit enough to carry a struggling fifty-pound child as he ran through a dark park, keeping her quiet the whole time. Mullany felt strongly he would be more like a combat veteran than a Peeping Tom. Besides all that, if he was as young as they thought— draftable during the ongoing Vietnam War—the odds that he had served in the military were good.

He'd thrive in solitary jobs where he needn't interact with other workers. Everybody has three different lives: professional, personal, and secret. Deeply disturbed criminals work hardest to protect their secret lives. The UnSub would have been most vulnerable among coworkers and bosses who'd constantly watch him, possibly detecting clues about his deepest, darkest secrets. So he'd avoid that kind of exposure by working alone.

He had likely stumbled on the tent in the campground where Susie Jaeger was snatched. But he quickly began planning his next move, probably savoring the risks it might require.

He lived in the area. In fact, he was well-known to local folks but regarded as odd. The UnSub had to know the park's layout and the places he could hide Susie. His boldness suggested he didn't fear getting caught by local law enforcement, whom he knew well enough to regard as Keystone Kops. An outsider wouldn't have been so confident. Also, the possibility that Sandra Smallegan's disappearance almost eight months later was related made them think the UnSub didn't look like a stranger to locals who thought they knew everybody. Confidence in his own invisibility might cause mistakes. Arrogance would ultimately be his worst enemy, the profilers told Dunbar.

Socially, the UnSub was *friendly but never truly companionable.* While not genuinely aloof, he wouldn't inject himself unnecessarily into any social situation. He'd float around the edges of any group. He probably didn't even realize that people considered him odd.

The deeper they dug into Dunbar's box, the more complicated their UnSub became. Mullany and Teten talked endlessly about him, and they even brought in a fledgling agent named Robert Ressler as an apprentice in their nascent undertaking. They schlepped the case file around to other agents in Quantico, and called Dunbar at all hours of the day with enigmatic questions that seemed, to him, to create new mysteries where there were none. The more questions they asked, the more they sensed he was starting to question whether this "profiling" thing was meaningful crime fighting or just concocted bunk.

They weren't sure themselves. Yeah, Dr. Brussel had hit the bull's-eye on George Metesky twenty years before, but nobody had succeeded so spectacularly since then, or even tried. They were in uncharted territory, and failure in this case could unravel their grand experiment entirely with their bosses. Hoover's ghost would win.

Dunbar's discomfort wasn't unexpected. Even though he'd sought their help, his trust remained in conventional police work—

just like with Brussel and the NYPD. At least Dunbar was open to the potential of profiling as a crime-solving tool, although he seemed to be questioning it now.

Teten and Mullany couldn't look back. They couldn't afford to fail. Their only option was to forge ahead as if they'd done a million criminal profiles—instead of never having done one before.

The profile in Susie Jaeger's case needed to be more robust, they decided. And their work had to be fast.

Over the next few weeks, they bored deeper into a mind that existed only in *their* minds.

And what they found—or imagined—was disturbing.

The UnSub had probably killed before. The snatching of Susie Jaeger was too sophisticated, too flawless, for a skittish beginner. He wasn't experimenting. And when he killed, it was to maintain his control, superiority, and dominance.

His mother was domineering, and his father was absent or unknown. Ed Kemper—who shot his grandparents and later slaughtered his own mother, decapitating her, cutting off her hands, and stuffing her dismembered larynx down her sink's garbage disposal— was their aptest model. He'd made them believe that every psychopath was damaged by one or both of his parents in some way, whether by abuse, abandonment, or, oddly, too much affection. Such a psychopath's victims were often vulnerable, innocent, accessible surrogates for the person he really wanted to kill: Mom or Dad . . . or both.

He was fascinated with body parts. It was becoming increasingly common for psychotic killers, such as Kemper, to retain pieces of their victims. In fact, Teten and Mullany told a skeptical Dunbar, if the UnSub was ever arrested, investigators would likely find ugly "souvenirs" he had taken from his corpses. Why? Again, it was about his need for power and control. As long as he owned their body parts, he owned his victims, too. In his mind, even death didn't free them from his domination.

He'd find a way to insert himself into the investigation. He wanted to know what the cops knew, and he loved the thrill of being right in front of their stupid eyes, like a moth dancing defiantly in front of the flame. He might even try to lead them astray, Teten and Mullany warned. At any rate, he'd be reliving the high he got from the murder and playing a secret game that showed *he* was in control, not them. The UnSub's ultimate goal of control included fostering and maintaining a sense of mystery about himself. Revealing his truth would diminish the enigma he was. He was, in short, a narcissist who believed he was smarter than them.

And risk turned him on. How could they presume anything else about a man who'd snatch a child in the dark while she slept in a tent inches from her siblings, surrounded by a dozen other campers?

There might be a "God element." It might show up as twisted zealotry or distorted religious anger—or it might not—but in any case, the UnSub probably grew up in the area, which was devoutly Christian. Teten and Mullany couldn't be sure church played a role, but they agreed it wouldn't surprise them.

And, finally, this was a very emotional crime for the UnSub. In fact, his intense connection to the abduction and to Susie meant that he'd reach out to her family, probably on a date that was important to him. Maybe the date of her abduction or the exact time he had killed her.

Why? He would want to extend his crime to the family. He was still deriving pleasure from it. He wanted to mock and torment the family as a kind of celebration of his cunning.

So Mullany and Teten advised Dunbar to attach a better FBI tape recorder to the Jaegers' home phone in Farmington Hills, Michigan, and to be ready to quickly trace any incoming calls.

Dunbar seemed relieved. Finally, something that sounded like real police work.

TETEN AND MULLANY WANTED to tip the scales in their favor. They couldn't rely on chance. If the UnSub was the narcissist they believed he was, he'd be aroused by reading his name in a newspaper story acknowledging that he'd outwitted the best investigators in the world for a whole year—and if he was the sadist they believed he was, he'd be even more stimulated to torment the Jaegers at a vulnerable moment.

Coaching Marietta to say the right words was easy. Getting her words out to the world was harder.

Gone were the days when the government could strong-arm reporters. They'd once been useful pawns, but Vietnam had turned them defiant, and this current Watergate mess had galvanized them into open rebellion against the government, certainly the FBI. Even the director himself couldn't simply plant his own stories or browbeat editors like he did in the good ol' days. Teten and Mullany needed a different approach on this one.

Dunbar knew just the guy.

Hugh van Swearingen, the news editor in the AP's Helena bureau, had followed Susie Jaeger's story from the beginning. He'd rushed the seventy miles to Headwaters State Park before dawn on the morning after Susie vanished. He'd interviewed Dunbar a few times. He was a good reporter who did what he had to do, but he clearly felt the Jaegers' pain. Hugh wouldn't take orders from the FBI, Dunbar knew, but he might take a suggestion.

Van Swearingen was a Montana guy who'd earned his bachelor's degree in English at a small college up in Great Falls. Journalism was one of the few ways he could be compensated for his poor choice of major, so he'd knocked around a few Montana papers before the

Associated Press recruited him in 1968. After a couple of deployments in cold, dreary bureaus like Butte and Bismarck, the AP sent him to the capital bureau in Helena. He was thirty-six now, married, and the father of two young girls a little older than Susie Jaeger.

In early June, Dunbar phoned van Swearingen, ostensibly to update him on the investigation, but also to plant the seed of an anniversary story. Dunbar figured reporters loved anniversary stories, because all they needed was a phone and a good news morgue.

Deep down, though, van Swearingen was reluctant to interview the Jaegers at such a tender time. He already knew they had good days and bad days. Every time he talked to them, they appeared impassive and resolute, but he sensed their guilt as much as their anguish. He didn't like intruding on their grief. And he knew people believed it was typically ghoulish of a reporter to scrape open wounds just to sell papers.

But he also knew that people continued to wonder what had happened to Susie while they'd been dealing with another year in their normal lives. Such features allowed an exploration of layers and complexities that the headlong rush-rush of daily news reporting didn't. And they stood as a kind of memorial.

Van Swearingen was conflicted, but hell, journalists often found themselves in conflicted positions. It all came down to the story, and van Swearingen finally decided little Susie Jaeger's was worth telling again.

So on Wednesday, June 19, 1974—just six days before the first anniversary of Susie's abduction and time enough to get the story on the wires for most papers' Sunday editions—van Swearingen dialed the Jaegers' number in Michigan, as they'd arranged a few days earlier. Marietta and Bill remembered him from the early days in Headwaters Park, and their voices were unexpectedly serene. He asked if they minded his recording the conversation for accuracy, expressed his sympathy, and wished they were talking about something happier. Then the interview began.

Marietta did all the talking. Van Swearingen scribbled in his notebook that she was very articulate and in control of her emotions. Right off the bat, she revealed something he didn't know: Shortly after they returned from Montana last August, a man had called their home, made taunting remarks, and identified Susie by a unique characteristic that Marietta didn't explain—exactly like the man who'd called the deputy's house after the abduction. The Jaegers and the FBI were certain it was Susie's abductor.

"He said he had not completed plans for an exchange [of ransom money for Susie] and we would be contacted again, maybe in a week or two or a month," she told van Swearingen.

In the ten long months since, the call had never come.

Has the FBI tapped your phone in case the call comes?

"I don't believe they have," she said. "It wouldn't do any good. We think he would probably call from the western states, and it has to go through Chicago. It would take hours to trace."

But that didn't mean their phone wasn't ringing. They accepted all collect calls, and their phone bill was astronomical. One caller was eventually arrested for extortion after falsely claiming he could lead them to Susie. Since then they'd gotten dozens of calls, none malicious but none productive, either.

Do you believe Susie is still alive?

"I have nothing to go on," Marietta said. "I just feel she is still alive. I cannot give up hope until I have proof."

She and Bill had been talking about going back to Montana, without the other kids, just to wander around, maybe see Susie's face in some small town.

"We just have to look for her. It's just something we have to do."

Do you worry about your other kids?

"They've resumed their normal lives. We have to protect them, but we must be fair [to them]. We can't be too overprotective."

How have you gotten through this past year?

"It's not tolerable on the human level," Marietta said. "You can only accept it with religion. It's just not God's time" for Susie to come home.

What are your feelings about Susie's kidnapper?

"I guess I feel sorry for him," she said. "Anyone who could do a thing like that can't be happy. I would like to talk to him, to find out why. I guess I'll never get the chance."

If the kidnapper calls, are you willing to secretly cooperate with him? In other words, would you keep the FBI in the dark if you thought they would put Susie at risk?

"I don't care if we never see who took her," she said. "All we want is for Susan to be returned."

A lot of people have called with tips about Susie. None have panned out. How do you feel about that?

"Until you can prove to me that she is dead, I will hope she is alive. There is always that big question: How is she? Where is she?"

Their grief drifted down eighteen hundred miles of phone lines. Van Swearingen was a tough newsman, but he wasn't immune to the sound of sorrow.

He just left it at that, and they hung up. He had a deadline. After a break from his desk and a cleansing deep breath, he tapped out his lede at one of the AP's fancy new computer terminals:

WHERE IS SUSAN JAEGER?

AP REPORTER HUGH VAN Swearingen didn't know it, but the FBI had eavesdropped on every sentence of his interview with the Jaegers.

The important words—the shape of which the profilers put in Marietta's heart—had been spoken: *Anyone who could do a thing like that can't be happy. I would like to talk to him, to find out why. I guess I'll never get the chance.*

The story went out on the AP wire that weekend, slugged as a Sunday special.

The *Billings Gazette*, Montana's biggest daily, published van Swearingen's story on page one of its Sunday, June 23, edition, the day when nonsubscribers in outlying towns were most likely to buy it at the news rack. It appeared under the headline "Susie Jaeger Mystery (and Hope) Survive a Year."

Over the next few days, several big American dailies ran it. But more important, the story was picked up in Butte, Missoula, Bozeman, and other far-flung Montana cities, in one of which the profilers were certain the UnSub was hiding somewhere in plain sight. Marietta's misery was seeping into his turf, but would it be enough to seduce him out of his shadows?

They waited.

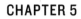

CHAPTER 5

VOICES

TUESDAY, JUNE 25, 1974
FARMINGTON HILLS, MICHIGAN

In the darkest hours after midnight on June 25, 1974—precisely one year since Susie Jaeger went missing—the phone startled Marietta Jaeger from her fitful sleep. She stumbled over a stool in the dark and picked up the receiver.

"Hello?" she said.

"Is this Susie's mom?" a male voice asked.

"Yes, it is."

"Can't hear you."

"Yes, this is," Marietta repeated, slightly louder. "I am Susie's mother."

His next words chilled her.

"Well, I'm the guy who took her from you," he said, "exactly a year ago to the minute."

Blood thumped in Marietta Jaeger's head.

She was suddenly awake and shaking. She stood in blackness.

"You did?"

"Yeah."

"Where is she now?"

"I can't hardly tell you that."

Marietta prayed the FBI's phone tap was rolling. And she prayed this was the kidnapper, not another cruel hoaxer.

"Is she alive?"

"Yes, she is, ma'am."

"Can we have her back? Can we have her back?"

Again, the caller demanded that she speak up. "I can't hear you."

"Can we have her back?" Marietta felt like she was almost screaming.

"Well, I am in a kinda awkward position to do that," he said, toying with her. "Actually, I have gotten used to her."

"I can't believe you that she is still alive," she pushed back as a mother of five. "How can you take care of a little girl?"

"Well, how would *you* take care of a little girl?"

"I have a home and I am here all day long."

The man turned cocky but defensive.

"I do also," he said. "And I probably have more money than you have."

"How can you support her, and how can you take care of her and go to work?"

"I don't have to work, ma'am," he said. "We have covered the West pretty well, just sightseeing. Me, I've gotten used to her."

Marietta sobbed, not much more than a sad whisper. *"Ahhh."*

Suddenly, the phone went dead. Marietta stood there in the dark, gutted and empty, as if her insides had all spilled out of her. *So close.* She wanted to hear anything she could cling to, even if it was . . .

Then the phone rang again. She snatched it up.

"Hello, ma'am," he said. "We musta got cut off."

"I thought you hung up on us."

"Nope."

"Why can't we have Susie back?" she asked, almost begged. "She is our child. She belongs to us, and we'll pay any amount of money. Ugh, you know."

"I realize that, ma'am, but I am in kinda an awkward position."

"Why is that?"

"Well, once I have turned her over to you," he said so utterly calmly, "she can identify me."

Marietta argued more confidently than she really was.

"Not in a court," she countered. "She is too young. They won't put a child in court to identify someone."

He scoffed.

"I know better than that. It don't need to be in a court anyway. Right now, as it is, I'm pretty safe because they have no suspicion of me at all . . . haven't even been contacted. 'Cause I'm pretty smart for them."

Marietta grew angrier.

"I don't believe that you really still have her," she said. "You are trying to play games with us, like so many other people."

"No, I am not playing games."

She called his bluff.

"Can you tell me a particular piece of identification about Susie?"

"I can tell you lots of things."

"All right, tell me."

"Well . . ."

She hoped it wasn't another late-night crank call. There'd been so many. Then there were the crazies who called at all hours with their tips. As he often did, Bill gently picked up the receiver in another room to listen.

But this call was different.

"Prove to me that you do have her," she said, hopeful but half convinced this was just one of those shams.

After a pause, he spoke again.

"All right, first of all, it was I who called the Denver FBI on Saturday, June 30, late in the afternoon. It is also I who called you, who called Mrs. Brown on July 2, sometime after ten thirty at night. It is also I who called you on September 24, early in the afternoon and you weren't home; later on, a relative of yours who spoke with me, and finally I talked to your oldest son, and if that is not enough—you are waiting, aren't you?"

"Yes."

"The nails of her first fingers are hooked."

Not good enough, Marietta thought.

"All right, what else can you tell me?" she said. "You are a little late with your call because it has been leaked. There are some people who know about that and who are able to tell us about that. But you are just trying to play games with us."

He was suddenly off-balance.

"As far as I know, it has not been leaked," he said.

"Tell me something else about her. If you have been with her and traveling around with her, if she is still really alive and with you, then you must know a lot of things about her. Has she talked to you about us? What has she told you about us? Surely you must talk?"

She'd unwittingly left the door open for more cruelty.

"Well, the thing is, I have been kinda workin' on her mind," he responded. "Almost got most of the memory of you, your home, and your other children wiped out of her mind through psychotherapy."

Marietta was more wounded than incredulous.

"How are you qualified to do something like that? I don't believe that is possible. She had a good home here, she was loved very much, and she was treated well. I can't believe you can erase those kind of memories."

The man paused a long moment.

"You better believe it."

She shifted away from the agonizing thought of Susie being turned against her own mother. She still wanted proof this was her kidnapper.

"How did you happen to take Susie? How did you know there was a little girl in our tent? Had you seen her earlier?"

"I came by the tent during the night, and I heard her and her sister talking," he said. "But I waited until they fell asleep again before I took her."

"Where did you take Susie when you were traveling? How did you keep her hidden?"

"I took her to Disneyland and to the San Diego Zoo," he said. "I only had to keep her hidden when I was at home. The rest of the time she was just a little girl with her father."

Marietta blanched but persisted.

"Did she mention what pets we have? Did she say the things we used to do?"

He was tired of the interrogation.

"Look, if you don't believe me, you'd just as well hang up, and you will never hear from me again."

"I want to believe that she is alive," the desperate mother pleaded. "I have gone the whole year hoping that she is still alive, just to know positively that she still is, but all you can tell me—"

"That is precisely why I called you. To tell you that she is."

"But you can't prove it to me. All you can tell me are the things you have done. Is that all—you called just to tell us she is alive?"

He regained the sadistic upper hand.

"I expect to get her back to you one of these days," he said. "Like

I said, I have been working on her mind, and I want to get her to wipe me out of her mind, just like she has wiped you out of her mind."

"Have you been good to her?"

"Yes, I have."

"Why did you take her?"

"Well, it's kind of a long story," he said. "I always wanted a little girl myself. . . ."

He choked up, and Marietta thought it was genuine. "Always wanted a little girl of my own," he repeated.

"Did you ever have a little girl of your own, your very own?"

"No."

"Are you married?"

"Not now."

"Has she been abused?" she asked. "Have you hurt her?"

"No, just that first night—I had to choke her some."

"When you took her out of the tent?"

"Yeah."

"Did she wake up?"

"Not right away," he said. "I grabbed her around the throat."

"How did you get away? No one could figure out how you possibly got away."

His voice was suddenly suspicious.

"Are you recording this?" he asked.

"No," she lied. Oddly, she felt guilty about it, but she had no choice.

"Are you sure?"

"How could I record it?"

"With a microphone on the phone."

"No."

He became the accuser now.

"You're lying to me."

Marietta thought fast.

"In the middle of the night, I should put a recorder on my telephone? No, I am not, but I am concerned about Susie. If you could tell me something to prove that she still really is alive and what you want us to do . . . because we will do anything you want us to do on our own without notifying the FBI, the sheriff, or anybody."

"I realize that," he said, "but what comes after that is bothering me."

"What can we do to help you? Do you know I've been praying for you?"

Silence.

"You can't move about as you like," she said. "How can she get an education? There's no way you can give her a normal life. . . . She's my little girl and no one can love her or care for her as I can. I brought her into this world. I am her mother and I have a right to her."

Silence.

"Where is Susie?" she asked.

"Up in my cabin sleeping."

"Where are you?"

"I'm not that far."

Marietta promised again they'd never tell anyone if he brought Susie home.

"Things like this just draw national attention," he sneered. "How would you let me go scot-free? Once the FBI finds that Susie's home, they'll come right after me. . . . That's why I'm doing the best I can to keep from being caught. I've some things to prepare, like how I do her hair. . . ."

"She's had a birthday."

"Yes," he said, "and we had a very nice party for her, too."

"What was the date?" Marietta asked, testing him.

"I'd like to give you the date," the caller said, "but if I give you everything I know about her, if I call again, there won't be nothin' left. I've got to have something to fall back on."

Marietta told him she still didn't believe him—although secretly she did.

"Now, look, I don't care if you believe me or not," he said angrily. "I just called to settle your peace of mind."

As any mother would, Marietta wanted desperately to know how he was treating Susie, if she was healthy.

"I take good care of Susie," he assured her. "She knows herself as a human, but not as Susie. It's not entirely forgotten. It's just not mounted in the back of her brain."

She implored him to return Susie, whatever the cost.

"I'll see what I can do, ma'am. You seem like a very nice person."

The parry and thrust continued, ultimately, for over an hour. Marietta continued to probe for evidence that Susie was alive, but he slipped away every time. In fact, he seemed to grow more dispirited, even depressed, as the call went on.

"I'd like to have this burden off my soul," he said, barely whispering.

What was his burden? Marietta wondered. But it was more important to her that he believe that she believed everything he said.

A sudden staccato of mysterious clicks rattled the phone.

"What was that?" he asked, spooked.

Marietta didn't know but made up some excuse. She needed to keep him on the phone.

"Who's listening?" he asked. "Who picked up the phone? I heard the phone click. Did you do that?"

He apologized for calling so late. He said he'd taken Susie to places where she could play with other children. He said he was a teacher and he schooled her at home. He showered her with tender affection. And he promised to call again soon, not another year. Sooner.

She finally confronted him confidently, accusing him of not having the courage to tell her that Susie was dead.

"Just tell me: Is she OK?"

"Yes, she is," the caller said. "I couldn't kill a little girl like that. When I took her that night, I tried not to, the best I could."

At the end, he was unable to hang up, and he begged Marietta to hang up on him. So Marietta ended the call by saying she felt sorry for him and would pray for him.

He whimpered, begging her to hang up.

"Won't you say goodbye so that I can say goodbye to you?" he pleaded.

Marietta refused. The voice on the other end of the line was flat, despondent.

"Oh, well . . ."

It was over.

She hoped throughout the whole conversation. She hoped that whatever magic happened in phone lines led the FBI to him. She hoped his anguish was real. But although Marietta had hoped for a year that her beautiful little daughter was still alive, the call left her with no doubt that Susie was dead.

THE EXTRAORDINARY CONVERSATION DELIVERED more clues than anyone imagined.

Without any law enforcement or interrogation training whatsoever, Marietta Jaeger had overcome her fear and grief to ask penetrating questions. She'd kept the caller talking for more than an hour, during which he unwittingly left an ominous trail of clues about his crime and his mind.

Dunbar nursed a glimmer of hope, however slight, that Susie was still alive, but as with Marietta, the long phone call convinced Mullany and Teten she wasn't. They were certain the caller was the UnSub, but nothing he said suggested Susie had survived for any serious length of time after she was taken.

There was always a snag.

Brief previous calls had been traced quickly, but the length of this call, thought to be a blessing, was really a curse. It was taking too long to trace. The telephone company transmitted long-distance calls through several different relays. The longer the time and distance, the more relays and the more likely that a trace would ricochet in some berserk direction.

In this case, the FBI's trace led to Sarasota, Florida. It raised the specter that the UnSub was a carnival or sideshow roustabout who crisscrossed America in summer, then wintered with the circus people down there. *The UnSub said he traveled a lot, didn't he?*

A few of the circus folks thought maybe, possibly they might have seen a fella with a little blond girl, but they couldn't be sure. Hell, at seven towns a week, they half-saw a million faces in a season and maybe fifty thousand of 'em were forgettable little blond girls. *The big top in Grand Island? No, maybe the midway in Yuma. Or the fairgrounds in Jonesboro.*

Weeks of exhaustive legwork, including high-tech forensics and hundreds of interviews, proved what Dunbar and the profilers feared: The FBI's trace had simply been detoured into an electronic dead end by a computer that couldn't give a damn about Susie Jaeger.

Now all they had was the Memorex cassette on which Marietta and the UnSub's conversation was recorded—and it was a profiler's bonanza. It couldn't identify the actual caller, but it conveyed a lot about him. The words he chose, the way he said them, and the timbre of his voice all meant something.

Teten and Mullany knew one thing above all: The UnSub was a sadist. They heard it in his words.

A sadist is stimulated by instilling dependency, dread, and degradation in his victims. This UnSub was confused but his psychopathy was clear: He was attracted to people younger than him so he could maintain control, superiority, and dominance.

In short, the profilers knew their UnSub was utterly capable of slaughtering a little girl or a young woman.

Most obvious of the call's characteristics was that it contained very little background noise. No traffic or street sounds, no distant trains, no passing voices . . . just a faint purl that sounded something like crickets. The call came from a very quiet outdoor environment, away from urban cacophony but not a soundproof room.

Somebody suggested that they send the tapes over to the National Security Agency. The NSA employed a whole unit of blind people who gathered intelligence purely by listening to voices on wiretaps and by their preternatural ability to detect nearly imperceptible noises in the background.

That was the best the FBI's technicians could do.

And it wasn't enough.

AGENT PAT MULLANY WANTED a second opinion, and he knew just where to seek it.

Dr. Murray Miron was a psychology professor at Syracuse University in upstate New York who specialized in psycholinguistics, a deep, computer-aided analysis of the relationship between language and criminal minds. In short, Miron believed he could use semantics to discern distinct personality traits. His portraits, he believed passionately, could be as robust and accurate as Teten and Mullany's evidence-based profiles.

What men said was as telling as what they left behind, Dr. Miron theorized.

All he needed were words.

He was a known—and respected—resource at the FBI. A few years earlier, J. Edgar Hoover would have barred the door to Dr. Miron's particular form of mind reading, as he'd done with Howard Teten and Pat Mullany's voodoo. But now, under Clarence M. Kelley, the new and less dogmatic director, the door was cracked ever so slightly. After all, these new "sciences"—which still required quotation marks in any serious discussions—hadn't proven themselves to be much more than forensic carnival sideshows.

That all changed on February 4, 1974, less than a week before Sandra Smallegan vanished. Newspaper heiress Patty Hearst was kidnapped by the Symbionese Liberation Army, a small but radical band of domestic terrorists. The FBI leapt into action, dubbing their investigation HEARNAP—a shortened version of "Hearst kidnapping"—but the sheer magnitude of this "special" case soon swamped the Bureau. America's front pages screamed; readers and nightly-news viewers clenched; politicians railed. Director Kelley was smart enough to know he needed help.

Dr. Miron's subsequent analyses of audio communiqués from the SLA's leaders helped agents understand the dynamics inside the radical cell. Eventually, his evaluation played an informative role in the final, bloody climax. And suddenly the FBI was more receptive to the idea of psychological sleuthing than it would have been even six months before.

So Mullany was eager for Dr. Miron to listen to the UnSub's late-night call to the Jaegers. His mission would be twofold: sketch the UnSub's mind and determine whether Susie Jaeger might still be alive. Whatever they might hear from Syracuse, Mullany assured his bosses, would be vetted by the FBI's newly christened Behavioral

Science Unit (which consisted of Mullany, Teten, and their fresh-faced helper, Bob Ressler).

Despite the FBI's new attitude about Dr. Miron's work, it took Mullany seven weeks to get the Bureau's imprimatur. Everything the profilers were doing was breaking new ground. The day Director Kelley signed off on the idea, Mullany rushed audio copies to the Psycholinguistics Center at Syracuse, requesting they be made a priority.

Two weeks later, Dr. Miron telephoned Mullany with an executive summary of a voluminous report to come later. Mullany recorded their conversation so he needn't wait for the official document:

The UnSub was closer to twenty than to forty.

He traveled a lot.

The caller's phraseology and word choice suggested he had at least a high school education and came from a rural background. It wasn't just his slight Western accent. He frequently used countrified and cowboy vernacular—colloquialisms like "it don't need . . ." and "kinda workin' . . . " and more.

The caller might have had his own daughter at one time.

He had a layman's knowledge of psychology, but nothing more. As such, he might once have been in therapy or been exposed to psychology in school.

He might be wealthy or at least own several properties out West.

But most frighteningly, the UnSub was extremely psychotic, a sadist prone to violence. He enjoyed the emotional torment he inflicted on Marietta. And his side of the conversation illustrated how he could *ascend* to swaggering bravado, then in the blink of an eye *descend* into weepy depression. When extreme highs and lows are so seamlessly entwined, he must resort to violence just to maintain his deluded self-image.

Dr. Miron was confident the UnSub would be described by others as outwardly mild mannered, not considered strong or aggressive at all. But when he called his victim's mother at the exact time and date of her abduction a year before, he exposed his sadistic traits.

In fact, based on certain key words, Miron believed the UnSub knew—or felt he knew—Marietta. His compulsion to talk to her was strong, and he wanted to impress her by saying Susie was alive.

The tapes also revealed to Dr. Miron that the caller was distinctly insecure around females. His occasional meekness toward Marietta suggested a vulnerability to—maybe even fear of—dominant women. As such, Dr. Miron proposed that if the FBI ever identified a good suspect, the Bureau should arrange an impromptu confrontation between Marietta and the off-guard UnSub. Use caution, he warned: He'd either wilt into passive aggression or explode with spectacular ferocity.

The disturbed caller also desired deeply to keep Susie, but he knew doing so was wrong. His personality was in conflict with his own guilty feelings—maybe about an untoward relationship with his mother, cruel fantasies, or possibly a prior killing—and he had perfected his personal art of repressing his guilt, Dr. Miron said.

Then the psycholinguist added one more crucial piece of the profile: When crossed, cornered, or arrested, this UnSub might lash out against cops, kill another girl, or commit suicide. If the UnSub was the merciless, controlling sadist they imagined, he might assume final control over himself. His death would be his choice, not theirs.

And then he sounded his last ominous caution.

Tread carefully, he warned Mullany. The UnSub was a tinderbox in search of a spark.

"Be careful," he said. "He can explode in a violent rage when you talk to him. Or he might commit some other bizarre violence. Just watch him very closely."

THIS AIN'T RIGHT.

Ranching in western Montana wasn't easy. Ranchers watched their pennies. One cow could make the difference between a store-bought Christmas and hand-me-downs under the tree. Ralph Green was one of those frugal cowboys who minded every expense, even the little ones.

So when June's phone bill came in July, it seemed a little high. There were only two toll calls. He recognized one but not the other, and it was a biggie. He was at the tail end of a five-family party line, but his wife sure hadn't made an hour-long call at three twenty-five a.m. on June 25. *Almost thirteen bucks! Damn near a day's worth of hay,* he thought. *Blasted phone company put somebody else's call on my bill.*

The next day, Green took his bill to the phone company in Bozeman, all ready to refuse to pay if they didn't forgive the errant charges. The girl in front sent him to the accounting department, which was just another girl in the back. While she was making a copy of the bill, she noticed that the recipient of the call was Mr. William Jaeger of Farmington Hills, Michigan.

Everybody knew that name. That was the father of the little girl who disappeared the previous summer from Headwaters State Park. But more important, the FBI had flagged the number for operators across America. If the UnSub called the Jaegers, agents could quickly narrow down his location.

In this case, the location was the Green Ranch, which happened to adjoin the Lockhart place. The proximity was too peculiar to be a coincidence.

Agent Dunbar paid Ralph Green a visit.

Everybody had been asleep in the house in the wee hours of June 25, Green said, like always. The doors and windows were locked, like always. Nobody could have used the house phone without him or the wife knowing, like always.

Wait. There was one other thing.

Ranchers see things in the earth that nobody else can. Green told Dunbar that he was headed out to the main road the next morning when he saw some fresh tire tracks in the dry summer dust. He knew they were made after four thirty the previous afternoon because they lay over the tracks made by his wife's vehicle when she came home from town. Around here, it paid to know your signs.

Anyway, those new tracks came off the main road and first pointed toward the ranch house but then veered off toward his wheat field, over a hill, and down a gulch where he and his son had slung a private telephone line out of sight from the main ranch house. The tire tracks went maybe twenty feet beyond the drooping wire and took a back way out to the main road. Whoever it was could have come and gone without being seen or heard.

Dunbar looked closely at the cable in the gulch. It wasn't worth a damn. The rubber sheathing had disintegrated in great long stretches, and the wires underneath were bare. It was a pure-D miracle the Greens could call a neighbor, much less dial a number halfway across the continent. That was the dark side of self-sufficiency: Things got done with expedience, not workmanship.

What if the UnSub knew these gullies so well that he could navigate in the dark without headlights? What if somebody tapped into that drooping wire with some kind of handset like a lineman used? What if he stood in the back of his truck, because the line sagged but was still more than ten feet up, higher than a man could reach?

Damn it. This wasn't Dunbar's first rodeo. He knew if the answer required a bunch of tangled-up "what-ifs," it probably wasn't the right answer. "Common things are common," they said at the Academy. "Look for horses, not zebras."

Oh, and another thing. Ralph Green had thought of something else.

He recognized those faint tracks. They were made by the same model as the spare tire in the back of his pickup: Goodyear Suburbanite. All-season traction treads. Damn good rubber for these parts.

And he knew a guy, a hired hand, who left a while back and who rode those exact tires on all four wheels. A young fella who hunted all over these hills and knew every ravine like the part in his hair.

A kid named David Meirhofer.

BACK IN BOZEMAN, DUNBAR called the manager of the local phone company.

The June 25 call had definitely come from Manhattan, Three Forks, or one of a handful of other small towns in two or three surrounding counties.

An operator in Livingston would have asked for the caller's number for billing purposes, then punched that number into a machine, without a lot of second thought. So it would have been "extremely unlikely" that an operator would remember where any particular call was coming from or going to. In fact, the three operators on duty that night had already been questioned. They recalled nothing.

"Could the caller have used a portable handset like a lineman?" Dunbar asked.

A "buttinski," the manager called it. And, yes, anybody with a buttinski and access to the line wouldn't have had any problem tapping into it and placing such a call. But it didn't even require a handset, which wasn't exactly the kind of thing you'd find in a local hardware store. Somebody who knew how phone lines worked could actually wire an ordinary home phone into the exposed wires and dial a number as if he were calling from the comfort of his own home.

AGENT PETE DUNBAR WAS back at square one, and the bedeviled David Meirhofer was there with him.

Meirhofer was snakebit. The poor guy was now everybody's bogeyman. *Somebody mentions his name one time and pretty soon the whole town is whispering.* If they were asked, every citizen in Manhattan would probably peg him for shooting Kennedy and hacking up the Black Dahlia, too.

Sure, he was a little odd, and that marked him automatically guilty in the eyes of everybody who considered themselves normal—which was the whole damn town. But he wasn't a psycho.

In some ways, Meirhofer's biography fit the damn profile, and in some ways, it didn't. In fact, Dunbar thought the profile was now hindering more than helping. They were trying to match the UnSub to the crime rather than evaluating the crime and matching it to the UnSub.

And it narrowed his view of the case as if he were squinting through a soda straw. He should have been seeing everything and considering everybody. Instead he had nobody.

And David Meirhofer was one of the nobodies.

He didn't snatch Susie Jaeger, he didn't abduct Sandy Smallegan, he didn't incinerate them, he didn't crush their bones, and he didn't scatter them like ghastly dust all over the Lockhart Ranch. Dunbar had a gut feeling David wasn't their guy, and the lie detector proved it.

Teten and Mullany felt different. To them, Meirhofer was either guilty as hell or the unluckiest son of a bitch in Montana. Since their theory—as untested as it was—didn't allow for coincidence, they seized on the former and dismissed the latter.

Dunbar had to run out every ground ball. Teten and Mullany had never talked to this kid, but they sat closer to the throne in Quantico. He'd take a critical new look at David and rule him out once and for all. He only hoped that while he was pissing in the wind the real butcher didn't steal another girl. At least the SAC couldn't say he hadn't followed up.

So in early July 1974—more than a year since Susie Jaeger was snatched—Pete Dunbar paid a visit to David Meirhofer. He dutifully informed David that he was among the prime suspects for the murders of Susie and Sandy and that he should probably retain a lawyer.

But still, Dunbar was fairly certain David Meirhofer wasn't his guy.

THE PROFILERS SAID THE UnSub had military experience. That was the easiest place for Dunbar to start.

Dunbar knew David had been a Marine, but that was about it. A lot of other western Montana kids served, too. Volunteers, not draftees. This wasn't a place where they burned draft cards.

All it took was one phone call. The next day, a teletype arrived from Washington.

David Meirhofer hadn't been drafted. He drove to Butte and

enlisted in the Marine Corps just two days after his nineteenth birthday—and barely ten days after they killed Bobby Kennedy in Los Angeles. He sat out the long, hot summer of 1968 in the Corps Reserve, waiting until they could fit him into a class of recruits for his desired job in communications.

On October 1, recruit David Meirhofer reported for boot camp in San Diego. Fourteen weeks later, he was assigned to his first training school, studying communications and electronics for three months in San Diego.

While many Marines in his recruiting class were being shipped off to Vietnam, David's first billet was the Marine Corps Air Station at Cherry Point, North Carolina, where he happily did any grunt work they'd normally assign to any green-boot PFC in the communications center. While he was there, the Corps granted him a top secret security clearance so he could handle sensitive records. Without hesitation.

Five months later, New Year's Eve 1969, David Meirhofer landed in Da Nang, South Vietnam. I Corps. *Indian Country.* The 5th Communications Battalion assigned him to be a switchboard operator and radioman at Camp Hoa Long, a concertina garrison wedged between the impoverished hamlet of Da Man—"Dogpatch" to the jarheads—and the tumbledown Sacred Heart Catholic orphanage just outside the northern wire.

The official report didn't go deeper, but when he wasn't working, David occasionally hung out alone at the "Beach Club," where they served up warm local beer and risqué entertainment that only titillated lonely Marines a million miles away from girlfriends, wives, and free-love hippie chicks who gave it away. So it wasn't especially shocking that some of his fellow grunts periodically sneaked off to Dogpatch to find some *coka* girls for boom-boom.

It wasn't David's scene. Not the beer, not the jiggling lady parts, not the boom-boom. He preferred to hole up in his hooch or do odd jobs for the nuns at the orphanage. Sometimes he slept outside in a truck just to avoid the profane ruckus of young males in a war zone.

He had enrolled in the USMC's basic carpentry course, a cakewalk because he'd already done more sophisticated carpentry back home. His handyman skills were a big help at the orphanage, where bad plumbing, busted beds, a perpetually leaking roof—and everything else—always needed attention. The old nunnery had more kids than it could hold, maybe two hundred orphans and street kids from infants to preteens. It was impossible for the nuns to keep track of them all, so it was unfortunately common for them to simply go missing in a war zone. Some just ran away, others were probably abducted by sex traffickers and slavers, and still others were pressed into the service of the Vietcong as errand boys or suicide bombers—and some simply vanished as collateral damage of war. It wasn't for nothing that the Mother Superior always slung an old Thompson submachine gun over her shoulder.

It was technically against orders to go outside Hoa Long's wire without a buddy, but David came and went alone at the orphanage whenever he had some time to kill. He loved to play with the kids, kicking a ball around or playing tag. *Hearts and minds.*

When a recon unit needed a radioman, somebody from David's battalion, often David himself, would be assigned to go into the bush. He saw some combat, but mostly stayed back at the base camp.

His military jacket showed him rising through the ranks, first to corporal, then to lance corporal, at the usual intervals. He stayed out of trouble, and his disciplinary record was squeaky-clean. He kept his profile so low that the mail sorter didn't know who he was.

Toward the end of his tour, the Corps promoted David to sergeant. In his subsequent fitness report, his company commander had high praise:

"If necessary [David] can be left in charge of the message center and the combat operation center with no hesitation at all by his seniors," the officer wrote. "[He's] a very versatile individual . . . with excellent growth potential and would be rated second among the five sergeants in the platoon. With more experience he will undoubtedly possess all of the requisite skills for promotion."

After almost a year in-country, David returned to the World. He was sent to Camp Pendleton, where he almost immediately asked for and received permission to "mess separately"—live off base. He moved into apartment seven at 509 South Pacific Street in nearby Oceanside, California, where he lived for seven months, literally a stone's throw from the shore.

In August 1971, as the war in Vietnam was ratcheting down, David asked for an early discharge so he could return home to Montana in time to help with the wheat and barley harvest. The Marines, who really didn't need him any longer and were sloughing off noncareer guys like old skin, agreed.

When his required exit physical found nothing beyond small scars on his chin and back, certainly no diseases or psychiatric problems, he was honorably discharged. He had earned three decorations, including bronze service stars for his role in three different combat campaigns. He'd given two years, ten months, and twenty-six days of his life to making the world safe from commies. He was a damn hero back home on Main Street in Manhattan.

OK, so the UnSub might be a veteran, Dunbar admitted, but David Meirhofer had been a consummate Marine, totally squared away . . . not like a lot of the dirtbags and headcases coming home from 'Nam, lugging more defective baggage than they took over there.

Dunbar shook his head. Nothing in David Meirhofer's immaculate service record suggested he was likely to speed in a school zone, much less kidnap and kill a child in the dead of night.

Except one thing.

A CAPTAIN AT THE US Marine Corps' communications school in San Diego got Dunbar's phone message and called back. The agent didn't go into a lot of detail, except that he had a former Marine with communications training who might have tapped into a rural phone line to make a call. *Could he have learned how to do that in the Marines?*

The Marines' basic communications-and-electronics course was indeed pretty basic, the captain said, teaching a radioman how to send and receive routine messages, never something as sophisticated as tapping into a live wire.

Back to square one, Dunbar thought. *Again.*

But the captain wasn't finished. There was a correspondence course called Basic Wire Comms that taught radio operators how to set up a complete communications center in the middle of nowhere, like a jungle or a desert. It definitely would teach somebody how to piggyback on even the most primitive wires or signals.

Dunbar flipped to the back page of David's USMC jacket and scanned the half dozen military classes he took.

One from 1970 stood out: *Basic Wire Communications.*

But anybody with modest technical skills, military or not, could figure it out, the captain quickly added. Even if the guy had the skills and the equipment, he wasn't the only one. Any guy with a ham radio in his basement was capable. It wasn't rocket science.

"If he had field experience with either a business telephone unit, a regimental-sized unit in Vietnam, or a Marine aircraft wing," the captain said, "then he would have had access to dial-telephone gear, which would have given him the practical experience to tap into a telephone system."

So the captain didn't rule David doubtlessly in, but he didn't rule him out, either.

DUNBAR WENT BACK TO David with more questions and another bold request: a different kind of lie detector test, in which he'd be questioned under the influence of a "truth serum."

David's patience had worn razor-thin. Here he was being falsely accused again. *What, a fourth, maybe fifth time?* No, he said emphatically, he wasn't involved with the little girl's disappearance or with Sandy Smallegan's apparent murder.

It was clear why the feds were here: Ever since he was a kid and pulled a knife during a fight, he'd been blamed for every mystery in Manhattan, and it pissed him off. *He was just a kid, fergawdsakes.*

Dunbar perked up. He wanted to know more, and David minimized it as a boyish tussle in which a knife fell out of his pocket. David himself was eventually stabbed with his own knife—*not the other kid!*—and needed a few stitches to close the minor wound. David was blamed because he was older. Nobody was arrested, but the kid's parents demanded David see a psychiatrist—or face assault charges. That was all. If Dunbar didn't believe him, David said, he could talk to the shrink. He signed more of their paperwork and walked away.

By mid-July, David Meirhofer was officially tired of the FBI's on-again, off-again doubts. He hired a Bozeman lawyer, Doug Dasinger, to keep him from being harassed and railroaded by the feds.

Dasinger was no callow country lawyer. Yes, he grew up in tiny Wolf Point, Montana, the son of Eastern Europeans who came down through Canada after World War I. He was a high school football star in an undermanned, underweight conference, but was good enough to be recruited by the University of Montana Grizzlies, where he became a second-team all-America lineman in his undergrad days. After college, Dasinger returned to Wolf Point and settled into his dream of being a high school football coach.

But his new wife planned a different life for him. She wanted to be married to a lawyer. Hectored into submission, he grudgingly enrolled in the University of Montana's law school, where—with the help of his genuine photographic memory—he graduated at the top of his class in 1967. It pissed off students who worked harder that he did so much better.

But that was seven years ago. Now Dasinger was cursed with an ex-wife and a photographic memory that wouldn't let him forget, smoked two packs a day, was too fat and prematurely bald, drove a barely legal compact car, and wore a mustache so bushy that it looked like a little animal nesting under his nose. He never had money, never had fancy cars, and never cared.

His laziness and self-indulgence extended to the courtroom. He tended to half-ass the cases that bored him, but when he latched onto a juicy case, he was a rabid bulldog.

He was especially keen on his rare death-penalty case. Like most of his fellow defense lawyers and liberal Democrats, he found capital punishment to be more monstrous than any killer.

Dunbar knew him. Dasinger had defended the accused teenage killer in a hopeless Manhattan murder case a year before. His unsympathetic client repeatedly stabbed his neighbor—a mother of four—in a frenzy of blood, booze, and anger. The boy was arrested when deputies followed a conspicuous trail of blood from the murder scene to the house next door. Miraculously, Dasinger not only kept his client off Death Row; he also convinced the judge to go easy on the kid.

Dasinger had already asked the FBI for a quick backgrounder on Susie Jaeger's case, and gotten it. After talking to David, he was sure his client didn't do it. Not in the way a defense lawyer is paid to believe. He genuinely believed in David. The FBI was hassling him because they had no other suspects.

David just wanted the FBI to stop coming around, and Dasinger was glad to help. He wasn't a fan of the heavy-handed feds, and he didn't like them poking around in any case he took. The sooner David was ruled out, the sooner he could get back to his life, free of perpetual suspicion.

Dasinger's belief in David's innocence was so deep he agreed to Dunbar's ballsy suggestion. He'd let David undergo "truth serum" questioning, even permit a full-scale search of David's property. Two conditions: The test would be administered at the state mental hospital by a certified psychiatrist David knew, not an FBI questioner. And Dasinger would be allowed to observe.

If David passed the test, Dasinger warned, the FBI's pestering had better end immediately.

What the hell? Dunbar wondered. He hadn't thought any defense attorney in the world would allow his client to be injected with a powerful drug that might induce him to confess to murder. Or let agents search every inch of his client's property. And no butterball attorney was going to tell the FBI what to do.

But it was another disheartening sign that David wasn't the UnSub. Would a seasoned criminal lawyer, without a warrant, gamble on a drug-induced confession if he didn't truly believe his client?

Sodium amytal was a barbiturate commonly used as a sedative or anxiety medicine, but for decades doctors believed that it also made people unable to censor themselves. In its "twilight sleep," patients could empty their memories into a cohesive narrative, telling a true story without all the conscious filters.

Teten and Mullany sounded a cautionary note, louder than Dunbar wanted to hear. Truth serum tests were tricky, at best. When this one was done, they cautioned, Dunbar still wouldn't know anything for sure.

"By disrupting defensive patterns, barbiturates may sometimes be helpful in an interrogation," Mullany wrote, "but even under the best conditions, the drugs will elicit answers contaminated by deception, fantasy, and garbled speech."

The idea was good in theory, but problematic in practice.

"Suspects under the influence of such drugs may deliberately withhold information, give untruthful answers, and falsely confess to crimes they didn't commit. Plus, the psychopathic personality in particular appears to resist the influence of these drugs."

"Narco-interrogation" had no reliable value, Mullany concluded. Forget judges and juries—it wouldn't even give investigators trustworthy leads to follow. Even drugged up, a psychotic suspect might concoct a fabulous wild-goose chase.

"It's likely any individual who can withstand ordinary intensive interrogation can hold out in narcosis."

Dunbar decided it was worth the risk. He was grasping at straws. David might not be his best suspect, but Dunbar had no intention of ruling him out permanently.

If David failed the truth serum test, the FBI would crawl up his ass. But if he passed, he probably wasn't the UnSub anyway.

Nothing to lose.

SA DUNBAR STOPPED FIRST at the office of Bozeman's only psychiatrist, Dr. William Prunty, who'd listened to seventeen-year-old David's account of the minor stabbing incident eight years before. "Listened" being the operative word, since David quit coming after only three sessions—about four hours altogether—and before Dr. Prunty truly counseled him.

At first, the psychiatrist wouldn't even acknowledge he'd ever met David Meirhofer, much less treated him. But when Dunbar showed him David's written permission to release his therapy record, Dr. Prunty described their brief interaction and what few conclusions he took away from it.

In the summer of 1966, the Meirhofers' family doctor in Manhattan referred David to Dr. Prunty to resolve a dispute over a bloody fight between David and a younger fourteen-year-old boy.

In his first session, David told his side of the story: Although he was a junior in high school, he had become extraordinarily close friends with a fourteen-year-old Manhattan middle schooler. In fact, they'd been so close that the kid's parents worried that maybe it had become homosexual.

David interrupted his story to assure Dr. Prunty that he had no sexual interest in the boy whatsoever, but that he "loved" the young man, who had told David he loved him back.

Anyway, another fourteen-year-old kid—David called him a "smart aleck"—intruded. The two younger boys began hanging out together, and it rankled David. He wasn't jealous, David emphasized to the doctor, but he was angry that the intruder might have an unhealthy influence on his young friend.

So David hatched a plan to teach this "smart aleck" a lesson. David drove him to a secluded spot south of town with the intention of "beating him up." The beatdown started as soon as they got out of the car, and a knife "just came out of my pocket," David said. In the ensuing struggle, the eighth grader wrested the knife away and sliced open David's back. The fight stopped as the boy administered haphazard first aid. Together, they rushed back to town, where a doctor stitched up David, who told a more innocent story about the wound.

The psychiatrist asked about the need for a knife, and David couldn't answer. He hadn't wanted to hurt the kid, only to "teach him a lesson. The knife . . . well, it just happened."

Both boys' families were enraged. They demanded that David stop seeing his young friend and that he stay away from the "smart aleck."

David refused, fiercely. He wouldn't end the friendship. Period.

So the kid's parents delivered an ultimatum: mandatory therapy or a lawsuit against the Meirhofers. David's divorced parents chose therapy, albeit reluctantly.

Dr. Prunty asked some uncomfortable questions about David's life, family, and secret thoughts.

David's parents had been busy. They'd had five kids over less than eleven years. David was the second born, wedged between his older sister, Cheryl, and brother Alan, who was about four years younger and tagged along with David a lot. A little brother and sister came several years later.

His indulgent parents were together most of David's childhood and even after their divorce, when David was thirteen. His father, Cliff Meirhofer, then forty-two, was the biggest businessman in town and, as far as anyone knew, an affectionate dad. Just not a very good husband.

Folks winked about Cliff's infidelities and weakness for younger girls. There was the barmaid out in Logan. And the ranch wife out at the Lockhart. And the time some nubile sunbathers caught him peeping from the riverside underbrush. Everybody knew that was just Cliff.

When Cliff and Eleanor Meirhofer finally divorced, Cliff took

David and Alan to Cookie's Café to break the news. David cried. He became more distant after that.

Now David lived with Cliff and his twenty-two-year-old step-mother, who'd been Cliff's teenage secretary at the implement store when they started their illicit affair four years before. David told Dr. Prunty he got along with them just fine. Same with his mother.

David had belonged to the Boy Scouts in his grade school days. By high school, he became the assistant leader of his father's troop. It was a good time in his life, when he had many good friends— almost all of them younger kids in the troop, including his middle school buddy. It hurt him deeply when the Scouts expelled him in April 1968 for odd, vaguely menacing behavior. It made the other boys skittish. Again, being a little strange didn't help.

Cliff Meirhofer attended only one of Dr. Prunty's sessions with David, but he heard enough to get the drift. "My son's no faggot!" he growled, and walked out.

David admitted he despised women. "They're domineering and controlling and can ruin a man's life by getting him to do any-thing that they wanted [sic] him to do." He swore he'd never get married.

He was quick to add: He hated women but he wasn't attracted to men, either. There just wasn't a place for sex in any normal life, he said. Sure, he'd masturbated when he was younger, but he stopped when he read in "a doctor's book" that it was hazard-ous. Besides jacking off, he'd never had sex of any kind. He was a virgin.

That was as candid as David ever got. He didn't talk about much more, or ever in depth. He described *how* he felt but not *why*. Whenever his feelings about other people came up, he grew very anxious.

"I was impressed that David's denial of any sexual interest was unrealistic," Dr. Prunty told Dunbar. "I also felt that his antipathy for the opposite sex was significant and very deep-seated."

David exhibited severe anxiety, especially for a teenager, Dr. Prunty said. But he gave off no incriminating vibe.

"My impression at the time I was seeing David was that there was indeed a homosexual meaning to his feelings for his young friend, but I was unable to get any verification of this from David. He was pleasant and cooperative but seemed to realize that if he admitted nothing his legal problems would take care of themselves. But I saw nothing to indicate that David was or had been psychotic. . . . There was nothing that would indicate David's involvement in the disappearance of Susan Jaeger."

The earnest psychiatrist mentioned one last thing to Dunbar. When the young Boy Scout Michael Raney was murdered at Headwaters State Park in 1968, less than two years after David's aborted counseling, Dr. Prunty secretly told Sheriff Andy Anderson that he should look at David Meirhofer. The good doctor's hunch was based purely on the involvement of a Boy Scout and a knife. David was subsequently questioned, passed the same lie detector test given to hundreds of scouts at the time, and was ruled out as a suspect. Dr. Prunty was now admitting he'd been wrong.

Dunbar deflated. David had passed two polygraph examinations in two, maybe three murder investigations, and now was voluntarily submitting to a third test. Dr. Prunty only added to the professional opinions about David Meirhofer's innocence that were rapidly piling up on Pete Dunbar's desk.

Maybe David was justified in feeling that he was a victim of harassment by the cops. Maybe they were all barking up the wrong tree. Maybe Dunbar was narrowing his pool down to the wrong one.

And maybe Quantico's mind games were just another post-Hoover boondoggle.

ON AUGUST 19, DAVID Meirhofer and Doug Dasinger showed up bright and early at the Montana State Hospital in Warm Springs, a state-owned patch of land near Anaconda, eighty miles west of Manhattan.

At the hospital—a bleak hundred-year-old asylum for desperately ill mental patients and the criminally insane—psychiatrist Dr. Lars Slette led David to a dark little room where he injected him with sodium amytal. Dasinger sat nearby and watched intently.

The drug took effect within a few minutes. When David had entered a state somewhere between tipsy and sleep, Dr. Slette asked a few control questions before getting into Dunbar's list—*Have you ever committed any crimes of any kind? . . . Do you have any knowledge of Susie Jaeger's disappearance? . . . Sandy Smallegan's? . . . Where were you on June 25, 1973? . . . February 10, 1974? . . . What were you doing? . . . Who were you with? . . . Have you ever telephoned Susie Jaeger's parents?*—and David answered them all like a morning drunk just this side of a six-pack.

The interview lasted less than an hour. While David slowly came out of his stupor, the psychiatrist had no doubt. The test was successful, he said, and David's answers showed no sign of guilt whatsoever. He simply didn't fit the "psychological pattern" of a miscreant who could abduct a child, much less butcher her.

Furthermore, Dr. Slette told Dunbar he personally knew David. He was a good son, a hard worker, a moral man. The FBI, the good doctor said, was barking up the wrong tree.

David Meirhofer was no killer.

THAT SAME NIGHT, A strange thing happened at Camp Silver Cloud, a lakeside Girl Scout campground in the forest just twenty-seven miles west of Warm Springs. Fifteen preteen girls and a few adult troop leaders camped there, a last summer outing before a new school year started.

After dark, two girls took a giggly walk down a wooded path. Suddenly, a man in a black hooded mask sneaked up from behind. He threw one girl down and began choking the other one with a rope. When another girl shined a flashlight in the direction of the scuffle, the shadowy figure fled. The girls reported it to their chaperones, who reported it to the Deer Lodge County sheriff, who only half believed the story and didn't believe a genuine crime had happened anyway. He assigned a deputy to check it out.

There wasn't much to go on except the say-so of a couple little girls. Hell, it wasn't even clear if it was a real assault or the little girls just saw a shadow. But the deputy had seen a couple teletypes about missing girls down in Gallatin County. *Something about Scouts, or camping, or some guy jumping out of the shadows, or some such.*

It probably wasn't related, but the deputy picked up the phone and called a deputy he knew down in Bozeman anyway. Better safe than sorry.

UP TO THIS MOMENT, Dunbar's investigation was proving the Warm Springs psychiatrist, the polygraph examiner, and everybody else right—everybody but the profilers.

David was, at best, a C student at Manhattan High School. He worked on the school paper and appeared in the senior play, but avoided sports games, dances, and all other after-school activities. He worked in the school cafeteria. His classmates described him as an introverted loner who could be invisible in a crowd. They didn't recall him at school dances or ever having a girlfriend . . . or any friends at all, really.

He wrote in one yearbook: *I'm not really much of a writer but there's only a little room left anyway. I'll just wish you the "best of luck" in your future. . . . Keep smiling and you'll have the whole world on your side. Good luck. David M.*

Many in the class of '67 recalled that David always carried a knife, which was a little off-putting. Still, while David was peculiar, he was friendly enough, clean-cut, and well-spoken, and he dressed more neatly than most boys out here.

Seven years out of high school now, he owned a few properties around Manhattan and Three Forks, some of which he'd renovated into apartments that he rented out. He was, by all accounts, a benevolent landlord. His creditors were all happy. The Town of Manhattan trusted him enough to hire him to build a new municipal shop.

Several people noted that David liked to play with children like an uncle, not a pervert. He'd get down on the floor and roll around with them. He communicated with them on their level, and they loved him for it. He just had a way with kids.

One of David's casual acquaintances told Dunbar that he'd once hunted antelope with David in the Horseshoe Hills. They bagged one, and when David started to gut it, he got sick. He really didn't want to disembowel the animal, but he felt goaded into it by another hunter. *Did that sound like a psycho killer?*

In this instance, the profile didn't fit Meirhofer. Mullany and Teten were fixated on the wrong elements, or David really wasn't the perpetrator. Dunbar's gut told him that both were true.

Even if David Meirhofer was the UnSub—*and he wasn't*—not one shred of hard evidence directly connected him with *any* crime, let alone two kidnappings, two murders, and the most macabre corpse dumping Dunbar had ever seen. Their only two leads? A couple tipsters who thought David was a slightly odd character in a town full of slightly odd characters (many of whom thought the FBI and cops were unfairly picking on David), and some tire tracks under a half-assed telephone wire in a dry gulch.

Still, the tips trickled in, more than a year after Susie was taken. Dunbar and Terry, plus a handful of deputies who chased leads when their regular duties allowed, followed every one, even a few of the wacky ones. More Volkswagens, more hippies, more hitchhiking convicts. Somebody reported a guy who was writing a book in a cabin near Bozeman and talked about crazy stuff like spirits and communicating with the dead. A Michigan man hired a personal clairvoyant who said Susie could be found in a town whose name started with an "L." A skittish sheriff down in Anaconda reported that two Girl Scouts had been physically accosted in their campground on August 19 by an unknown man who ran away when somebody turned on the lights.

Nothing led anywhere.

The profilers' psychobabble now chagrined Dunbar. Most of their profile was a wild-ass guess, didn't fit, or couldn't be known. Mullany and Teten were just a couple wannabe shrinks sitting on their asses in an air-conditioned office back in Quantico. They hadn't chased this ghost all over hell. They weren't following a thousand leads into blind alleys. They had never talked to David. They'd probably never set foot in Montana. How could they know?

Even Gallatin's podunk sheriff, Andy Anderson, called it "black magic."

No, the real UnSub was among the fifteen hundred people, near and far, whose names or descriptions had popped up in the past year. A lot of them, maybe most, had never been tracked down and ruled out. The UnSub was one of them, Dunbar was certain.

David's not our guy, the agent concluded.

"HE'S YOUR GUY," MULLANY told Dunbar on the phone that night.

An exasperated Dunbar pushed back. He ran down the list of what he knew about David—his grades, his upbringing, his manners, his stable finances, his work ethic, his spotless service record, supporters all over town who vouched for him, even the damn psychiatrist who injected him with truth serum—but Mullany countered with everything he knew about criminal minds.

"But he passed the lie detector with flying colors," Dunbar argued.

Mullany was unmoved.

A polygraph measured an ordinary person's response to specific questions by monitoring ever-so-slight changes in breathing, heart rate, blood pressure, and perspiration. But it was just an ordinary machine and psychopaths weren't ordinary people. They'd lied all their lives and they were good at it, he said. Or maybe they simply weren't physically aroused the same way by their lies. They might not even know where the truth ended and the lies began.

Finally, the rate of "false negatives," or tests that indicated a guilty man was innocent, wasn't insignificant. They could have been caused by a bad machine, an unfit examiner, or flawed questions.

Truth serum was no more reliable, maybe less. It was often difficult for the examiner to discern truth from untruth during "narco-analysis" because he simply couldn't know how fantasies might be entangled in a certain reality. Sometimes patients confessed to crimes they hadn't committed. Others developed such warm feelings for their interrogator, they said whatever they thought might please him, true or not. Worst of all, patients occasionally developed "false memories" after the test, jeopardizing any future testimony. Messing with the brain was risky, especially for cops.

Mullany and Teten also believed the polygraph and truth serum were especially useless with "severely antisocial" killers who mutilated their victims—as they suspected David Meirhofer to be. They just weren't wired right.

Bottom line: It proved absolutely nothing that David passed three lie detection tests. A fourth or fifth wouldn't matter. David could beat any test Dunbar gave, they said.

Dunbar expressed that for all the mind reading, the only way they were going to catch the UnSub—whether it was David or not—was through old-fashioned police work, beating the bushes and talking to people.

That was because he had no experience doing it a different way, Mullany told him.

Pete Dunbar hung up. He was weary of traveling somewhere and arriving nowhere.

FACT WAS, BACK AT the Behavioral Science Unit, the profilers were secretly as frustrated as Dunbar.

It wasn't just pushback from the boots on the ground. It was also an unshakable sense that they might be completely wrong. They'd never say so, but it was true.

Admittedly, some elements of their profile were educated guesses more than psychological insight—more "possibly" than "positively." By comparison with Brussel's extraordinarily detailed, almost magical sketch of the unknown subject that eventually proved to be George Metesky, theirs was generic and bland.

Maybe the distance between Quantico and Montana was too

great. They believed the criminal mind was knowable, but did the landscape itself also exert subtle influences? Were they just sideshow mind readers, carnival hustlers making the midway crowds ooh and ahh?

Maybe their profile didn't narrow the pool of suspects enough. Or narrowed it too much.

Maybe their lack of experience hurt more than it helped.

Maybe some "evidence" was not as it seemed and they were seeing only what they wanted to see.

Maybe it was more about what they wanted the UnSub to be instead of what he really was.

And maybe Pete Dunbar, a smart veteran field agent who'd looked his suspects in the eye, was right: David Meirhofer probably wasn't their guy.

But they couldn't just call the whole thing off now. They couldn't start over. They might not have been perfectly right, but nothing had proven them thoroughly wrong, either. Only busting the UnSub would validate their profile.

But things changed quickly.

The next day—August 20, 1974—Pete Dunbar, Bill Terry, and a few young agents out of Butte knocked on David's door. Lawyer Douglas Dasinger was there to watch as David freely granted Dunbar written permission to search his South Sixth Street house and garage, vehicles, Main Street warehouse, and any other properties Meirhofer owned.

He had nothing to hide, he said. Again.

For three hours, they sifted through a strange life. They found no smoking guns but seized some items that chilled them.

David was a scrupulous, maybe obsessive record keeper. His logbooks noted mileage, hours, paychecks, oil changes, fill-ups, motel stays, and even descriptions of the food he ate. He kept credit

Manhattan, Montana, in the 1920s looked very much as it does today.

In 1967 thirteen-year-old Bernie Poelman died of a single gunshot wound while climbing on the Nixon Bridge near Manhattan. His death was attributed to a stray shot.   RON FRANSCELL

The FBI circulated Susie Jaeger's 1972 school picture after her disappearance. FEDERAL BUREAU OF INVESTIGATION

The semicircular slice in the Jaegers' camp tent.

FEDERAL BUREAU OF INVESTIGATION

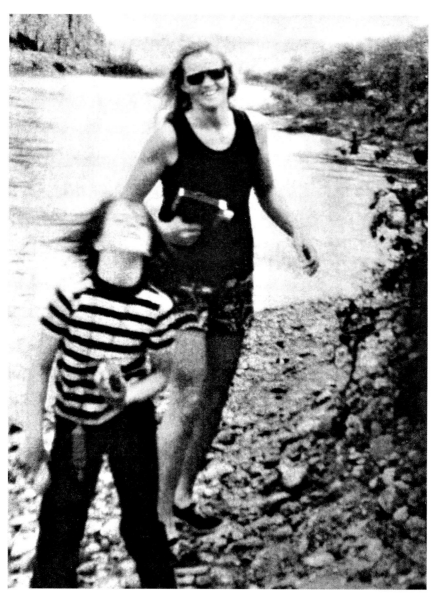

On one of the happier days of their 1973 family vacation, Susie romped with her mother, Marietta, beside a river.

The Jaegers' Western vacation made them closer.

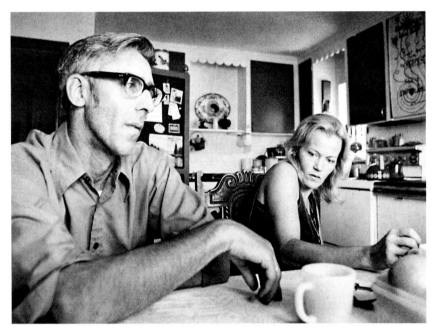

Bill and Marietta Jaeger talked to any reporters who would listen as they waited for word about Susie in their Michigan home.

The abandoned Lockhart Ranch. © *BOZEMAN DAILY CHRONICLE* (MT)

A deputy points to the general area near the Lockhart Ranch homestead where searchers first found pulverized bones. © *BOZEMAN DAILY CHRONICLE* (MT)

Tell the Jaegers to come back as soon as possible they can have Suzie back Friday the 27th. I don't want this in the paper or on T.V.

Hoaxers came out of the woodwork in hopes of snagging substantial ransom money.   FEDERAL BUREAU OF INVESTIGATION

Gallatin County Deputy Don Houghton.

COURTESY OF DON HOUGHTON

FBI profiler Howard Teten.
FEDERAL BUREAU OF INVESTIGATION

FBI profiler Pat Mullany.
FEDERAL BUREAU OF INVESTIGATION

FBI Special Agent Pete Dunbar.
FEDERAL BUREAU OF INVESTIGATION

Five-year-old Siobhan McGuinness.

Sandra Dykman was one of
the popular girls at Manhattan
High School.

David Meirhofer was peculiar and standoffish in high school. © OLIVER CAMPBELL

Meirhofer lived in a converted garage behind a large house he owned in Manhattan. © *BOZEMAN DAILY CHRONICLE* (MT)

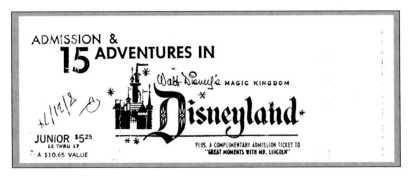

A child's Disneyland ticket book found in a search at Meirhofer's garage apartment.   FEDERAL BUREAU OF INVESTIGATION

THINGS TO DO TODAY

CAMP SILVER CLOUD
EAST OF SILVER LAKE
GIRL SCOUTS

TAKE STORM LAKE ACCESS
ROAD, TAKE 1st LEFT

DENSLY WOODED

August 13-19

FRIDAY, MAY 31, 1974

APRIL	MAY	JUNE
Su Mo Tu We Th Fr Sa	Sun Mon Tue Wed Thu Fri Sat	Su Mo Tu We Th Fr Sa
1 2 3 4 5 6	1 2 3 4	1
7 8 9 10 11 12 13	5 6 7 8 9 10 11	2 3 4 5 6 7 8
14 15 16 17 18 19 20	12 13 14 15 16 17 18	9 10 11 12 13 14 15
21 22 23 24 25 26 27	19 20 21 22 23 24 25	16 17 18 19 20 21 22
28 29 30	26 27 28 29 30 31	23 24 25 26 27 28 29
		30
151st Day	Patented	214 Days to Come

Meirhofer scribbled notes about a Girl Scout camp-out in his calendar.   FEDERAL BUREAU OF INVESTIGATION

A Salt Lake City motel receipt was key in the hunt for a psycho killer. FEDERAL BUREAU OF INVESTIGATION

After arraignment, Deputy Don Houghton *(left)* and Sheriff Andy Anderson led accused killer David Meirhofer to jail through a restless throng on Bozeman's Main Street. © *BOZEMAN DAILY CHRONICLE* (MT)

Mild
Mild with gusty westerly winds through Sunday, except for scattered showers in the extreme northeast portion Saturday night and Sunday. Highs both days 55 to 65, lows 30 to 40. More weather on Page 6.

The Billings Gazette

89th Year—No. 149   Billings, Montana, Saturday Morning, September 28, 1974   Single Copy 15¢

Eye opener
Advice to college students: Be kind to your parents. After they get through paying to send you, you're all they'll have.

Suspect charged with killing Jaeger girl

By ROGER CLAWSON
Of The Gazette Staff

BOZEMAN — A quiet Manhattan man was arrested Friday and charged with the kidnaping and murders of a 7-year-old Michigan girl and a Manhattan teen-ager.

David G. Meirhofer, 25, was charged in the abductions and deaths of Susan Jaeger and Sandra D. Smallegan, according to Gallatin County Atty. Thomas A. Olson.

The Jaeger child was kidnaped from a tent in Missouri Headwaters State Park near Three Forks June 25th, last year. The FBI took jurisdiction and launched a massive manhunt for the abductor of the 7-year-old Farmington, Mich., girl.

The investigation intensified when Sandra D. Smallegan, 19, of Manhattan was reported missing Feb. 9.

MRS. SMALLEGAN'S car, and later her charred bones, were discovered at an abandoned ranch house northwest of Three Forks by Gallatin sheriff's deputies and Bozeman police.

On Sept. 17, a single bone was found in an outhouse pit on a Manhattan ranch only a few feet from where Mrs. Smallegan's bones were found. It went to a lab in Washington, D.C. and the report back to Montana authorities said the bone was that of a 6-to-8-year-old child and was "slightly more likely to be female than male."

Officials had previously given no indication that the Jaeger girl had been slain until Friday.

Documents filed in Bozeman District Court indicate that Meirhofer's arrest followed the screening of numerous telephone calls made to the Jaeger residence by the main purported to be Susan's kidnaper.

The Associated Press quoted Olson as saying Susan's parents, Mr. and Mrs. William Jaeger, identified Meirhofer's voice as that of a previous caller who had demanded ransom.

EVIDENCE USED in charging Meirhofer included recordings of three telephone calls placed to the Jaegers' home. Olson's seven-page statement of evidence said the caller in the last conversation expressed anger that the previous

calls had been recorded and turned over to the FBI.

On August 26, Meirhofer consented to join in a group call to the Jaeger home. A number of persons, including Meirhofer spoke to the Jaegers. The Jaegers identified Meirhofer's voice as that of the previous caller, the statement said.

Other calls had been placed by a man to the Denver FBI office and a Gallatin County sheriff's deputy.

The first came three days after the Jaeger girl's disappearance, demanding $25,000 in ransom. A week later the caller demanded $50,000.

A YEAR AFTER the first call to the Jaegers, a man called saying he had their daughter but could not return her.

In a prepared statement, officials said Mrs. Jaeger met with Meirhofer personally for more than an hour last Thursday, and again last Friday.

Authorities said that during a telephone conversation Tuesday, the caller told the Jaegers they would never see

(Turn to Suspect on P. 6)

SANDRA SMALLEGAN   SUSAN JAEGER

Powder dam is proposed

Policies, advisers

David Meirhofer's arrest in September 1974 was big news in Montana.

© *BILLINGS GAZETTE* (MT)

The cell where Meirhofer hanged himself.

© *BOZEMAN DAILY CHRONICLE* (MT)

Three-year-old
David Meirhofer
on Christmas
Day 1952.
**COURTESY OF THE
MEIRHOFER FAMILY**

By the time he
graduated from
Manhattan High
School in May
1967, David had
already murdered
at least one child.
**COURTESY OF THE
MEIRHOFER FAMILY**

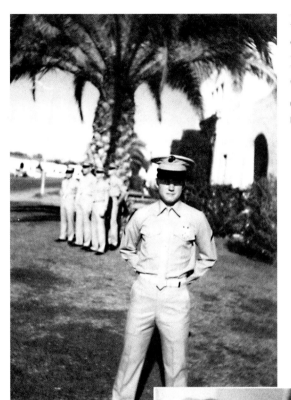

Marine boot camp in Camp Pendleton, California.

Despite the darkness already inside him, a teenage David in a lighter moment.

Susie Jaeger's grave in Bozeman's Sunset Hills Cemetery.
RON FRANSCELL

Sandra Smallegan's grave in Meadow View Cemetery in Manhattan.
RON FRANSCELL

Despite David Meirhofer's murder confessions, he got a military burial in Three Forks, Montana.   RON FRANSCELL slips, register receipts, diner stubs, and hardware invoices. One of them was a $193 sales slip from a local Goodyear store for four new Suburbanite tires in October 1973. Another was a guest check (No. 0532) from the Husky truck-stop diner in Cheyenne, Wyoming, dated September 24, 1973.

Old Bozeman newspapers, all from the past summer, were stashed in his pickup truck, with the picture of a young Butte girl named Karen Smith that David had clipped from one of them. On his page-a-day calendar, David had handwritten some directions to a Girl Scout camp near Anaconda, with a description of the surroundings as "densely wooded." Below it all, he'd scribbled: *August 13–19.* Dunbar made a note to himself to follow up on the puzzling notation.

More intriguing, in David's warehouse they found some bed linens stained with what looked like smeared blood in splotches much bigger than a nosebleed.

Eerie, yes. But a desk drawer contained the eeriest bits, things even harder to explain for an awkward bachelor carpenter in a small Montana town.

Agents found two unused Disneyland ticket books—one for an adult and one for a child. A little girl's delicate chain necklace with a silver heart. A schoolgirl's blue blouse. And a tube of Cashmere Bouquet lipstick.

Neither the Jaegers nor the Dykmans recognized any of it, so nothing proved to be a direct link to Susie or Sandra. It'd take time for the FBI lab to determine if it was blood on the sheets and whose it might be. Gas receipts showed David had been at the diner in Cheyenne on the same day somebody phoned the Jaegers' home from there and talked to Danny. Cryptic notes, necklaces, lipstick, and random newspaper clippings raised more questions than answers. Who was Karen Smith? *And Disneyland tickets for a kid? What the hell?*

David Meirhofer explained everything—or tried. He found the stained sheets and the girl's blouse in the warehouse when he bought it. He found the necklace on the sidewalk. The lipstick was a forgotten leftover from a high school hazing ritual in which upperclassmen smeared lowly freshmen in embarrassing ways. A fellow Marine gifted David the Disneyland tickets when the buddy was shipped overseas. He drove all over the Rockies delivering his dad's farm machinery, so he wore out his tires quickly and carefully planned his travel in advance. He'd dropped off some suspicious hitchhikers at the Husky truck stop in Cheyenne, where he grabbed a quick bite before hitting the road again. He was a big newspaper reader and everything was in neat piles.

Dunbar didn't buy any of it.

In three chaotic days, the wind had shifted. Dots couldn't yet be connected but they were certainly lining up. Evidence of *something* was mounting, and Dunbar's gut now told him David Meirhofer wasn't what he seemed.

Maybe he was a sex pervert. Maybe a psycho killer. Maybe both.

But David no longer looked like an innocent kid with unlucky stars. If he was the UnSub, he had eluded the FBI and local cops for more than a year. A deceptively familiar darkness in broad daylight, like a shadow. There but not there. Sometimes in front, sometimes behind, sometimes invisible.

Catching a shadow wouldn't be easy. Dunbar needed more than his gut.

Dunbar picked up the phone and dialed Mullany's desk in Quantico.

THE PROFILERS HADN'T YET exhausted their bag of tricks.

Pat Mullany had a brainstorm.

As a social scientist, he wasn't sure about this whole experiment. But the FBI field agent in him still liked Meirhofer for Susie Jaeger's kidnapping and near-certain murder. A lot.

Sandy Smallegan floated in the shadowy background like a specter. The only evidence that directly linked her to David Meirhofer was one date in a small town where most of the boys probably dated most of the girls. It was possible—maybe even likely—that Sandy's and Susie's corpses were butchered, burned, and scattered in the same place by the same killer, but there was no forensic proof. Mullany suggested that Dunbar launch a new search at the Lockhart Ranch. Fresh eyes might see something overlooked.

So far they had connected many more dots in the Jaeger case. Meirhofer's link to the phone calls—although circumstantial—was powerful. His proximity, military training, age, job, relationship status, and vaguely off-kilter personality put him in the right ballpark, but none of them definitively pinpointed him as the UnSub. The physical evidence seized in Dunbar's search fascinated them. Meirhofer was guilty of *something* weird . . . but it proved nothing beyond a reasonable doubt.

However, what about the UnSub's voice? It was the only piece of real evidence he'd left behind so far. Could it connect Meirhofer or anybody else to Susie?

The FBI wasn't high on voiceprinting, which presumed that certain speech characteristics could be almost as unique as fingerprints. But it was an evolving forensic tool. One of the Bureau's most reliable analysts, a psychologist at an upstate New York college, was being sued, and there were just too many variables to produce a report that would stand up in court. As such, the FBI lab would examine voice samples for "investigative guidance only."

What if we arranged a voice lineup? Mullany asked. Marietta and

Bill Jaeger had both heard the caller's voice. Maybe they could discern it from among several men's voices.

Dunbar thought it was worth a shot.

THE PAINSTAKING SEARCH OUT at the Lockhart Ranch had continued off and on—mostly with little success—for seven months since Deputy Don Houghton and Town Marshal Ron Skinner had found Sandy Smallegan's car.

But now the Smithsonian's meticulous anthropologists had puzzle-pieced together the tiny bone chips and shards to rebuild much of a young woman's skull, almost certainly Sandy's. Undoubtedly some of the missing pieces remained scattered across the abandoned ranch. With winter coming, they urged SA Dunbar to take a last look.

So Dunbar mobilized a whole new team of searchers and sent them to the Lockhart Ranch. He wasn't sure what they might find that two dozen cops on their hands and knees hadn't seen. Right now, though, the Smithsonian guys' hunches couldn't be any crappier than his own.

And those two dozen cops had crawled over the *surface* of the earth. They hadn't looked *under* it.

While a half dozen men walked the whole place again, literally kicking every rock, somebody found a small white vertebra under a sagebrush. It might have been a piece of a dead coyote's spinal column, an abandoned fawn's, or maybe a little girl's, but it didn't seem big enough to be a full-grown woman's. It was bagged and tagged.

Closer to the house, Gallatin County Deputy Jim Jordan dug into the soft, ashy dirt of the old firepit.

It wasn't deep, no more than a foot down. He'd turned only a couple spadefuls of earth when he found an oddly shaped bone. It didn't look familiar to anybody, even the seasoned hunters. It was caked with grayish dirt, patches of red mold, and clots of congealed fat. Scraps of toilet paper appeared to have been wrapped around it while it was wet. A fringe of dried-up ligaments trimmed the edge, and a few beetle cocoons clung to it. They recognized, though, the cleanly hacked edges.

A few days later, Smithsonian anthropologists identified it as a child's sacrum, a triangular bone where the spinal column attaches to the pelvis, from which the tailbone dangles. A few vertebrae were still attached. It wasn't freshly buried; it had been in its hole for up to a year. The dry dirt and ash had retarded decay, effectively mummifying the nerves, tendons, and cartilage still adhering to it.

The Smithsonian people estimated the sacrum belonged to a female child between six and eight years old. In fact, they said, she would have been closer to her seventh birthday.

It had literally been hacked out with a large knife, or maybe a machete, while there was still flesh on the body. The slices across the bone were deep and clean. Sandy Smallegan's bones had been cut with a handsaw, but this little girl's had not.

The anthropologists saw no hesitation marks. The butcher had known what he was doing. He had carved a little girl in half at her lower back, slit her upward through the crotch, then hacked off her legs. To finally dislodge the bone, he had stabbed a knife directly up between the child's legs.

The sacrum definitely wasn't Sandy Smallegan's. It was probably Susie Jaeger's . . . but what if it was a different little girl's?

Suddenly, there rose a specter of more slaughtered children—unknown children.

JUST THREE DAYS AFTER David Meirhofer skated through a truth serum test at the state hospital, FBI Special Agent Pete Dunbar stood in Doug Dasinger's cramped Bozeman law office. It was really just a manufactured home on a downtown lot where piles of paper and dog-eared law books seemed more like part of the furniture than temporary turmoil. The cheap little pigsty stank of stale cigarettes.

Dunbar had come to propose Mullany's idea: Five different anonymous men, including David, would call the Jaegers on a lineman's handset tapped into Ralph Green's jerry-rigged phone wire. Identified only as No. 1 through No. 5, each would recite the same four-page script: the mysterious caller's sixty-eight verbatim comments and responses during the late-night phone call exactly one year after Susie's disappearance. Marietta's part of the conversation would be left out.

On the other end of the line, FBI agents from the Detroit field office would monitor and record the five monologues so they could be compared with the so-called "anniversary call" in the lab.

Marietta and Bill Jaeger would also listen to the calls in different rooms, unable to communicate in any way—even with a glance—about what they were hearing. They were forbidden to speak or react out loud to anything they heard. Afterward, they'd be asked separately by agents if any of the voices sounded familiar.

It was an old-fashioned police lineup, except that the witnesses wouldn't look at faces; they'd listen only to voices. Dunbar's plan was to re-create the conditions of the "anniversary call" as precisely as possible, just to eliminate any sound variations that would render the lineup meaningless in court or in the Jaegers' minds.

Would your client do that? Dunbar asked.

Surprisingly—again—Dasinger readily agreed. Just like with the truth serum test and the voluntary search, he believed in David's innocence, and he'd do anything to get federal agents off his client's persecuted ass. The real killer was still out there someplace. After a little minor wrangling over who and how, the agent and the lawyer agreed to run the blind voice test the next Wednesday, August 28.

David himself suggested one of the callers be a guy he knew whose voice he believed sounded similar to his own. Maybe even the man they were hunting, he said. Dunbar consented, then convinced David's father, brother, and uncle to participate in the unusual reading, too.

On a hot morning five days later, a phone-company technician clamped the handset onto the wire. Agents sat tight with their fancy recorders in the Jaegers' Michigan home. Defense lawyer Dasinger stood by in a remote Montana wash. And it began.

One by one, the men spoke the FBI's text into the handset in Ralph Green's gully. David was No. 2. For almost two hours, the familiar words were recited five times by five different men while Marietta and Bill listened intently. On his end, Dasinger listened closely, too.

"Is this Susie's mom?"

"Can't hear you."

"Well, I am in a kinda awkward position to do that. Actually, I have gotten used to her."

"We have covered the West pretty well, just sightseeing. Me, I've gotten used to her."

"Well, the thing is, I have been kinda workin' on her mind. Almost got most of the memory of you, your home, and your other children wiped out of her mind through psychotherapy."

"I took her to Disneyland and to the San Diego Zoo. I only had to keep her hidden when I was at home. The rest of the time she was just a little girl with her father."

And so on.

Marietta relived each painful line five times. But one of the voices stood out. It was slightly stilted. It lacked inflection, or variation, or whatever strange energy animated words. But the resonance and tone, the way the speaker formed his words . . . too familiar.

In the other room, Bill Jaeger heard one voice that he thought he recognized, and four he didn't. It wasn't by process of elimination, but a strong feeling that one voice was the same one he heard that awful night. *Yes,* he told the agent, *I'm sure.*

Marietta and Bill, in their separate rooms, unable to see or communicate with each other, were both certain that the caller—and probably their beautiful little girl's killer—was No. 2.

THAT WAS THE FINAL straw for Dunbar.

Too many roads led straight to David Meirhofer. Dunbar saw them now. The voice lineup, the surreptitious phone call from a remote ranch, the tire tracks matching Meirhofer's truck, his Marine training with phone communications, a receipt proving he'd been in Cheyenne at the exact place and time of the UnSub's call to the Jaegers' home . . . the preponderance of evidence pointed at David Meirhofer.

The profile lined up, too. Dunbar still couldn't explain how a guilty man could pass both lie detector and truth serum tests, but the profilers were confident that a miswired psycho could fool their meager science.

Dunbar's gut had been wrong all along. It wasn't easy to swallow, but at least he finally had a target after fourteen months. Nevertheless, the case against Meirhofer was all circumstantial, and they still had no weapons, no confessions, no witnesses. Dunbar needed to turn up the heat and hope a rattled Meirhofer made a mistake.

Three days after the Jaegers recognized David's voice, Dunbar drove from Bozeman to David's South Sixth Street bungalow in Manhattan. It was really just a renovated garage behind a timeworn three-story prairie Victorian he'd refurbished into a triplex that he rented out. It was also half a block from Sandy Smallegan's apartment over his father's farm-implement dealership.

Their conversation was short and unvarnished. Dunbar told him that the Jaegers had identified his voice as the anniversary caller's and he was officially the prime suspect in Susie Jaeger's kidnapping. It was only a matter of time.

Meirhofer protested. His voice rose an octave. He had never called the Jaegers. He knew nothing about their daughter. And he sure as hell didn't snatch her or know where she was now. It was unfair for Dunbar to target him and a waste of manpower to watch him. Period. End of story.

Dunbar kept his voice low. He warned Meirhofer that he was being watched 'round the clock and he shouldn't go too far from Manhattan. Then he left.

If control was Meirhofer's compulsion, he'd just lost it.

SA PAT MULLANY ITCHED to crack Meirhofer wide open, too.

The Jaegers were slowly making peace with the likelihood that Susie was dead, possibly butchered. Their trust in the FBI ran so deep that they had not a shred . . . a sliver . . . a whisper of doubt about who had done it. They wanted justice, and they wanted to hear Meirhofer admit, out loud, that he had killed her. They knew that the profilers had predicted the UnSub's suicide attempt, and they hoped to their wounded core that the FBI wouldn't let Meirhofer die before he confessed, if only to them.

While Dunbar shook Montana's bushes to see what might slither out, the profiler was flat-footed. Up to this point the profile had held together, but now they'd hit a brick wall. Yes, it had narrowed the pool of suspects, but it couldn't connect all the dots. Only old-fashioned police work could do that.

Mullany knew he needed to throw David off-balance. If he believed he was losing control, as if he were tipping toward a fall, he'd likely screw up while he struggled to regain equilibrium. If he did, Dunbar would be there to catch him.

But so far, Meirhofer had built impenetrable walls around himself. There seemed to be no tunnel into his head. At no point had Dunbar or the local cops breached his defenses, and he'd shown no cracks in his shell.

Except once.

On the phone with Marietta, the caller had revealed his Achilles' heel.

Assertive, confident women unnerved the UnSub—now presumably Meirhofer. As his emotional reaction to Marietta had shown, a strong woman might disarm him.

Dr. Miron, the psycholinguist, had already proposed a brilliant idea. The way to upset Meirhofer's perfect balance might be for a strong woman to confront him.

Mullany pondered how he could make that happen.

Marietta Jaeger was ideal for the assignment, but she was also a vulnerable civilian. He considered sending a self-assured, strong-willed female FBI agent to pose as Marietta, but she couldn't possibly *be* Marietta. Why shouldn't they assume that Meirhofer had seen news photos of her? He'd likely recognize an impostor. And what if Marietta herself wasn't willing to confront David Meirhofer?

Mullany needn't have worried about that. Dunbar reached out to Marietta and she liked the idea. But her eagerness didn't forestall Mullany's other questions about the operation.

Where should it happen? When? Would Meirhofer's lawyer agree to it? What would this spontaneous whim cost? Did they genuinely think he'd just blurt out a confession? Would they ever get a second chance?

Not without some help . . . and some luck.

The bigger problem was, no cop had ever tried this unusual

tactic. Placing a grieving mother inches from her young daughter's alleged killer was fraught with danger. Not just physical danger— might he kill her . . . or she kill him?—but also real legal issues. What if some unforeseen violation of his civil rights compromised his eventual prosecution? What if a murderer walked free because of a makeshift scheme that was more speculative than scientific?

"Should we surprise him on the street?" Dunbar asked. "Just walk up to him?"

No, Mullany said.

"Surprise isn't an essential ingredient," he told Dunbar. "It would be preferable if Meirhofer is forewarned. The potential anxiety of meeting his victim's mother will tend to ensure success and achieve the desired purpose—the location of his victim."

Mullany was sure about only one thing: He'd need approval from the top, maybe from the new director himself. Sure, Clarence M. Kelley was more of a progressive believer than Hoover had been, but even Kelley couldn't be certain the plan was valid. The risks were many—failure would destroy the program and send the whole idea of criminal profiling back to its sideshow days, among other things. So nobody was more surprised than Mullany when the higher-ups granted their permission two days later.

More miraculously, Meirhofer's lawyer, Doug Dasinger, would allow Marietta to meet David if the meeting would be secret and take place in Dasinger's law office, and if David's security was guaranteed by the FBI. For its part, the FBI wanted only to record the conversation and to search David for weapons beforehand. Dasinger protested, and Dunbar agreed to let the lawyer himself frisk David, which was better than letting the opportunity slip away.

Other than that, they agreed, it would just be a grieving mother begging for answers and a falsely accused guy begging to be left alone.

The deal was done.

Dunbar immediately made plane reservations for Marietta and Bill Jaeger from Detroit to Bozeman on September 18. The six-hour flight would cost the Bureau $236.55, to be paid from a secret fund. To save money and offer a degree of security, Dunbar invited the Jaegers to stay at his Bozeman home.

That night, Dunbar prepared Marietta. The meeting would start at ten thirty a.m. the next day, September 19, in Dasinger's untidy little office. Dunbar and Dasinger would be in the meeting room, but Bill must wait outside. Dunbar described David Meirhofer to her, just so she wouldn't be suddenly speechless upon seeing him for the first time.

But she was more than ready to face the man she believed beyond the faintest shadow of a doubt had taken Susie and maybe killed her.

David held her answers.

IF THE IMPENDING ENCOUNTER distressed David Meirhofer, the lawmen who were following him around didn't notice.

His daily life unfolded as it always had. Routine trips to the lumberyard, stops at the hardware store, days working on his old houses, lunches at the diner (often sitting down with some of the deputies who'd been watching him), and visits to his mom's house.

In fact, four days before he was to meet Marietta, he attended a church potluck with one of his homemade deer-meat casseroles and chatted with his neighbors as if he hadn't a care in the world. And maybe he hadn't. The Bible told him so. *"Bring me venison, and make me savory meat,'"* he recited earnestly—from memory—to a fellow churchgoer at the potluck, *"so we can eat and be blessed.'"*

He didn't get the verse precisely right, but what did it matter if a few words were changed?

To the FBI, a few words apparently mattered a lot.

About that same time, the FBI's special agent in charge in Butte decreed a minor paperwork change that was, in fact, more symbolic than clerical.

For more than a year, the subject line on all FBI teletypes and correspondence in the Susie Jaeger investigation followed the Bureau's inflexible protocol for identifying the case to which the document referred. During that time, when nobody knew exactly whom they were looking for, the header on all official communiqués was:

```
UNSUB;
SUSAN MARIE JAEGER, AKA-VICTIM
KIDNAPPING
```

Now one word was changed. Starting immediately, in every subject line on every document related to this case, the word "UnSub" would be replaced by "David Gail Meirhofer."

CHAPTER 6

MYSTERIOUS SKIN

THURSDAY, SEPTEMBER 19, 1974
BOZEMAN, MONTANA

The Jaegers arrived early at Doug Dasinger's law office, followed by Agents Dunbar and Terry. After some brief pleasantries, the lawyer seated Marietta in a big chair at one end of his conference table, himself at the other end with a tape recorder, and Dunbar on one side. Bill Jaeger and Terry waited in the cramped little office outside.

An empty chair, less comfortable than Marietta's, waited across from Dunbar. David Meirhofer was late.

Marietta whispered a little prayer before David came through the door. He apologized politely for being tardy. Dasinger performed a superficial pat down—mostly for Dunbar's benefit—and introduced each of them. Neither Marietta nor Dunbar stood to shake David's hand.

The first thing Marietta noticed was David's bottomless black eyes. *Those eyes* . . . They were the color of shadows where anything might have been hiding. Dunbar had described him to her, but now here he was, right in front of her. Flesh and blood, not just a voice on the phone. Any mental picture she might have had before this moment vaporized.

David Meirhofer was short, only slightly taller than Marietta at five foot four.

She found him unexpectedly nice-looking, although not classically handsome. He was trim and well-built, like a ranch hand or carpenter would be. When he spoke, he sounded intelligent and articulate, even friendly. His voice was pleasant, almost gentle.

In fact, under different circumstances, she might have found him attractive.

The man before her—the man she genuinely believed had stolen her Susie—didn't scare or disgust her. She believed he was profoundly sick, but she wasn't frightened. A bit of her fearlessness came from her faith that God protected her, but she also guessed Dunbar was carrying a hidden handgun.

Marietta wanted to like David. That might make her appear concerned and sympathetic. She didn't want to turn him off or chase him away before he told her where Susie was.

The conversation that followed consisted of Marietta repeatedly telling, asking, accusing David of taking Susie . . . and him denying it. She never cried or raised her voice. As always, she was very controlled on the outside, knotted up on the inside. She simply didn't want any of those men in the room—Dunbar, Dasinger, or David himself—to think she was a hysterical, out-of-control woman.

Throughout, David's tone was calm and earnest, almost submissive. He knew only what he'd read in the paper. He'd never do such a thing, because he loved children and he was a good man. He didn't know anybody who would. He couldn't imagine Marietta's grief, but he wasn't the kidnapper. He knew nothing about any phone calls to Michigan. He hoped Susie came home safe someday.

For an hour and a half, the meeting went nowhere. No tense words, no small talk, no confessions, no veering from Marietta's central accusation that David took Susie . . . and his insistence that he didn't.

Dasinger sat quietly through it all, never once interrupting or intruding until he abruptly announced, "This interview is done."

When everybody stood to leave, Marietta held her hand out to David, and he shook it.

Marietta didn't want to let go. Not because she believed his denials, but because she *didn't* believe them. She knew David was her last, best connection to Susie.

"David, I know you're the man who took Susie," Marietta told him, now holding his hand with both of hers. "And the authorities will be able to prove it in court. But it would be so much better for you if you admit it now."

David locked his deep black eyes on her.

"I'm really sorry, Mrs. Jaeger," he said. "I wish I could help you, but I don't know anything about your little girl. I hope you find her."

Then he walked out.

Afterward, in the outer room, she hugged her husband, Bill. She was drained and disappointed. Whatever answers David Meirhofer might have offered walked out of that room inside him.

"Should I go after him?" Bill asked. She knew what he meant.

"No," she said.

"WE'RE DONE, RIGHT?" DASINGER asked Dunbar when they were alone.

Not quite. Dunbar had a plan B.

He wanted Marietta to confront David away from his lawyer, where he might feel more vulnerable and respond differently. But the US attorney for Montana had warned Dunbar that David's attorney must know the FBI might approach his client. Dasinger didn't forbid it—David wasn't under arrest and possessed no useful information—but he had already strongly advised David not to speak to the Jaegers or the FBI without him present.

That night, a little before nine thirty, Marietta dialed David's home phone from Dunbar's office in the Bozeman federal building. David had just come home from bowling at the Manhattan alley.

For eighty-four minutes, their earlier conversation repeated itself . . . accusation and denial, pleading and deflection, questions and claims of ignorance. At one point, he asked if somebody else, namely the FBI, was listening to their conversation, and she told him they were alone. The longer they talked, the more impatience, then indignation, she heard in David's voice.

Just before eleven, they were both spent, but Marietta posed a final question: *Would David meet her one last time? Face-to-face. Just the two of them. No cops or lawyers or tape recorders. Wherever he wanted.*

David agreed. He had nothing to hide, he told her.

They arranged to meet after lunch the next day at the city shop where David was building a float that the town council had entered in Manhattan High School's homecoming parade, only a week away.

At one thirty p.m. on September 20, the sky was dirty gray but the temperature hovered between summer and winter. Marietta needed no coat.

Various cops in civilian clothes had taken up inconspicuous positions in the neighborhood, just in case David made any aggressive moves. Manhattan's night cop, Ron Skinner—who'd been at the Lockhart Ranch when Sandy Smallegan's Cortina was found—sneaked into the shop early that morning and perched above the john with his shotgun. His assignment was to keep it trained on

David, his old classmate, the whole time. Seven years before, they had appeared together in the senior play, *Twelve Angry Men*, about a kid falsely accused of murder. Secretly, Skinner wasn't sure he could shoot somebody he knew, and he prayed he didn't have to.

And down the street, Marietta saw her husband, Bill, slumped down in the front seat of his half-hidden rental car, watching from a safe distance. *Stay in his line of sight,* she told herself.

Marietta knocked on the shop's front door. David opened the door, but he didn't ask her in. He just stood there. Neither of them crossed that threshold.

David wondered, out loud, if Marietta was wired. She assured him she wasn't.

She asked him about the Disneyland tickets, the necklace, and the lipstick FBI agents had found in his house the month before.

"Did you kidnap Susie to replace the girl you knew in California and that you had taken to Disneyland?" she asked him out of the blue.

He visibly blanched but said nothing.

She asked about Sandy Smallegan. Again, nothing.

She asked about the Girl Scouts on the night of the truth serum test. Nothing.

"I wish I could help you" was all he said.

She told him—again—that she knew he took Susie and he denied it—again. Over and over, in one way or another, their abortive earlier conversations repeated for forty minutes there on the sidewalk.

"I forgive you, David," she told him. "And more than that, God forgives you, whatever you've done . . . if only you will accept it."

David listened but remained leery.

"Please acknowledge Susie's death," she said, feeling herself start to beg, "so you can receive the help you need . . . to become the man you were created to be, not unhappy and lonely like you are now."

"I don't need any help," he responded calmly. "Nothing's wrong with me. I'm not sick."

Their brief conversation was no longer than any chance Friday meeting between neighbors on a small town's Main Street. When she ran out of words to speak, Marietta again shook his hand and left.

And it was no easier to walk away a second time. She was even more convinced he had kidnapped and probably killed Susie, but she felt as if she'd failed her family, Pete Dunbar, God . . . and Susie. David was a broken soul, and in her mind, God required that she ache for him.

She also knew he wasn't telling something. And it saddened her to know he might never tell.

WHEN MARIETTA JAEGER HAD confronted the man she truly believed had killed her little girl, she walked away with power over him. Pat Mullany knew that if Marietta's sixth sense about David Meirhofer's wickedness was wrong, he'd want to stay as far from her as he could. But if the profilers were right and if strong women paralyzed the UnSub, Meirhofer would try to recapture his power. It wouldn't be pretty.

In late August, the profiler called SA Pete Dunbar. He and Teten had recently agreed that if every calculation in their new science became part of the FBI's permanent records, they might unwittingly be educating future criminals about how to literally get away with murder. So while their request to omit most of the Behavioral Science Unit's communications from case files tumbled slowly through the bureaucratic bowels in DC, they did much of their work by phone.

Mullany told Dunbar the UnSub wouldn't melt back into the

shadows. He'd show himself again. And again, as with the anniversary call, he'd likely select a meaningful time and date. Problem was, Mullany admitted, that time and date might be meaningful only to the UnSub.

He suggested that Dunbar coordinate with the Detroit field office to intercept, record, and trace any incoming calls at the Jaeger home and to alert agents immediately about unusual mail or lingering strangers. And he warned that they should be especially watchful over the Jaegers' other daughter, thirteen-year-old Heidi.

Finally, if the call came, Mullany advised Dunbar to find Meirhofer before it ended. That was one way to rule him out—or in.

They could do nothing else but wait. The UnSub must make the next move, and it probably wouldn't be long.

CHAPTER 7

A DEEPER DARK

TUESDAY, SEPTEMBER 24, 1974
FARMINGTON HILLS, MICHIGAN

At ten minutes past noon, the Jaegers' phone rang.

Marietta was home alone. Bill was at work, the kids at school. Marietta's parents, who were visiting from Arizona, had parked their trailer out back. Her dad had gone on an errand, but her mother was sitting at the trailer's little fold-down table, sewing.

Marietta pressed a button on the recorder and picked up the receiver.

"I have a collect call for anyone from Mr. Travis," the operator said. "Will you accept the charges?"

"Yes, I will," Marietta said.

"Is this Susie's mom?" a man on the other end asked.

"Yes."

"I'm the guy that kidnapped Susie."

Marietta recognized the voice.

"Yes. Hello, David."

"Mr. Travis" was momentarily startled.

"David who?" he asked as if he'd stumbled over some unseen crack. "What are you talking about?"

"You know who I mean, David."

"I don't think so."

"Yes, you do."

"Tell me what you mean."

Marietta persisted. "You know what I'm saying."

"I don't know what you're talking about," he said, seeming to try to regain his footing. "I have your daughter Susie."

"Is she safe?"

"Yes, she is."

She nudged him a little off-balance again.

"Can you prove it to me, David?"

"What? What do you mean by calling me David now?"

"I know that's your name."

"Then how . . . how do you know my name is David?"

"We met together," Marietta said. "We talked."

"OK, what are you talking about?" the mysterious caller replied without an outright denial. "Have you been lying? Did you lie to me?"

"When?"

"The last time I called you. I'll bet you taped that conversation, didn't you?"

"What do you mean, did I lie to you?"

"You told me you weren't taping it."

"I wasn't."

"Well, I never have given you my name."

"Yes, you did."

"Well, you evidently found out somebody else's name."

"Don't you remember just a few days ago when we met?"

"No, no, no," he insisted, again trying to take control of the conversation. "I have Susie and you don't even want proof of it."

"What proof can you give me?"

"Well, I was the one who called you on the anniversary at this number and this is also an anniversary date, of the last time I called you."

"And talked to my son?"

"Yes."

"Have you come up with arrangements for the exchange of a ransom?"

"Now, uh, I don't know. Are you taping this again?"

"David, what else can you . . . ?"

"Mr. Travis" turned suddenly angry.

"Quit calling me David!"

"All right," Marietta said, backing off. "Can you identify Susie?"

"The nails of her first fingers are humped," the caller said. "You told me last time that the story was leaked. Has it?"

"Well, there is an awful lot of people who know about it."

"I have her right here," he said. "Would you like to hear her?"

"Can I talk to her?"

"No, no. I'm not going to let you talk to her."

"How do I know it's her if I can't talk to her?"

"You probably know her voice, don't you?"

"Please let me talk to her."

"I can't do that."

"Why not?"

"Because I'm . . . like I told you, I'm working on this psycho-therapy, and if she recalls your voice, or you mention anything about your family, it's gonna hinder it."

"I don't believe you can do that."

He ignored her comment.

"Evidently you've called the FBI onto this, huh?"

"They only want Susie back."

"How do you . . . how do you expect me to get her back to you when you got the FBI?"

"If you would . . ."

"If I would arrange a drop, you'd have the FBI there, wouldn't ya?"

"No. We just want Susie."

Marietta heard a muffled, not-quite-familiar noise in the background. *Maybe a phone booth door creaking open?* Then something like a faint voice a mile away, followed by a long pause. Then a little girl spoke into the phone.

"This guy, he's nice," she said.

Marietta was stunned. She couldn't speak for a moment. The girl sounded about Susie's age but the voice . . . it just wasn't right, in a way only a mother could know.

"And I'm sitting on his lap," the little girl continued.

Marietta heard more stifled noises, and then "Mr. Travis" came back on the phone.

"Did you hear her?"

"It didn't sound like her."

The caller turned cruel.

"Oh, I'm sorry, but that's the only girl I've got to give ya."

"Her hair." Marietta pressed for more. "Tell me about her hair."

"It's long right now."

"How tall is she?"

"About four seven."

"Does she talk about us?"

"No."

"Has she been sick? Is she well?"

"No. She gained weight," he said, then turned sarcastic. "How could she lose weight and grow?"

"She must be scared."

"She don't have to worry like you."

"Please, David, do you understand? We just want our Susie home. Is she safe?"

"Yes."

"Is she happy?"

"Very much."

"Can we please have her back?"

"Nope."

"Why did you take her from us?"

"Now we're getting back to where we was that night of the call last summer."

"What's going to happen now?"

"I told you before. We've got to get out of here now."

"Will you take her?"

"Yes."

"Why?"

"Well, well, what . . ."

"Please, David," Marietta begged. "Please let her come home."

"What . . . what . . . what about this David business?" He was clearly tense. "Who's this David you're talking about?"

"David, I know it's you. I told you in Montana. I know. . . ."

"You're never gonna get Susie back."

"Why?"

The line went suddenly dead. He'd banged the receiver down. "Mr. Travis" was gone.

"David? David?" Marietta pleaded, hoping she still might say whatever magic words he wanted to hear.

The UnSub—David Meirhofer or whoever he was—had taken back his control.

LONG BEFORE "MR. TRAVIS" hung up, Agent Pete Dunbar scrambled his team.

Bill and Marietta had prearranged a signal with her parents. They'd slap a fluorescent orange card in the window, easily seen from the trailer, if they needed help in a hurry. Marietta prayed her mother would look up to see it, even as she spoke calmly to Mr. Travis.

She did. In an instant, her mom bolted from the trailer and ran into the house. As soon as she understood what was happening, she ran to a neighbor's house to call Dunbar in Bozeman.

Before the call ended, Dunbar launched a lightning search for David Meirhofer. Astonishingly, David had vanished from his home, despite close overnight surveillance. He was now in the wind, considered to be armed and dangerous.

Dunbar was pissed. How could a guy go into his one-room house under the supposedly watchful eyes of several cops and slip away like some shadow in the dark without anyone seeing him?

FBI agents and local cops swarmed over Manhattan, the Bozeman bus terminal, car-rental offices, the Amtrak station, the city's little regional airport, even several ranchers' private landing strips. One deputy hurtled through the rugged Horseshoe Hills toward the Lockhart Ranch; others rousted anybody who might know where he was. David's lawyer, Doug Dasinger, told agents he had no idea his client was even missing, much less where he'd gone. In fact, David had missed an appointment at Dasinger's office after lunch.

At the same time, an urgent all-points bulletin went out to all police agencies in Montana and surrounding states about any new cases of missing children.

Meirhofer's Jeep pickup was found in a Bozeman repair shop, where it had been since the day before. Wherever he was, he hadn't driven his own vehicle there.

Nobody had seen David in the past eighteen hours, since four o'clock Montana time the day before.

Less than an hour after Marietta accepted the collect call from Mr. Travis, Mountain Bell reported the call definitely hadn't originated in Montana. It might have come from anywhere, so Mountain Bell's regional office rushed out a top-priority teletype to all of its western switchboards. The phone company warned it might take some time to trace the call.

It didn't.

Within two hours, Utah operators reported that the call had been placed from the Salt Palace Travelodge, a twelve-dollar-a-night motel just two blocks west of the big Mormon temple in downtown Salt Lake City. With no long stops, Salt Lake was six hours from Bozeman for a driver in a hurry, seven hours at a legal speed. So there would have been plenty of time for Meirhofer to make the run. One problem with that scenario, though: His truck never left the shop.

If Meirhofer had rented a room, he didn't register under his own name or any known aliases. Still, agents boxed up all the night's receipts for the FBI lab.

And nobody perfectly matching Meirhofer's description had checked in the previous night, according to the night clerk, who didn't recognize Meirhofer's photo.

The only suspicious guy all night was a rumpled, terribly smelly guy who checked in around five a.m. on the day of the call. No visible car, no luggage. He said he'd ridden a bus all day from Portland, Oregon, on his way to Danvers, Massachusetts. Then the weirdo told the clerk that he had a girl with him, but she never appeared.

Probably a hooker, the kid reckoned, although five in the morning wasn't the usual time for a quickie.

The clerk assigned him Room 122 and the guy paid $12.72 in cash. Then he went to his room. By the time the FBI agents showed up later in the day, the bedraggled traveler was long gone. And none of the downtown cabbies recalled giving the guy a lift.

While federal agents from the Salt Lake City field office crawled all over the Travelodge, FBI crime technicians in Washington, DC, analyzed the taped phone call from Mr. Travis. The man's voice was a near match to that of Meirhofer, who had been recorded during Marietta's first confrontation in Dasinger's law office.

The little girl's voice had been unfamiliar to Marietta, but the girl clearly wasn't close to the phone when she spoke. Mr. Travis didn't allow Marietta to interact with the child, and high-tech audio equipment picked up a very faint click when the child stopped speaking, but the human analysts couldn't say for certain if it was a tape recorder button they heard or just some fluky acoustic artifact.

Other than that, there was no detectable background noise that might have offered clues to Mr. Travis's location. He'd chosen a very quiet environment. But the audio specialists heard something else that Dunbar might use: When Mr. Travis abruptly hung up on Marietta, the receiver bounced audibly in the cradle, suggesting he'd called from a phone on a desk or table, not a wall . . . more like a motel room than a phone booth.

One complication: The call definitely came from the Travelodge, but there was no record of any such call going through the motel's switchboard.

Listening to the Salt Lake agents on the phone, Dunbar worried that Meirhofer had used his communications tricks to lead them on a wild-goose chase. *Could he have been in one place and made it seem like he was someplace completely different?*

Not necessarily.

Calls from the pay phone in the lobby would bypass the switchboard, the manager said. He never saw anybody using the phone that night anyway. Unfortunately, maids had cleaned the phone early that morning, before the Travelodge folks had had any inkling they might have hosted a very bad man.

And if a guest had placed a collect call, as "Mr. Travis" had, it would have gone directly to a phone-company operator, and the motel would have never known.

Crime-scene technicians dusted every phone in the Travelodge, especially the one in room 122, but found nothing useful.

Mr. Travis, whoever he was, had come and gone without a trace. Not a name on a guest register, not a fingerprint, not anyone who recognized him, not even a wrinkled bedspread.

Maybe he'd never been there at all, Dunbar feared.

Another shadow.

THAT LITTLE GIRL'S VOICE on the phone chilled Tom Olson, the Gallatin County Attorney. The former Marine officer had been a judge advocate general during the Vietnam War and had been Gallatin's chief prosecutor for four years. He was tough but was especially intractable about crimes against children.

Could it possibly have been Susie Jaeger? Had "Mr. Travis"—presumably David Meirhofer—abducted another living, breathing child? Was it a tape recording? If it was a recording, what had happened to the child who had recorded it? And if it was not a recording . . . *what had happened to that child?*

Nobody knew for sure.

While Olson set about drafting his summary of the case and an affidavit of probable cause to arrest Meirhofer, Agents Dunbar and

Terry paid David a last visit. Although David had been under constant and unconcealed surveillance for a while, there were moments when his movements went unobserved—*where was he the night before and the day of the Mr. Travis call from Salt Lake City?*—and maybe he'd slip up. It was worth a try.

Around four o'clock on Thursday afternoon—September 26—Dunbar and Terry pounded on the door of the city shop where Meirhofer attended to the final details on the town's float for the next day's homecoming parade. David answered.

The agents followed the FBI's strict protocols: They introduced themselves as if Meirhofer had never met them, reminded him that he'd previously been told he had certain rights even though he wasn't under arrest, and Mirandized him for at least the sixth time. They'd lost count.

David said he understood his rights with crystal clarity.

"So, can you tell us, David, where you were last Monday and Tuesday?" Dunbar asked him directly.

He told them in precise detail.

On Monday night—September 23—he went bowling. He left the alley around eleven thirty. On his way home, he said, he saw night cop Ron Skinner, who he believed was watching him. A couple minutes later, he said, he entered the renovated garage where he lived behind a bigger house he owned on South Sixth Street. He was there alone all night, he said. He made no calls, had no visitors. He rose around eight thirty Tuesday morning—September 24—dressed, ate breakfast, then walked over to the shop he was building for the town council. He worked, he said, for thirty to forty-five minutes. Then he walked to his own Main Street warehouse, where he worked until lunchtime. He went home for a sandwich. After less than an hour, he went back to his warehouse, where he said he worked until about three o'clock. Then he walked over to the city shop briefly, and back toward the center of town, where he waved at night cop Ron Skinner, who was again watching him. Other than seeing and being seen by Skinner, David said he never saw or spoke to anybody he knew.

And where was his vehicle? Dunbar asked.

The whole time, he said, a Bozeman mechanic was servicing his Jeep pickup. He had no wheels and walked everywhere.

So from eleven thirty Monday night until three o'clock on Tuesday afternoon, in the small, tight-knit town of Manhattan, Montana, where everybody watched everybody else, nobody saw David walking back and forth around the little downtown area. He didn't answer his door when agents pounded on it. He passed nobody familiar on a pleasant fall weekday when the local shops would have been conducting their usual business before the big homecoming parade (and Potato Festival) on Friday. To hear him tell it, he barely cast a shadow on the sidewalk. *Was it possible to be there and be invisible?*

Dunbar and Terry walked away more convinced than ever that David Meirhofer was their guy.

BACK AT THE FEDERAL building in Bozeman, a phone message awaited Dunbar.

A forensic anthropologist at the Smithsonian had called. The small vertebra found at the Lockhart place a week before was definitely human and belonged to a child. It was all preliminary, of course, but he knew Dunbar would want to know as quickly as possible.

Together with a little girl's hacked-out tailbone, the vertebra had been found in a place where it should never have been. Dunbar was simultaneously satisfied and sickened.

He dialed Marietta's number. He'd come to know her heart, and it was strong enough for the awful news he was about to deliver.

The previous week, they'd damn near torn down the old Lockhart Ranch looking for more evidence, he explained to her. "We took the place apart," he told her. They found . . . things . . . and sent them to the Smithsonian in DC, he said.

"This morning, Marietta"—his tone was somber—"we received a report that in the last parcel we sent, there were bones positively identified as being from a young child. I'm so sorry."

The details were new, but Marietta had known a long time ago what Dunbar was really saying. Susie was gone. A little part of her, way deep, still believed Susie could be alive, wanted to believe the caller who told her Susie was well. Her mind—at least some still-faithful corner of it—swirled with alternative circumstances that would allow Susie to come running back into her life . . . their lives.

But she no longer set a place for Susie at the dinner table. She no longer expected her to run from the school bus, smiling. She'd known for a long time.

Finally, she wept. She wept until she had nothing left inside. No tears, no anger, no hope.

A Catholic calendar hung on her bedroom wall. She usually flipped the pages only on the best days, but this was the worst day. And the scripture printed on this particular day was from Psalm 126: *Those who sow in tears shall reap with shouts of joy! He who goes out weeping, bearing the seed for sowing, shall come home with shouts of joy.*

To her, in that empty moment, it wasn't just a verse randomly chosen to fill a space on a church's free wall calendar.

It was a promise.

A WEEK BEFORE, ON the very day that Mr. Travis called Marietta Jaeger in Michigan, almost at the exact same moment sixteen hundred miles away, a sophomore English teacher at Manhattan High School collected creative-writing projects. They were ordinary compositions from ordinary kids on ordinary topics the teacher had come to expect from tenth graders, year after year: homecoming romance, sports glory, being noticed, dream cars.

But one was . . . not ordinary.

One fifteen-year-old girl whose father happened to be Manhattan's most prosperous businessman turned in a frightful ghost story. It was a spine-tingling tale about buried jewelry, a man's severed head and limbs hidden in the freezer at an abandoned house, and human bones pickled in canning jars.

The awful yarn's language and phraseology immediately struck the teacher as beyond the girl's normal proficiency. Her subject matter was beyond most small-town kids' imaginations, and this girl hadn't previously shown any dark tendencies.

The words, syntax, and style were far more mature than she was. But it wouldn't have been the first time an older sibling or even a parent had done a lazy child's homework. Not the first time a child embellished a story she'd been told. And certainly not the first time a kid tried to shock her teacher. Still, being a Meirhofer wasn't a free pass to cheat.

Then again, except for the creepy nonsense about frozen body parts, the story seemed to have been inspired by crime stories in the local paper (and whispers around town) about the two girls who had gone missing and ended up scattered all over the Lockhart Ranch. *Well, impressionable kids heard that stuff, too. Right?*

The teacher set it aside. Maybe she'd talk to the girl after class someday, but she didn't feel the need to tell anyone else. It was just a kid being a kid, trying to shock the old fogies. The teacher didn't know what any of it meant.

TOM OLSON MADE ONE last call that morning.

In his mind, if an execution was ever demanded, it was now. Dunbar felt the same. As every new, terrible detail had emerged in this case, they'd both become ever more convinced that this killer, whoever he was, should die. Now they knew the killer's name: David Meirhofer. The charges were drafted; an arrest was only a few hours away. His trial would be a mere formality; his date with the hangman up in Deer Lodge was unscheduled but definite. Olson and Dunbar might even enjoy watching him dangle.

The devout Dykmans, John and Betty, didn't oppose Olson's seeking the death penalty. But his conscience needed one last blessing.

He called the Jaegers' home in Michigan.

Marietta answered.

He told her he planned to charge David with four crimes, two of which—Sandy's aggravated abduction and murder—were new Montana crimes that both carried mandatory death sentences. In other words, if David was convicted by a jury and there were no mitigating circumstances, a judge would have no options except hanging.

Susie's kidnapping and killing happened before the new law, so life in prison was the most severe sentence allowed for those atrocities.

But the hangman wouldn't care which wickedness released the trapdoor.

How do you feel about the death penalty? Olson asked.

Marietta hadn't ever thought much about capital punishment, although she'd sometimes imagined what damage she might do to the man who took her Susie. But her bloody fantasies of revenge were secret and distressing, especially to a good Catholic girl.

Susie. She thought about Susie. How would she want her memory to be served?

In that instant, Marietta decided that her sweet, lost girl who smiled and laughed all her short life wouldn't want someone, even her own pitiless murderer, to be executed in her name.

There should always be a chance at redemption. At renewal. At forgiveness. If David was executed, there'd be no such chance. She remembered the priest who'd come to her in Montana after forgiving the man responsible for his own family's massacre; if he could forgive, why not her? She wasn't quite ready to forgive David Meirhofer, but neither could she be complicit in his death.

No, she said almost apologetically, she couldn't give her blessing to his execution, because Susie wouldn't have wanted that.

THE THIN AIR OF fall carried a whisper of woodsmoke and the distant drums of a marching band.

It was homecoming, a kind of holiday for most small towns out here. Traditionally, homecoming football games celebrated a team's return to its home field after a string of long road trips, but the Manhattan Tigers seldom went far. No matter. There was always a parade and it was always a big deal, even though Manhattan's Main Street was only eight blocks long.

The morning parade had passed a few hours before, and the afternoon game against Manhattan High's unbeaten rival, the Three Forks Wolves, was already under way. This wasn't the Tigers' season. They'd won only one game. The halftime band played better.

Still, almost everybody went to the game. Only a few folks milled around Main Street, mostly sweeping up cigarette butts, wads of gum, and stray hard candies. One of them was David Meirhofer, who sat on the town's parade committee and didn't much like crowds anyway. Even now he kept his distance from everybody, frequently visiting his warehouse.

All morning, he'd watched the cops watch him. Three, maybe four scattered around the crowd. They'd been shadowing him for weeks, not even trying to hide. Hell, it was a small town. There weren't many places to hide, and he knew them all. Once, when night cop Ron Skinner had been staking him out, Meirhofer had walked up and asked him for a lift to Bozeman because it didn't make any sense for them to drive separate cars with gas prices so high.

Around two thirty p.m., Meirhofer emerged again from his warehouse. The sidewalk was empty as he walked west with purpose, past Thompson's Hardware toward his mother's resale shop in the Morros' old liquor store adjacent to the Rexall. But he never got to her front door.

Whether he'd grown complacent or his focus flickered for an unlucky moment, he never saw it coming. Suddenly, two plain-clothes cops blocked the sidewalk ahead. Materializing out of nowhere, Deputy Don Houghton stood beside him. The profilers had warned them all that the UnSub, when cornered, might prefer to die in a spectacular, violent spasm than to be captured. For the safety of bystanders and lawmen alike, they had waited patiently until Meirhofer was alone and out in the open.

"David, you're under arrest for murder and kidnapping," Houghton said. Meirhofer averted his eyes but he looked stunned as Houghton cuffed him. "You have the right to remain silent. . . ."

And he exercised his right. He put up no resistance. No spectacular and no violent anything. He went down like a whipped pup.

Meirhofer said nothing on the short, tense trip to Bozeman in the backseat of Houghton's unmarked county car. Because it was a Friday, somebody called ahead to suggest to irascible District Judge W. W. Lessley that he might want to stay late.

The brassy, taunting, stealthy David Meirhofer was gone. He no longer controlled what would happen next. He had outsmarted them for a long time, and it was beginning to look like they'd never catch him. Now he was a shadow of himself, silent and blank.

In the jailhouse's cramped booking area, a jailer read Meirhofer's Miranda rights to him again, then fingerprinted and strip-searched him. His pockets contained a wallet, car keys, a ticket stub, some loose change, and a scrap of letterhead from a Salt Lake City motel—from the kind of marketing pad every motel drops near its room phones—on which was jotted only an unfamiliar phone number and a name: Mr. Travis. Whoever wrote it had obsessively traced again and again over the letters until the lines had nearly carved through the paper.

The jailer had no idea what any of it meant. Not his job. He just dumped it all in plastic bags, logged the items on a sheet of paper, then locked them in a jailhouse vault.

Throughout the booking process, the prisoner kept silent, except to insist he wouldn't answer any questions without his attorney present. For his part, Dasinger had requested that David remain dressed in his street clothes until he returned from court, hoping his first impression on the judge and, more important, the throng outside wasn't instantly that of a criminal. So the guard set aside Meirhofer's jail-issue white jumpsuit, slippers, and personal bath towel for now.

Around four p.m., the freshly accused killer was led to the holding cell—really, just the drunk tank—to cool his heels until the judge was ready to see him.

Dunbar didn't want Eleanor, his old high school flame, to hear it from anyone else first. He knocked on the door of her little house, and when she answered, he told her as gently as he could that her son had been arrested for two murders. "He did it! He did it!" Eleanor Meirhofer cried out in anguish, as any mother would feel, while her sixteen-year-old daughter, Julia, ran to her room, slammed the door, and threw herself facedown on her bed, screaming, "No, he didn't! No, he didn't!"

Eleanor composed herself and scurried through her house, collecting magazines and fruit that she then rushed to the jail for her son David.

Barely twenty feet from Meirhofer's cell stood the jail's ancient gallows, a relic of the days when Montana's county sheriffs executed their own outlaws (for counties that couldn't afford their own gallows, the state of Montana maintained a traveling scaffold and even printed invitations for public executions). Gallatin County had used its gibbet only once, back in 1924, when it hanged a local man for killing his fishing buddy and the buddy's wife. Seventy years later, the unlucky convict's widow confessed on her deathbed that she had killed the couple herself. At any rate, the state had taken control of executions in the 1940s, so Gallatin County's dusty scaffold just stood there silently as a kind of cautionary presence.

But in Meirhofer's case, death by hanging—Montana's method of execution, legal and otherwise, since the 1800s—wasn't just possible. It was likely.

BEFORE DEADLINE AT THE *Daily Chronicle* and in time to make the evening AP wires, SA Dunbar hand delivered the news in Bozeman. Dunbar and Prosecutor Olson had slapped it together in a half hour, run it past the SAC in Butte, then typed it up on official FBI letterhead.

September 27, 1974

PRESS RELEASE

David G. Meirhofer, 25, a Manhattan, Montana, resident, has been arrested and charged with the kidnapping and murders of Susan Jaeger and Sandra D[ykman] Smallegan.

. . . The arrest was the result of a massive investigation which was launched June 25, 1973, when Susan Jaeger, a 7-year-old Farmington Hills, Michigan, girl, was kidnapped from a tent at Headwaters State Park near Three Forks, Montana.

The investigation intensified when Sandra D. Smallegan, 19, of Manhattan, was reported missing on February 9, 1974. Her automobile and bones identified to be those of Sandra Smallegan were found at a remote and unoccupied ranch northeast of Three Forks.

. . . Meirhofer was arrested on the basis of numerous telephone calls to the Jaeger residence by the purported kidnapper. . . .

Only reporters needed official press releases. Nobody else waited for them. Word spread like a prairie fire across Gallatin County. A barber in Bozeman heard it sooner than the director of the FBI himself.

Even before Houghton delivered Meirhofer to the jail, a few folks milled around outside. Soon enough dozens of onlookers gathered on the sidewalk outside the courthouse and the jail next door.

Within the hour, hundreds spilled off the curb and into Bozeman's Main Street, as passing cars slowed for the spontaneous spectacle.

The gawkers clustered close to catch a glimpse of the killer, and to be near this fleeting moment of history. It might even make the national news, and the folks of Gallatin County were still provincial enough to take a certain amount of pride when the names of their towns popped up in the big papers outside Montana.

Judge Lessley called for the prisoner at a quarter past five that Friday night.

Sheriff Anderson and Deputy Houghton debated their next step, literally.

The sheriff wanted to escort a handcuffed Meirhofer through the restless, thrumming crowd outside, which had grown to more than a gang, but was not yet a mob. Not yet. They came to see a killer, and with an election coming up, Andy wanted them to know he was keeping citizens, some of whom were coincidentally voters, safe from such monsters.

Houghton, though, was thinking like a cop who wasn't running for any office. He considered there might be somebody so angry out there that he'd take a shot at Meirhofer or the deputies escorting him. Like Houghton.

Jailers never took suspects to the courthouse on the sidewalk outside. Instead, they always walked prisoners through a dimly lit underground tunnel between the jail and the adjacent courthouse. If a prisoner tried to escape, where would he run? Into the heavily locked doors at either end? But a hundred unexpected things, some of them fatal, might happen outside. The tunnel was not only more efficient; it was safer.

Houghton won.

They handcuffed Meirhofer in his cell and led him through the county's dark passage to Judge Lessley's third-floor courtroom.

Known around town simply as "the Judge," Lessley had grown up on a Gallatin County farm. He had gone off to college and law school in the Depression, then walked away from his law practice to enlist in the US Army Air Corps in World War II. He flew the perilous Burma Hump, where weather crashed more planes than the Japanese, and in three years he rose from buck private to major, winning the Bronze Star along the way. He came home to Bozeman and was soon elected Gallatin County's top prosecutor. On the day he became a district judge, his farmer father told him, "When you've finished this job, I want you to be able to look anyone in the eye and tell them to go to hell." In other words, everybody knew Judge Lessley was a tough son of a bitch who tolerated no theatrics or legal stunts. You didn't tell him. He told you.

Meirhofer's arraignment was short and cold.

The four serious charges against him were read. He stood accused in the kidnapping and first-degree murder of Susan Marie Jaeger, charges under an old Montana law that allowed sentences up to and including execution. But for the counts of "aggravated kidnapping" and "deliberate murder" of Sandra Smallegan, he faced possible mandatory death under the new law. *Do you understand?*

Meirhofer spoke softly. Yes, he did.

Because of the heinousness of the charges, Lessley ruled that no bond would be allowed. *Do you understand?*

Yes, Meirhofer said.

Dasinger then asked if the rest of his client's arraignment might be postponed for a week—until October 7—to allow more preparation than a mere three hours afforded him. Lessley agreed.

Without a doubt, this promised to be the most sensational case of the Judge's career on the bench, and he wasn't about to let it squitter out of his control. His final order was a gag: Nobody—not some seventy court staffers, lawyers, law enforcement officials, witnesses, or the defendant himself—was to speak about the case publicly, except for the barest facts to satisfy the public's right to know. Any violation would be considered contempt of court, and Lessley didn't like being embarrassed. *Do you understand?*

And just like that, in less than ten minutes, David Meirhofer had received more mercy and justice than Susie or Sandy ever got from their killer. From here on out, every time he stepped into a courtroom or jail cell he'd be protected by God, the law, and the light of day more than those two girls were. His presumed innocence would shield him; theirs doomed them.

And maybe sooner rather than later, he might breathe free again. They never would.

After court adjourned, Prosecutor Olson and Agent Dunbar followed the Judge to his chambers, where he approved the warrant for a second search of Meirhofer's properties and vehicles. While they could seize anything incriminating, they were specifically looking for a dainty turquoise ring worn by Susie Jaeger at the time she vanished, the "buttinski" handset Meirhofer might have used to place the anniversary call from Ralph Green's gully, and any receipts or other documents that might prove Meirhofer's whereabouts on the night of the Mr. Travis call.

During the court proceedings, Sheriff Anderson informed Pete Dunbar that he intended to take Meirhofer back to jail through the crowd out front. Assassins be damned, Andy wanted to give the folks what they came to see, maybe get a few votes. Dunbar protested but told Andy that if he insisted, the FBI wanted Deputy Houghton front and center. He'd been present at every major turn in this case, literally from the first morning fifteen months earlier to Meirhofer's arrest just a few hours before. He deserved at least as much credit as Andy.

The sheriff cuffed his suspect and choked his left arm above the elbow. Houghton grabbed his right. Surrounded by a phalanx of other deputies and state troopers, they strode out the courthouse's front door and waded directly into the rabble, which was now so big that it stopped Main Street traffic dead. Houghton kept a keen eye out for any guns or sudden movements in the gauntlet of jostling spectators. In the scrum, a photographer from the *Bozeman Daily Chronicle* snapped a few frames of the accused killer.

It seemed like a rugged mile to Houghton when, in fact, it took less than a minute to arrive at the safety of the jail's front door.

The jailer quickly finished Meirhofer's booking, took mug shots, and watched as he changed out of his street clothes into his requisite jail jumpsuit. He issued David his bath towel and led him to the lockup in back. Four long-term cells sat two and two on either side of a little exercise corridor, slightly hidden from the drunk tank and the guards going about their chores. They were also the darkest, loneliest, and farthest from any doors. If the Gallatin County jail had anything remotely resembling solitary confinement, David's cell was it.

Dunbar asked the jailer for David's personal effects. He wanted to examine his wallet and see what other things his suspect had carried in his pockets. When he saw the letterhead from the Salt Palace Travelodge with the Jaegers' phone number and "Mr. Travis" scrawled on it, his heart leapt. He hurried out to Olson's office. He'd found his smoking gun, finally: Mr. Travis had taken Susie . . . and David Meirhofer was Mr. Travis.

The dreadful dots were finally connected.

At the same time, Doug Dasinger returned to his cluttered office neither buoyant nor hopeless. The criminal case against David was sickening but, as far as he knew, entirely circumstantial. A hundred other good suspects existed, a thousand reasons to doubt that the FBI had the right guy. For every grieving mother who supposedly recognized his voice, there was a polygraph that declared him innocent; for every tire track that led to David, another led away; for every yokel who found him "odd," there were two who described him as a hardworking, modestly intelligent, genial son from a good family.

Dasinger didn't know what any of it meant.

But he knew the mob on Main Street—his future jury—might not care. Luckily, the street wasn't a courtroom.

And at that moment, he *didn't* know what else the FBI might find.

AT THAT SAME TIME, a swarm of Gallatin County deputies and Bozeman city cops was ransacking Meirhofer's truck and warehouse and the spartan garage-apartment where he lived. The FBI's earlier search had been relatively gentle, involving opening a few drawers and peeking in glove boxes. But now local cops were ripping apart a suspected killer's hidden spaces like hunting dogs on the trail of fresh blood. Each one of them hoped not so secretly that he'd find the piece of evidence that would hang David Meirhofer.

They couldn't find Susie Jaeger's turquoise ring, but hidden on a shelf behind some oilcans they found a yellow and black telephone lineman's handset—a "buttinski"—that might well have been used to place the anniversary call from Ralph Green's ranch line.

Wadded up in the back of a dresser drawer they found a homemade black mask, crudely stitched together from a thin material like a woman's blouse and with jagged eyeholes cut out—which might well have been used during the abortive abduction at the Girl Scouts' Camp Silver Cloud.

Lying open on Meirhofer's nightstand was a Bible—one of several they found. As a deputy leafed through the well-thumbed pages, he found two passages underlined and read them out loud before he really had a chance to absorb them. The first was from Hebrews chapter 9:

And almost all things are by the law purged with blood;
and without shedding of blood is no forgiveness.

The second was in Mark chapter 9:

And if thy hand offend thee, cut it off: it is better for thee
to enter into life maimed, than having two hands to go into Hell,
into the fire that never shall be quenched: Where their worm dieth not,
and the fire is not quenched.

The searchers stopped cold, silent, but there was more. Meirhofer's Bible required the spilled blood to be innocent, pure. Shedding guilty blood wouldn't work. Only innocent blood could be sacrificed to properly purge the sin.

Blood . . . fire . . . mutilation? Not in their churches, where butchery wasn't exactly included in Sunday school lessons.

For God's sake, was Meirhofer justifying his cruelty under the guise of religion? Did he actually believe that without bloodshed there could be no absolution? Did he think God had commanded him to hasten his victims' forgiveness by shedding their blood? *Did he see himself as some kind of sick purifying archangel?*

There wasn't time for ecclesiastical polemics. They were searching a likely killer's most intimate space. Seeing the invisible meaning in two-thousand-year-old words was what the FBI's mind readers back in Quantico, Teten and Mullany, got paid to do.

So Denny Thompson, a scrupulous Bozeman cop helping the

searchers, opened Meirhofer's refrigerator and looked inside. Aside from the usual stuff a bachelor would keep in his fridge was an uncovered plate with a raw, rancid steak that looked as if Meirhofer had intended to cook it for a dinner he'd never eat now. The spoiled meat didn't look like beef, so Thompson asked a couple of his buddies to look at it. Deer? Elk? They shrugged. Meirhofer was known to be a hunter who butchered his own game, so it might be anything. All they knew for sure was that it was rotting.

Maybe the meat mystery could be solved. Thompson opened the freezer compartment, where he found a bunch of home-wrapped packages of meat stacked inside. Meirhofer had scribbled "elk" on some of them, and six were labeled "deer burger" on one side and "SMDS" in smaller letters on the other. Maybe it stood for "suet, meat, deer sausage"? This also might be anything. Not unusual for a hunter in these parts.

A small chest freezer sat beside the fridge. Thompson opened it, too. More of the same, just a bunch of white freezer-paper packages.

But an unmarked and oddly shaped package sat off to one side. He picked it up and gently squeezed, noting that it felt like a hardened bird carcass or a halved squash, which was odd because neither of those things would commonly be frozen. He untaped the white freezer paper just enough to see what was inside.

He gasped and reflexively pitched it back into the freezer.

A DEPUTY RADIOED A dispatcher, who patched him through to Sheriff Anderson, who called Pete Dunbar, who called County Attorney Tom Olson, who called defense lawyer Doug Dasinger and asked him to meet them all at Meirhofer's bungalow in Manhattan.

Dunbar and Olson were already there when a rumpled Dasinger pulled up in his junker. He'd already spent a few hours earlier in Manhattan hovering around the searchers, but their warrant was broad and he was powerless to intervene, so he'd returned to Bozeman. His presence had served only as a reminder, however feeble, that his client still had rights and was still presumed innocent.

In fact, Dasinger still believed very strongly in his sclerotic heart that his kid was innocent.

Now here all the sheriff's men were looking for some otherwise meaningless tidbit to prove they were right. David had passed their lie detector tests and allowed them to pump so-called truth serum into his veins. He'd answered all their questions every time they bushwhacked him on the street. He submitted himself to the humiliating accusations of a grieving but deluded mother. The FBI had crawled up his ass and found nothing. Dasinger had heard the Bureau's shrinks were foisting some mystical juju bullshit that nobody—even they—truly understood. Even the big-time "Special Agent" Dunbar himself wasn't convinced that David Meirhofer was anything more than a hapless kid whose only real crimes were stealing socks from the Marine Corps and being slightly different.

Dunbar and his federal goons had found no smoking guns in their last search, just random stuff—Disneyland tickets, dirty old bedsheets, a necklace nobody recognized, and some lipstick, fergawdsakes—that required some real investigative gymnastics to sorta, maybe, possibly connect to two missing girls . . . crimes that might not even be related. These hayseeds weren't that smart.

Every shadow comes alive if you just squint.

Olson met Dasinger at the front door. The prosecutor handed him a copy of the search warrant and he glanced at it. Dunbar then informed Dasinger that they had found important evidence, although he didn't describe it.

What circumstantial crap had they found now? Dasinger

thought. A sharp steak knife? More newspaper clippings? A box of matches? These Barney Fife buffoons watched too much *Columbo*.

They led him to the kitchen area. Dunbar opened the freezer and pulled that odd-shaped package out. He unwrapped it for Dasinger, close enough to his face for the lawyer to see what it held.

It was a human hand, a right hand, cleanly sawn at the wrist and shriveled like a witch's claw. It was strangely delicate, with long nails painted red.

And clutched in its frozen palm, two bony fingers, also with painted nails.

"Oh, fuck!" Dasinger blurted. He dropped the warrant and went white as he rushed toward the door. He hadn't gotten more than a few steps outside before he puked.

Pretty funny, the smirking deputies outside thought as they watched the defense lawyer lose his lunch. *Pretty funny.*

DUNBAR GINGERLY PACKED THE uncovered steak and twenty icy packages of meat from the freezer into a foam cooler. When the severed hand and fingers had thawed just enough, fingerprints were taken. Then Dunbar dispatched a deputy to rush the whole cooler to Dr. John Pfaff, the pathologist at Great Falls' Columbus Hospital who had first identified the human bones at the Lockhart Ranch. Great Falls was more than two hours away, even in a speeding cruiser all lit up.

Pfaff's preliminary results were quick but unholy. Six of the packages labeled "deer meat" contained human flesh mixed with suet, a cow fat usually added to wild game to make it taste better. Another contained long strips of human muscle tissue cured like jerky.

The meat in one package contained type A blood, another type

B. Sandy Smallegan's blood had never been typed, but the blood types of her parents indicated she'd likely have had type AB. Susie's blood had never been typed, either, so the FBI asked Detroit agents to draw Marietta and Bill Jaeger's blood for comparison. Dr. Pfaff said he'd try to get a blood type from the frozen hand to compare to the wrapped meat, but it'd take a little more time. Until then, maybe it wasn't Sandy's, maybe it was Susie's, maybe the tests weren't precise enough . . . or maybe it was someone else's entirely.

The fingerprints definitely matched numerous latent prints lifted from Sandy Smallegan's Cortina and apartment. So, without a doubt, Dunbar's Montana expert in Helena said, the hand was Sandy Smallegan's.

And that solved another mystery.

The initials "SMDS" on the underside of the meat packages?

Sandra Mae Dykman Smallegan.

DOUG DASINGER WAS ENRAGED, embarrassed, and literally gut sick.

As he coaxed and prodded his rattletrap back to Bozeman, that severed hand haunted him. It wasn't just the grisly reality of how or why a young woman's hand and fingers had been hacked off and deep-frozen, not to mention the corpse of a little girl Meirhofer had likely cremated, hammered into unspeakable bits, and scattered like vile seeds on bad earth.

It was also a shocking piece of evidence too revolting for any jury to ignore. He was a damned good lawyer, but not so good that he could make a mutilated girl disappear. There was no longer any question in Dasinger's mind that David Meirhofer was a killer. Being so utterly deceived made him want to puke again.

A bigger problem existed. Montana's new capital-punishment laws, less than a year old, had been crafted to execute exactly this kind of depraved killer. No jurisdiction in the whole state would take pity on him. His suddenly loathsome client's chances of avoiding Death Row were less than zero. If David Meirhofer sickened his own defense lawyer—once his truest believer—an angry, nauseated jury wouldn't hesitate to hang him.

Dasinger fervently opposed capital punishment. He called it state-sponsored murder, even when deep down in the secret pit of his gut he quietly admitted to himself the earth would be better without that one evil person. Even if David Meirhofer was Satan himself, Dasinger felt a kind of sacred duty to save him from Montana's hangman. But when the prosecutor held up a photograph of that hand found in David Meirhofer's freezer . . . Dasinger would have nothing.

He drove straight to the tiny Gallatin County jail, where there wasn't any special room where a lawyer could confer privately with a client. Ron Brown, the deputy on duty that night, led Dasinger to Meirhofer's new cell at the farthest end of the jail.

Dasinger erupted. His fury and mortification spewed out, loud enough to be heard outside the confines of the little cellblock. Meirhofer said nothing.

Dasinger described the angry mob outside. Twelve of them would be jurors. And even a change of venue wouldn't help, because the horrid news was spreading in newspapers and radio broadcasts all over Montana. Meirhofer said nothing.

Dasinger explained, as best he could through his rage, how Meirhofer was screwed. How that frozen hand would close his coffin and drive in the final nail. Still, Meirhofer said nothing.

The last, best hope was a bargain. The odds were stacked a mile high against an acquittal, but they might take the death penalty off the table by negotiating a deal with the prosecution. The problem at the moment was that Tom Olson, for the rest of his life, would probably never take an easier or more appalling murder case into a courtroom. He knew a conviction was in the bag and a death sentence as certain as the human heart would allow. Dasinger, on the other hand, had no leverage. *Jesus Christ, why would a sane prosecutor strike a deal to save an innocent girl's butcher from an all-but-certain noose?*

Then Meirhofer said something.

What if there were others they don't know about?

CHAPTER 8

"TO FEEL HER"

After midnight, Doug Dasinger hollered for Deputy Ron Brown to let him out of Meirhofer's cell, which had suddenly grown claustrophobic.

As the steel door slammed behind him, Dasinger asked Brown if he could use the jail's phone to call County Attorney Tom Olson, who had returned from Manhattan and planned to spend the night at the courthouse collecting himself.

It must be urgent, Brown thought, since Olson's office was just next door.

It was urgent, all right.

Dasinger spoke in a low, grave voice. Brown overheard only his half of the short conversation.

Something has come up. . . .

Yeah, something big . . .

Can we talk . . . ?

A deal . . .

Now . . .

Maybe take the death penalty off the table . . .

Yeah, he'll confess. . . .

Other murders . . .

I don't know. . . .

First thing tomorrow . . .

Those two girls . . . and at least two more.

Olson hung up and caught his breath. He hadn't slept since dawn the day before and his body didn't feel like it belonged to him. But now he was wide-awake.

He'd been around. He'd heard more than his share of suspects' bullshit. Most wanted to trade nothing for something, but Olson always needed something for something. Incontrovertible details or no deal.

His mind raced. His tendency to disbelieve was undeniably suspended. Might David Meirhofer—the mild-mannered hacker of hands and cremator of corpses—reveal other such unimaginable atrocities? Was it all a delaying tactic or was an honest-to-God mass murderer sitting in the Gallatin County jail right now?

Olson called Dunbar, who was up late, too, cataloging the horrid, haunting evidence found the day before at Meirhofer's converted garage. The news had convulsed Dunbar's gut. Three times, Meirhofer had popped up on Dunbar's radar as a viable suspect . . . and three times, Dunbar had ruled him out. He believed the kid had been a victim of his own quirks. He believed Meirhofer's explanations. He believed the lie detector didn't lie and the truth serum told the truth. He just believed . . . at the exact moment he shouldn't have.

Now Meirhofer sought to trade his own all-but-certain death for dirty stories about other deaths. A future swapped for a past. Dunbar, like Olson, was trapped between vengeance for a killer and justice for his victims. And because he knew what agony the Jaegers and the Dykmans had endured, he had no doubt that some as-yet-unknown families out there wanted answers, too.

Morning would break soon. Neither Dunbar nor Olson doubted that David Meirhofer deserved to die sooner rather than later, but they agreed to hear Dasinger's proposal before deciding whether Hell must wait a little longer.

BY MIDMORNING, DAVID MEIRHOFER had told Dasinger everything, angering him even more. But the defense lawyer—and Meirhofer— knew these gruesome details about the murders of four innocent people might actually save his life. It would be an uphill battle. Only a prosecutor who cared more about decency than convictions would even give Meirhofer and Dasinger a chance.

Dasinger met Olson and Dunbar at the Gallatin County Attorney's office shortly after eleven a.m. Saturday. For the next two hours, they debated Meirhofer's fate.

Dasinger opened the bidding.

He offered Meirhofer's detailed confession to four murders, not two. Not just the unspeakable specifics of what he had done to Susie and Sandy, but also his other victims.

In return, he asked that Olson recommend to the judge that his client should not be executed, but should spend the rest of his life in prison. The possibility of parole was a bridge too far, and Dasinger never raised it.

One more thing: Meirhofer insisted that the graphic details of his confession remain secret to protect his parents and siblings from a small town's cruelties. If Manhattan ever learned his true monstrosity, the rancorous whispers and sidelong glances would isolate them in the only home they knew. They were innocent, Dasinger said, but they'd be worse than lepers, the walking dead.

Olson had another theory: Meirhofer feared that his father and mother would know once and for all that they'd raised a sadistic monster. If the profilers were right, one of them held the ultimate power over him.

If Olson agreed in principle to this deal, then—and only then—Dasinger would reveal names, dates, and places of those other crimes so Dunbar could verify them before the interrogation.

After that, Meirhofer was prepared to plead guilty to all four murders in court on Monday—just forty-eight hours from that moment.

Not so fast, Olson said.

First, he didn't give a shit what a child killer *insisted*.

Second, he and Dunbar needed more time to consider Dasinger's offer. They wanted to confer with the victims' families, the sheriff, and Dunbar's FBI team, including the profilers Teten and Mullany. It wouldn't be long, but it would be necessary.

They arranged to meet again before noon to hammer out a deal, if such a deal could be made at all.

It was a Saturday and already midafternoon back East when Dunbar called Mullany at home. He described the arrest in broad daylight, the search, and the staggering possibility that David Meirhofer had more victims than they had imagined. He wanted to know Mullany's thoughts on what came next.

Mullany told Dunbar he already knew most of what he needed to know.

David was deeply mentally ill, and his freezer contained all the proof anyone needed. Sadly, souvenir body parts and cannibalism were not really surprising.

For a long time, the outside world saw a friendly, well-dressed, articulate, slightly awkward but harmless fellow. It was just a mask. He removed the mask only in the dark. *Prepare to see a very different individual,* Mullany warned, *probably unrecognizable as the David Meirhofer you thought you knew.*

Look at unsolved cases. *Unless David was just getting started,* he said, *there are probably more than just four victims.*

Watch for a kind of progression in his killings, as if he was learning from each one.

The risks he took in his two known crimes were a big part of the thrill he got from them, so look for similar risk-taking in his other crimes. Abducting and murdering are a sport to him, and he likes to be up close.

He'll admit to some of his crimes, but don't expect long-winded descriptions or explanations. He's keeping those memories to himself for as long as he can. *You want it,* he told Dunbar, *so he holds power over you as long as he doesn't give it to you.*

His shell is impenetrable unless he chooses to reveal more. It will take time to learn just how sick he is, maybe weeks or months. So be patient.

Just before Dunbar hung up, Mullany shared one last thought.

Continue to take extra precautions with him, especially now. *He is a caged beast. He is cornered. And he is still dangerous to you and to himself.*

DUNBAR, OLSON, AND DASINGER reconvened that afternoon in Bozeman, all of them still bleary.

Olson accepted most of Dasinger's proposed deal—except keeping Meirhofer's confession secret. The anxious crowd at Meirhofer's "perp walk" was just a taste of the public uproar to come. There'd be an angry uprising if the details of his crimes were withheld from them.

Dasinger pushed back. If the transcript of their interrogation were to be made public, David might withdraw completely. His chances with a jury might be slim, but he'd take them. And two families—the Raneys and the Poelmans—would never know.

Would Meirhofer rather die than allow his secret sins to be known? If it was a bluff, it was a good one, Olson felt.

The confession would be used only to support the charges, Olson said. If Meirhofer pleaded guilty as promised, the county attorney wouldn't release the sicker details. But a single evasive or deceptive answer would end the conversation and send him straight to Death Row.

Dasinger nodded.

Olson added one final demand: If he accepted Dasinger's deal, Meirhofer could not claim to be guilty by reason of insanity. Yes, he was spectacularly insane, Olson believed, but not in the eyes of the law. The killer had gone to extremes to hide his crimes. He knew the difference between right and his abhorrent wrongs. An insanity defense would only muddy the waters and drag out justice.

And deal or not, Dasinger needed to know that this confession wouldn't close the books on David Meirhofer. Other investigations into other crimes couldn't be stopped. Anything he said could be used against him. Olson held no sway over prosecutors beyond Gallatin County's borders.

If the killer's body count piled up, the hangman might be a more relentless negotiator than a small-time county attorney.

Olson summarized:

If he didn't seek the death penalty but strongly urged the judge for a lesser sentence . . .

If Meirhofer waived all his rights to remain silent and agreed to answer all of the prosecution's questions . . .

If Meirhofer's confession remained confidential . . .

If there'd be no insanity defense . . .

If Dasinger understood the deal didn't apply to any other crimes that might surface . . .

Then David Meirhofer would freely confess—in painful detail—to four murders, and would plead guilty to all of them in district court on Monday morning.

Dasinger agreed, and they shook hands. Olson himself would draw up the formal paperwork, and as soon as Meirhofer understood and agreed to the deal, they would begin the interrogation, no matter the hour. The sooner the better.

After Dasinger left, Dunbar and Olson began drafting their questions. Dunbar already had a list of Montana's unsolved murders, but none were in Gallatin County. Surely Dasinger wouldn't let him confess to a murder that fell outside of Olson's jurisdiction, would he?

It was past midnight when all of them were prepared for the literally gory details. Sheriff Anderson arranged for Olson, Dunbar, Dasinger, and Meirhofer to meet around the small conference table in his private office at the jail.

They gathered somberly there at about three a.m. A jailer led Meirhofer into the room, wearing his white jail coveralls and looking hollow. No small talk. Dunbar placed a battery-operated tape recorder in the center of the table and slid in a fresh tape labeled "Meirhofer confession 9/29/74."

Precisely at three twenty a.m., when they had all settled uncomfortably in their straight-backed steel chairs, Dunbar pressed "Record."

SA PETE DUNBAR: I am with the FBI. You know Mr. Olson?

DAVID MEIRHOFER: Yes.

DUNBAR: County Attorney of Gallatin County. Your defense attorney, Douglas Dasinger, is here, right?

MEIRHOFER: Yes.

DUNBAR: It's now three twenty a.m., OK? Now, David, I have told you this before and I'm going to repeat it just so there's no doubt. Before we ask you any questions, you do know you have the right to remain silent, that anything you say can be used against you in court. You have the right to talk to a lawyer, who is here now for advice, and to have him present, which he is during this questioning. If you decide to answer our questions now with your lawyer present, you will and can do so, but you also will have the right to stop and not answer any questions until you do confer with your attorney, Mr. Dasinger. Now, do you understand this?

MEIRHOFER: Yes.

DUNBAR: The next thing, David, I am going to ask you if you know that this is in accordance with the Fifth Amendment, and if you do answer questions, you are waiving a right, so I would like you to consult with your attorney and know that you understand this and knowingly waive this right and go ahead and we can talk about things, OK?

MEIRHOFER: Yes.

DUNBAR: And if Mr. Dasinger will read this, explain it to you, and I would like him to have you sign it, with his having read it.

DEFENSE ATTORNEY DOUG DASINGER: Pete—Mr. Dunbar—has handed me what is called a "waiver of rights." You and I have discussed this matter, and under my advice, I have advised you that I feel it is in your best interests, under all the circumstances, to waive your rights under the Fifth Amendment and to make the statements and answer questions that are about to be asked. And I am advising you at this time to sign the waiver of rights, which means that you are, in effect, waiving your right to refuse to testify against yourself, and that's what I am handing you now.

MEIRHOFER: Do you have to have a written guarantee [that the details of this interview will remain secret if I plead guilty]?

DUNBAR: Yeah. Everything, David, that we are talking about is being recorded, OK?

MEIRHOFER: I mean, guarantee for what . . .

DASINGER: For what we talked about?

MEIRHOFER: Yeah.

DASINGER: That will be there, and this will be transcribed, if necessary.

DUNBAR: Would you put the time in, too, David? It's three twenty-three a.m.

MEIRHOFER: Bozeman?

DUNBAR and DASINGER (simultaneously): Yes.

DUNBAR: Can I go ahead, Mr. Olson and Mr. Dasinger—and state all the things we talked about, or do you want to do this?

DASINGER: Let me make a brief statement . . .

DUNBAR: Please do, yes.

DASINGER: . . . as to my understanding of this, and then I'd like to have Mr. Olson, unless you'd rather state first. I have conferred with David. We've discussed some matters. We have also discussed . . . I have also discussed with the county attorney, Mr. Olson, and with you, Mr. Dunbar, the fact that in return for a guarantee from the county attorney that he will strongly recommend against the death penalty in any of the charges, that David would be—I would advise David and he would be—willing to make a statement, uh, regarding the two crimes for which he's charged and other events. Uh, that he would be willing to answer questions—and again this would be based on the guarantee of the county attorney that he would recommend against any death penalty, and that, uh, I have also advised David that in my opinion the death penalty is applicable only in the case of *State of Montana v. David Meirhofer*, re: Sandra Smallegan, that in any other case we are discussing here, it is my opinion that the death penalty is unconstitutional and could not be applied to him. I have further advised him that I feel that under the circumstances of the evidence of which I am aware and all of the factors, that he, uh, is in grave danger of being convicted, and in my opinion it is almost a certainty he would be convicted and that under our law, the death penalty is mandatory unless there are mitigating circumstances. That is my understanding.

COUNTY ATTORNEY TOM OLSON: This is Tom Olson, the Gallatin County Attorney, speaking. I concur with Mr. Dasinger's and Mr. Meirhofer's understanding. I will strongly recommend to the district judge that the death penalty not be imposed on the condition that the defendant, David Meirhofer, make a full and complete statement concerning the Sandra Smallegan case, concerning the Susan Jaeger case, and concerning any other case that will be brought up at this proceeding. In addition, the defendant will waive any plea of not guilty by reason of insanity and would enter a plea of guilty to the two cases I have mentioned that have been filed in court and any other case that would be filed as a result of this conference.

DASINGER: Turn off the tape.

OLSON: Uh, the tape will now be shut off at the request of the defendant's attorney.

[*Tape resumes after a private discussion between Dasinger and Olson.*]

DUNBAR: OK, now both the county attorney and the defense attorney have made their statements. Now I am talking to you, David, as the investigating agent, Pete Dunbar with the FBI. You know me as such, right?

MEIRHOFER: Yes.

DUNBAR: Are you now willing, David, and will you answer questions that I pose to you?

MEIRHOFER: Yes.

DUNBAR: OK, do you realize, David, that this is on the record?

MEIRHOFER: Yes.

DUNBAR: Being very, very blunt, very truthful, cutting this to the bare essentials, did you on June 25 take Susie—Susie Jaeger—from a tent in the Headwaters State Park at Three Forks?

MEIRHOFER: Yes.

DUNBAR: Did you cause Susan to be hurt, and if so, why?

MEIRHOFER: Yes, I had to choke her.

DUNBAR: Was she killed when you choked her?

MEIRHOFER: No.

DUNBAR: When was she killed?

MEIRHOFER: Uh, a little later.

DUNBAR: All right, let's start, David. I know this is difficult but it's the only way I know to do it. When you took her from the tent and choked her, where did you take her?

MEIRHOFER: Uh, it was about a hundred yards north and then over to the highway fifty yards back across the highway up on top of the hill, where the monument is, down the road on top of this hill about half a mile to my pickup, which was waiting alongside the river.

DUNBAR: Did you put her in the pickup?

MEIRHOFER: Yes.

DUNBAR: And then where did you take her?

MEIRHOFER: Went out to the ranch.

DUNBAR: The Lockhart Ranch, right? Did you then nail her in the closet? I mean, put her in the closet and nail the door shut?

MEIRHOFER: No.

DUNBAR: Well, what happened, then?

MEIRHOFER: Well, I undressed her and then, uh . . . well, uh . . . I proceeded to feel her body and she got pretty wild, I guess, and I choked her. She died.

DUNBAR: She what?

MEIRHOFER: She died.

DUNBAR: OK, and then did you conceal her body?

MEIRHOFER: Yes.

DUNBAR: Where?

MEIRHOFER: Uh, I cut her up.

DUNBAR: And where is the body located?

MEIRHOFER: Well, not much left of it.

DUNBAR: What's left? Where . . . where did you put the pieces?

MEIRHOFER: I put her head in that outhouse behind the ranch and all the rest of it was burned.

DUNBAR: And what did you burn it with, David?

MEIRHOFER: Just wood.

DUNBAR: Pardon?

MEIRHOFER: Just wood.

DUNBAR: With wood and . . . ?

MEIRHOFER: It was done in different places on the ranch.

DUNBAR: And where did you spread these pieces?

MEIRHOFER: Well, the . . . uh, the main part of the torso . . . the upper torso . . . was burned alongside a culvert on the road between the Lockhart Ranch and Menard.

DUNBAR: And Menard?

MEIRHOFER: Uh-huh.

DUNBAR: And was it spread along or was it in one area?

MEIRHOFER: No, it was all . . . It was all right there. It . . . I had wrapped it in a bunch of blankets and stuff.

DUNBAR: Where . . . where could it be found for . . . for burial purposes?

MEIRHOFER: Well, it was burned completely.

DUNBAR: Just with wood? Is that correct? Just with wood?

MEIRHOFER: Yeah.

DUNBAR: OK. What did you use, David, as an instrument to cut the body up?

MEIRHOFER: My hunting knife.

DUNBAR: Just the knife?

MEIRHOFER: Yes.

DUNBAR: No saw or anything else?

MEIRHOFER: Yes.

DUNBAR: OK, now, David, did, uh . . . did you or will you tell us what happened to Sandra Smallegan?

MEIRHOFER: Yes.

DUNBAR: And in your own words, just the same way you did with Susie. Go ahead.

MEIRHOFER: Well, I went up to her apartment about two o'clock in the morning of the tenth.

DUNBAR: Of February. Is this correct?

MEIRHOFER: Yes.

DUNBAR: OK, pardon.

DASINGER: Year?

DUNBAR: 1974, OK?

MEIRHOFER: And, uh, I . . . she was sleeping and I jumped on her and choked her and then tied her up and put a piece of tape around her mouth and then I was gonna . . . While I was putting some of her clothes and stuff in the car, she evidently died. She couldn't get any air through the tape.

DUNBAR: She was dead, then, before you left Manhattan?

MEIRHOFER: Yes.

DUNBAR: OK, and then what happened?

MEIRHOFER: Then I put her in the car, too, and went out to the Lockhart Ranch.

DUNBAR: OK, and then what?

MEIRHOFER: And I proceeded to cut her up, too.

DUNBAR: With what?

MEIRHOFER: My hunting knife.

DUNBAR: Nothing else?

MEIRHOFER: I think I did use a saw.

DUNBAR: What kind of saw, David?

MEIRHOFER: A handsaw.

DUNBAR: OK and, uh . . . what did you do with her pieces?

MEIRHOFER: Well, I burned them right there at the ranch.

DUNBAR: With what?

MEIRHOFER: With wood shingles and stuff that were piled alongside the buildings.

DUNBAR: Nothing else?

MEIRHOFER: No.

DUNBAR: Where . . . where would Sandra's remains be?

MEIRHOFER: Right in that campfire beside the house.

DUNBAR: Nowhere else? OK, did you, David, have occasion to hurt in any way a Boy Scout at the camp in Three Forks where Susie was?

MEIRHOFER: Yes.

DUNBAR: And do you know his name?

MEIRHOFER: Michael Raney.

DUNBAR: Did you know him before this happened?

MEIRHOFER: No.

DUNBAR: OK, then what happened with Michael Raney?

MEIRHOFER: Well, I went to the park where the Boy Scouts were camped and I was going to get somebody, and I opened this tent and I saw this little boy, and I couldn't force myself to take him, I guess, so I stabbed him in the back.

DUNBAR: And then did you hit him with anything on the head?

MEIRHOFER: No, I did not.

DUNBAR: This was just a stabbing. Is that correct?

MEIRHOFER: Yes.

DUNBAR: You did not hit him with a club or your fist or anything?

MEIRHOFER: I did not.

DUNBAR: Just stabbed him? And what happened then?

MEIRHOFER: Well, I ran back to my truck.

DUNBAR: Did you know whether Michael Raney died until you read it in the newspaper?

MEIRHOFER: I did not, until I read it.

DUNBAR: David, do you know or do you recall having caused injury to a boy on the bridge directly behind Manhattan, or north of Manhattan across the Gallatin River? Is it the Noxon or Nixon Bridge?

MEIRHOFER: Nixon Bridge.

DUNBAR: And did you know this boy by name?

MEIRHOFER: Yes.

DUNBAR: Like before, what happened then? In your own words.

MEIRHOFER: Well, I had been up in the hills and came down past the bridge and the two boys were . . . I seen them playing there and I went down the road and parked about a hundred, hundred fifty yards and walked out around with my rifle—.22-caliber—into the bushes on the other side of the river. Then I saw Bernie

Poelman climbing up on the pillar of the bridge and then I shot him.

DUNBAR: Did you see him fall into the river?

MEIRHOFER: Yes.

DUNBAR: Did you know he was dead?

MEIRHOFER: I didn't know for sure.

DUNBAR: In other words, you shot him and saw him fall into the river . . . and what happened then? Did you leave the area?

MEIRHOFER: Yes. The other kid took off running and I went back to my truck and went back up through the hills and come out at Logan.

DUNBAR: You knew who you shot then. Is that right?

MEIRHOFER: Yes.

DUNBAR: All right. Now I'm going to ask you a couple of other questions, David, which your attorney perhaps does not know and I think it will resolve something just . . . which you, too, would want to resolve. Did you go over to Silver Cloud Camp and attack a young girl and be startled during the attack and leave? Recently, in August?

MEIRHOFER: Silver Cloud Camp?

DUNBAR: Yeah, over by Anaconda.

MEIRHOFER: No.

DUNBAR: Now, if you did this, David, it would . . . You have admitted many things and everything would indicate that you probably were the person who went into the Girl Scout camp and were in the process of bending over a girl and tying a rope around her neck and choking her when the light came on, and then left. With what we have said, there would be no reasons that I can see—and I hope your attorney would agree—if you did do it, uh, we should know it. It's the same camp that you had the map drawn of, in the same area, in August of this year.

DASINGER: This would be the same day that we went over to Warm Springs to take the sodium amytal test.

DUNBAR: The same day that you took the sodium amytal [*truth serum*] test.

MEIRHOFER: No, I wasn't over there.

DUNBAR: You were not? OK, we'll drop it. I just felt if you did, this would be the time to say so. OK?

MEIRHOFER: Yeah.

DUNBAR: If, David, you are responsible for any of the other persons who have been attacked around Montana, we should know about it now. Do you agree?

MEIRHOFER: Yes.

DUNBAR: Are you responsible?

MEIRHOFER: No, I am not.

DUNBAR: I am specifically asking now, and I will go point by point, OK? Two girls missing in Marion, Montana, on July 31—Jessica Westphal and Karen Tyler—three days after you delivered your combine to Kalispell?

MEIRHOFER: No.

DUNBAR: OK, Siobhan McGuinness, a little girl who was attacked in Missoula, taken from Missoula to a culvert east of town and put in the culvert.

MEIRHOFER: No.

DUNBAR: OK, Donna Pounds, a woman who was tied in her home at Missoula, bound, sexually attacked, and killed?

MEIRHOFER: No.

DUNBAR: Mr. and Mrs. Bernhardt, killed in their home in Missoula, Montana, or—I'm sorry, David—Billings, Montana.

MEIRHOFER: No.

DUNBAR: Peggy Lee Harstad, killed in July 1974, uh, near Conrad, Montana.

MEIRHOFER: No.

DUNBAR: OK, Donna Lemon, killed somewhere between July 4 and July 8, between Bozeman and Idaho Falls, Idaho? Or her body was left in Idaho Falls.

MEIRHOFER: No.

DUNBAR: Do you know her?

MEIRHOFER: No.

DUNBAR: OK, now, if we can go back—again, this is not for publication; this is for our own purposes—just to fill in details. We'll go back to Susie, OK? When you took Susie from her tent, if I'm correct, death occurred actually at the time when you were starting, as you say, "to feel her." This is when she became wild and you killed her. Is that correct?

MEIRHOFER: Yes.

DUNBAR: What caused death?

MEIRHOFER: Strangulation.

DUNBAR: Was she sexually attacked?

MEIRHOFER: No.

DUNBAR: There was no sexual intercourse?

MEIRHOFER: No.

DUNBAR: Was this at the Lockhart Ranch?

MEIRHOFER: Yes.

DUNBAR: When you strangled her and she died, she had not yet been cut up. Is this correct?

MEIRHOFER: Yes.

DUNBAR: In other words, after death you cut her up?

MEIRHOFER: Yes.

DUNBAR: Am I correct, David, that you spread her legs apart and cut from the top side down, or the front rather than the back?

MEIRHOFER: Yes.

DUNBAR: How many cuts did you make?

MEIRHOFER: Well, I cut her legs off, and her arms off, and her head.

DUNBAR: The head is in the outhouse now. Is that correct?

MEIRHOFER: Yes.

DUNBAR: Is it in one piece?

MEIRHOFER: As far as I know.

DUNBAR: Her legs. Where are they?

MEIRHOFER: They were burned.

DUNBAR: Did they completely dissolve with burning?

MEIRHOFER: Yes.

DUNBAR: Were there any bones left?

MEIRHOFER: No.

DUNBAR: Did you know that Susie had a unique fingernail? On the index fingers?

MEIRHOFER: Yes.

DUNBAR: Where are those fingernails?

MEIRHOFER: They were on her hands.

DUNBAR: Where are her hands now?

MEIRHOFER: They were burned, too.

DUNBAR: In the same place that the legs were burned?

MEIRHOFER: Yes.

DUNBAR: Did they dissolve completely?

MEIRHOFER: Yes.

DUNBAR: The torso, now, if I am correct, is between the Lockhart Ranch and Menard. On the regular road?

MEIRHOFER: Yes.

DUNBAR: Could you take us to where the torso is?

MEIRHOFER: Yes.

DUNBAR: This is just the upper . . . ?

MEIRHOFER: Yeah.

DUNBAR: And it is burned, too?

MEIRHOFER: Yes.

DUNBAR: Is there anything left of it?

MEIRHOFER: No.

DUNBAR: Completely dissolved?

MEIRHOFER: Yes.

DUNBAR: Only the head exists. Is this correct?

MEIRHOFER: Yes.

DUNBAR: Then, now we know and you know that the lower tailbone, the sacrum—I may not be pronouncing it right—exists. How does that exist? It was in the outhouse, too?

MEIRHOFER: I don't remember quite. When I cut the legs off, it was hanging down there.

DUNBAR: Did you put it in with the head?

MEIRHOFER: No. Maybe the firepit.

DUNBAR: Nothing was left but the head and that bone?

MEIRHOFER: Right.

DUNBAR: You're sure?

MEIRHOFER: Yes.

DUNBAR: Is there anything we can find other than the head?

MEIRHOFER: No.

DUNBAR: And the head is not in the house. It's in the outhouse. It's in the outhouse separate from the house. Is that right?

MEIRHOFER: It was in the outhouse outside.

DUNBAR: OK, how deep?

MEIRHOFER: It should be in the same depth as the other bone [*that was in the firepit*].

DUNBAR: No lime, no burning, no nothing?

MEIRHOFER: No.

DUNBAR: OK, in the case of Sandra Smallegan, you went to her house at two a.m. Did she see you?

MEIRHOFER: No.

DUNBAR: You . . . you choked her and covered her mouth without her knowing it?

MEIRHOFER: Well, yes.

DUNBAR: How did you get her into the car?

MEIRHOFER: I had her tied up.

DUNBAR: And carried her?

MEIRHOFER: I carried her, yes.

DUNBAR: To her car? Did you drive her car?

MEIRHOFER: Yes.

DUNBAR: To the Lockhart Ranch?

MEIRHOFER: Yes.

DUNBAR: Did you take the route from Manhattan to the Lockhart Ranch, or did you go by way of Logan?

MEIRHOFER: I went through Logan.

DUNBAR: To the ranch?

MEIRHOFER: On the interstate. Not through Logan, but on the other side of Logan.

DUNBAR: In other words, you didn't go straight north of Manhattan on that road.

MEIRHOFER: No.

DUNBAR: But you do know that road?

MEIRHOFER: Yes.

DUNBAR: OK, you took her directly to the Lockhart Ranch. Is that correct?

MEIRHOFER: Yes.

DUNBAR: She was dead.

MEIRHOFER: Yes.

DUNBAR: Where did you actually cut her up?

MEIRHOFER: On the floor of the house.

DUNBAR: On the floor of the house?

MEIRHOFER: In the Lockhart Ranch.

DUNBAR: How did you cut her? By this I mean, was she lying on her back?

MEIRHOFER: No.

DUNBAR: On her stomach?

MEIRHOFER: Yeah, on her back—excuse me.

DUNBAR: OK, how many cuts were made there?

MEIRHOFER: The same. I cut off the arms, the legs.

DUNBAR: The head?

MEIRHOFER: And the head.

DUNBAR: Where is the head?

MEIRHOFER: It was burned.

DUNBAR: Did it dissolve?

MEIRHOFER: Yes.

DUNBAR: Where was the burning?

MEIRHOFER: Right alongside the house.

DUNBAR: Of everything?

MEIRHOFER: Yes.

DUNBAR: You only burned in one spot. Is that correct?

MEIRHOFER: Well, it wasn't all put on at once.

DUNBAR: How . . . how long did this take?

MEIRHOFER: Well, I had to go back there the next night and burn the rest.

DUNBAR: You took her on Saturday night or early Sunday morning, really. You came back and changed oil for your neighbor in his car.

MEIRHOFER: Yes, I was back in town by eight o'clock.

DUNBAR: Had any of the burning taken place by then?

MEIRHOFER: Yes.

DUNBAR: How much?

MEIRHOFER: The head and the upper torso.

DUNBAR: And then you went back to finish.

MEIRHOFER: Yes.

DUNBAR: Is there any of Sandra located anywhere except the Lockhart Ranch?

MEIRHOFER: Yes.

DUNBAR: Where?

MEIRHOFER: I don't know where they are at now.

DASINGER: Tell him what he's indirectly talking about.

DUNBAR: Pardon?

MEIRHOFER: I had one of her hands and a couple of her fingers in my freezer.

DUNBAR: This . . . this is correct. Is there anything of Susie located anywhere that we could locate and identify for the family, other than the head and that bone?

MEIRHOFER: No.

DUNBAR: You have nothing of her in your home?

MEIRHOFER: No.

DUNBAR: What I'm getting at, David—and I'm sure you know this. When we searched your house—remember?—and your warehouse, the sheets and the bedspread that we picked up—remember?—all had human blood on them in great quantity. What were they used for? Sandra or Susie?

MEIRHOFER: I don't know. I didn't use them.

DUNBAR: There is a great deal of human blood on them.

MEIRHOFER: I did not use them. They were in that building when I bought it, and they had been.

DUNBAR: What you told me before was completely correct? Is that right?

MEIRHOFER: Yes. They was in that cooler in there when I got it. I did not use them.

DUNBAR: There is nothing that we can find of Sandra, then, except what we have already found. Is that correct?

MEIRHOFER: That's right.

DUNBAR: You probably know about as well as we do what has been found. There is nothing else. Is that right?

MEIRHOFER: Right.

DUNBAR: Except the hand that was located today.

MEIRHOFER: Right.

DUNBAR: OK, now, is there anything of Susie that we can find?

MEIRHOFER: No.

DUNBAR: Other than what you have told us. We can find the head, right?

MEIRHOFER: Yeah.

DUNBAR: You can take us to the head and show us where it was?

MEIRHOFER: Yes.

DUNBAR: It isn't put in lime or isn't burned or anything?

MEIRHOFER: No.

DUNBAR: OK, now, going to the boy Poeler—is that his name?

MEIRHOFER: Poelman.

DUNBAR: Poelman. Where is the gun that was used to shoot him?

MEIRHOFER: I have no idea.

DUNBAR: It's your gun, right?

MEIRHOFER: No.

DUNBAR: Whose gun was it?

MEIRHOFER: It was my gun at the time.

DUNBAR: What did you do with the gun?

MEIRHOFER: Well, I traded it in.

DUNBAR: To who?

MEIRHOFER: Uh, Beaver Pond [*a gun shop*]. That one out here . . .

DUNBAR: Here in Bozeman? OK, uh, you did see the boy fall and go into the river. Is this right?

MEIRHOFER: Yes.

DUNBAR: You assumed he was dead. Is this correct?

MEIRHOFER: Yes.

DUNBAR: I mean, in the absence of newspaper stories or anything, you assumed that you had shot him and killed him. Is that correct?

MEIRHOFER: Yes.

DUNBAR: Did you stay to see what happened?

MEIRHOFER: No.

DUNBAR: How did you leave?

MEIRHOFER: In my truck.

DUNBAR: A Jeep, right?

MEIRHOFER: Uh, yes, but . . .

DUNBAR: Your older Jeep?

MEIRHOFER: Yes.

DUNBAR: What year?

MEIRHOFER: '64.

DUNBAR: And you returned to your home?

MEIRHOFER: I, uh, no. I went back up through the hills, come out at Logan, and went and talked to a friend of mine. Jim, uh . . . Jim Gregson.

DUNBAR: When you say "up into the hills," you went north into the Horseshoe Hills?

MEIRHOFER: I went to Manhattan, drove to the Lockhart Ranch.

DUNBAR: By the Lockhart Ranch and out of Logan. Is that correct?

MEIRHOFER: Yes.

DUNBAR: The normal road through the Horseshoe Hills.

MEIRHOFER: Yes.

DUNBAR: OK, going to the Raney boy, was there anyone else with you?

MEIRHOFER: No.

DUNBAR: Was this caused by problems that happened a day or two before? [*Meirhofer's expulsion from his father's scouting troop*]

MEIRHOFER: No.

DUNBAR: What caused you to go to the camp?

MEIRHOFER: Well, uh . . . I wanted . . . I wanted to get that little . . . to get a little kid.

DUNBAR: A kid. Did you . . . you were not looking for the Raney boy. Is this correct? A boy or any child?

MEIRHOFER: Anyone.

DUNBAR: What caused you to stab him rather than take him out of the tent?

MEIRHOFER: I wanted to. I was going to choke him like I done to . . . like what happened to Susie, but I couldn't get in just right to do it, and I was scared.

DUNBAR: But you did not hit him.

MEIRHOFER: I did not.

DUNBAR: Did you know he was dead until you read it in the paper?

MEIRHOFER: No, I didn't. It was three, four days later.

DUNBAR: Right. Did you, um, then leave the area after you . . . after he was stabbed?

MEIRHOFER: Yes.

DUNBAR: Where is the knife?

MEIRHOFER: It's, uh . . . it should be in my Jeep.

DUNBAR: Your present Jeep?

MEIRHOFER: Yes.

DUNBAR: Is this the same hunting knife you used for Susie and Sandra?

MEIRHOFER: Well, uh, the same one for Susie, I think. I think I used another one, a different one, for Sandy.

DUNBAR: Where is the knife you used on Sandy?

MEIRHOFER: It should be in the Jeep, too.

DUNBAR: There should be two hunting knives in the Jeep, which were used to cut these people. Is that correct? Where is the saw that was used?

MEIRHOFER: Uh, I'm not sure which one it was. There's two in the back of the Jeep, in the camper.

DUNBAR: What kind of saw?

MEIRHOFER: What kind of saw? A wood saw.

DUNBAR: I mean, a hacksaw or a regular crosscut saw?

MEIRHOFER: It's a crosscut type.

DUNBAR: Not anything special?

MEIRHOFER: No.

DUNBAR: Now, David, we have, as you know, come a long ways. Is there anything else that we should know now? We have made certain assurances to you. In return, I feel that if there is anything else that you should tell us about, there is nothing to gain by not telling us. Are there any other events that have happened that you were involved in that are of concern to families or people?

MEIRHOFER: No.

DUNBAR: You definitely, absolutely, without reservation state that the only things you were involved in were the stabbing of Michael Raney, the shooting of the Poelman boy on Nixon

Bridge near Manhattan, the kidnapping and killing and cutting of Susie Jaeger, [and] the kidnapping and killing and cutting of Sandy Smallegan. Is this correct?

MEIRHOFER: Yes.

DUNBAR: There is absolutely nothing else?

MEIRHOFER: Yes.

DUNBAR: Nothing else?

MEIRHOFER: There's nothing else.

The confession had petered out but hadn't ended.

Dunbar asked Meirhofer several times again if he committed any other crimes that the law should know about, and each time Meirhofer said, "No." Those four murders "were all, as far as I know," he said. *As far as he knows?*

Meirhofer refused to talk about—even to acknowledge—any slayings he might have committed outside of Gallatin County: elsewhere in Montana, Southern California, Vietnam, and God knows where, all places where he still might face execution. Dunbar believed there might even have been more in Gallatin County.

The killer explained how he'd eluded deputies the night before his "Mr. Travis" call by turning off all the lights in his house and slipping through a bathroom window into the shadows. He had planned it all carefully. He put his pickup truck in a Bozeman shop to set up an alibi. For his overnight dash to Salt Lake City and back, he'd "borrowed" a friend's car stored in his warehouse. He seemed proud of his cunning.

But he wouldn't talk about the little girl's voice. Dunbar and

Olson let it slide. Mullany had counseled patience, so Dunbar didn't press. He had many more days ahead, days when he would have sharper wits, to explore those awful details.

Finally, Dunbar mentioned the formal statement Meirhofer would make to a law enforcement officer of his choosing later that day.

MEIRHOFER: What would be the reason for this thing?

DUNBAR: The reason for this, David, is that the people of Gallatin County have somewhat a feeling that our law enforcement has not done their job, and I would like their efforts in this case to be known. This will be sworn to secrecy, but when you plead guilty, it will be an acknowledgment that this agency is responsible [*for Meirhofer's capture*].

Olson watched Meirhofer closely. The longer the interrogation went, the more the killer shrank. It was just exhaustion. It was as though someone had let all the air out of him.

Olson and Dasinger had no further questions . . . at the moment. The interrogation formally ended at four o'clock Sunday morning when Dunbar shut off the recorder and the jailer came to take Meirhofer back to his cell. Less than two days after his arrest, David Meirhofer had confessed to four killings and would never breathe a free breath again.

Just like that, at the dark beginning of a Sabbath morning, it was done.

The long nightmare ended.

SA PETE DUNBAR, COUNTY Attorney Tom Olson, and defense lawyer Doug Dasinger had been awake, except for fitful catnaps, for almost three days. The accused butcher David Meirhofer had slept more than they had. Only the horror of it had kept them focused this long.

Their first, most important mission was accomplished: As he'd promised, Meirhofer confessed to his four Gallatin County murders. He was halfway to prison forever.

Dunbar and Olson had the rest of that Sunday, the rest of the week, the rest of Meirhofer's macabre life, to dislodge answers to a thousand more questions. Dunbar made a note to call Howard Teten and Pat Mullany first thing Monday. But right now they all needed sleep.

Early Monday morning, Meirhofer and Dasinger would go before District Judge W. W. Lessley to plead guilty to all four slayings. For his part, as he'd agreed, Prosecutor Olson would ask the court to sentence Meirhofer to life in prison and to keep the transcript of the killer's confession secret.

Questions hung thick in the air. How had Meirhofer gotten back to Manhattan after dumping Sandy's car at the Lockhart Ranch? Did he have help? Had there been others?

But for now their interrogation was done. Olson arranged with Dasinger to continue questioning Meirhofer after court on Monday. FBI teletypes would go out nationwide within hours. Questions would soon be coming in from sheriffs elsewhere in Montana about their own cold cases. Cold-case detectives everywhere else would call. Marine Corps investigators—first alerted when Dunbar dove deep into Meirhofer's military background—had their own questions. Reporters were already en route and would arrive to find a more grotesque story than they'd imagined.

A deputy escorted Meirhofer forty paces from the sheriff's office back to his cell, and locked him in for the rest of the night. The sun would be up in less than three hours.

Dunbar briefed Sheriff Andy Anderson, who'd waited just outside in the jail until the interrogation ended. Andy didn't want rumors about Meirhofer's other crimes to leak out prematurely, so he chose not to say anything to the night jailer, a guy Andy pegged as a gossip.

The citizens of Manhattan and the rest of Gallatin County who thought they already knew?

They didn't yet know what they didn't know.

CHAPTER 9

DESCENT INTO HELL

SEPTEMBER 29, 1974
BOZEMAN, MONTANA

And then David Meirhofer died.

Just like that.

Less than six hours after he unmasked the monster inside himself, a jailer found him hanged in his cell.

Suicide.

Handyman Meirhofer's last project was to split his jail-issue bath towel down the middle and twist the pieces into a makeshift rope. From his cell's top bunk, he tied one end with a simple overhand knot around the highest crosspiece between the bars. He looped the other end into a terry cloth noose that he snugged around his neck.

Then he simply plunged headfirst from the top bunk.

The short fall wasn't enough to break his neck. Meirhofer wasn't as tall as the drop. Doubtlessly he kicked ferociously for a few seconds, while some tiny veins in his eyeballs burst and his front teeth clamped down on his swelling tongue. Once he passed out, he convulsed spastically for a couple minutes as his brain, heart, and lungs competed for his arteries' last life-giving oxygen. Foamy spittle dribbled down his chin. In the last few seconds of David Meirhofer's savage life, he pissed himself and shit his pants. His blood-engorged penis reared up, spiritless.

Then he died, just twenty-five years old

His feet dangled barely off the floor. Turned out, David Meirhofer's trip to Hell was only two inches.

One guard had seen Meirhofer alive around eight a.m. He hollered, "How's it going in there?" and the confessed killer's reply was, "Not so good."

Another guard sauntered past the killer's cell at ten twenty-five a.m. and noticed that his bunk was empty, but didn't think much of it. Then something—*maybe the smell of fresh human crap or just dead silence*—made him look back over his shoulder. Meirhofer's motionless corpse dangled against the bars. The stunned jailer had no key. Deputies eventually rushed to cut him down and tried to resuscitate him, but he'd been dead too long. Five minutes later, Sheriff Anderson himself delivered the stupefying news to SA Pete Dunbar.

Back at the federal building, Dunbar dashed off a painfully abrupt teletype to Director Kelley and to the Detroit field office, which would, in turn, dispatch an agent to notify the Jaegers:

```
SHERIFF L.D.W. ANDERSON ADVISED AT
10:30AM THAT JUST PRIOR TO THAT TIME,
SUBJECT HUNG HIMSELF IN JAIL CELL, AND
    IS DEAD.
```

Sinister and sad stuff would stay forever locked up tight in Meirhofer's airless brain.

Every secret he kept.

Every mercy he never gave.

Every apology he might have offered.

Every comfort he might have given.

Every answer to every unasked question.

Every remnant dreg of his unfinished soul.

Every memory of a time when he wasn't this way.

Every idle thought that wasn't monstrous, if there were any.

And every chance that somebody might finally gain control over him.

All dead and long gone.

CHAPTER 10

SHADOWS GO

SAME DAY
FARMINGTON HILLS, MICHIGAN

An FBI agent from Detroit personally delivered the news about the suicide to the Jaegers that Sunday morning.

"Oh, no, no, no!" Marietta cried.

After fifteen months, she didn't know what she had expected from—or for—David Meirhofer, but not this. His ending came too fast. She didn't want the story to end like this.

At the same time, the sheriff called to inform Sandy's parents, John and Betty Dykman, who had just come home from church with Reverend Roger Hill.

John hung up and turned to the pastor. The grieving father asked if Reverend Hill would accompany him to the home of his boss and best friend, Clifford Meirhofer, at the edge of town.

Why? the preacher asked.

"Because Cliff has lost his son" was all John said.

ON THE THIRD DAY after he hanged himself—October 2, 1974—
David Gail Meirhofer was buried beside a dirt road in Three Forks'
Fairview Cemetery.

Bozeman's hospital pathologist had performed a hasty autopsy
and found nothing surprising about the cause of his death, although
the Gallatin County coroner, Dr. Robert P. Myers—a fine local
veterinarian—initially ruled the manner of death to be "undeter-
mined." Within a day or so, he scratched it out and squiggled "suicide" in the little box on the form.

Profilers Howard Teten and Pat Mullany had already phoned
SA Pete Dunbar with a special urgent request: Ask the autopsist to
closely examine Meirhofer's skull and brain, then report any visible
abnormalities, no matter how small. The pathologist saw none, but
this particular psycho's abnormalities were shadows nobody could
see, like Meirhofer himself.

When Meirhofer was arrested, the US Marine Corps had
scrambled a team to question him about any kidnappings or murders he might have committed while living off base in Oceanside,
California, or in Vietnam. Those unused kiddie tickets from Disneyland suggested something grim. But when the Marine detectives
got word of the suicide, they canceled their hop.

Meirhofer's corpse had been embalmed in Bozeman's big-city
mortuary, then quietly delivered to a mom-and-pop funeral parlor
for burial. But the tiny cemetery in Manhattan refused to take him,
so they hauled him up to Fairview, where they found a spot for him
on the margins of the graveyard. Small-town burial grounds are just
a different kind of small town: Nobody is ever very far from everybody else. In this case, the killer's grave was only about a hundred

paces from his first known victim, Bernie Poelman. But maybe they were both past caring.

Finding a grave is one thing. Finding a minister is something else entirely. At least three local clergymen declined to speak at the killer's funeral. A Presbyterian preacher finally agreed to say a few reassuring words, albeit reluctantly and quickly, because a traumatized family needed to hear them more than David Meirhofer did. Small towns can be cruel.

The afternoon of the graveside service—a Wednesday—was hotter by almost twenty degrees than most fall days in these parts. The trees were turning, yet the air simmered like summer. The cemetery reeked of ferment and funeral flowers. It'd freeze three days later, but nobody up here was surprised by capricious weather.

Only the killer's family came, and not even all of them. They didn't want to be there, either. None offered personal tributes or memories, although David's mother was clearly shaken. The whole goodbye lasted only fifteen minutes, and then they were gone.

Some old soldiers from the American Legion carried his casket. In time, a military headstone would mark the spot. Every Memorial Day, the caretaker still plants a little American flag at David Meirhofer's grave. Respect for a Marine sergeant's wartime service, he'd say, not for a psychotic butcher.

Not long after his jailhouse suicide, the FBI redesigned its lie detectors—and maybe its polygraph examiners—recalibrating them to catch the next David Meirhofer. For years, his name was invoked whenever any agent extolled the virtues and accuracy of those machines.

Eleanor Meirhofer, David's mother, listened to the birthday cassette of her dead son singing "Mama, a Rainbow" every year until she was in her eighties and dementia made him a stranger. It was found among her personal effects in her nursing home room after she died at age ninety-three in October 2020. And for all of her cognizant days, "David's china" was used only at Thanksgiving and Christmas. Today, it sits, still perfectly unbroken, safely in boxes at a daughter's house.

She never denied what her son had become, but she remembered what he'd been. Eventually she remembered none of it, which might have been a blessing.

A few days after David's suicide became big news, a Manhattan High School English teacher showed the FBI a strange homework horror story written by his sixteen-year-old sister a few weeks before. It paralleled David's crimes so closely that it chilled Dunbar. But David's crimes were solved and the case was behind Dunbar. He wrote a one-page report for the case file and didn't follow up.

Decades later, David's sister didn't remember writing the story and wasn't aware it was given to the FBI, but she was absolutely sure David didn't write it. It's possible, though, she says today, that she was blocked and David "prompted" her with a frightful but supposedly fabricated story. In any case, she is chilled, too, by her fantasy's similarity to David's reality.

Where Main Street crosses Broadway in downtown Manhattan, such as it is, there sits a monument to the town's World War II servicemen. None from World War I, Korea, Vietnam, or later conflicts. So Marine Sergeant David Meirhofer's name isn't memorialized anywhere but on his safely distant tombstone.

David's name was deliberately omitted from the 2009 obituary of his father, Clifford, too, because in the end his family knew they'd raised a monster, and there was no reason to remind everybody. They all knew there was a good David and a bad David, but they couldn't talk about one without mentioning the other, so they just didn't.

Most days now, a turnbuckle clanks like a death knell against the flagpole down at the American Legion. David Meirhofer's memory is a putrefying, foul wound in Manhattan, but it endures. Better people have been forgotten.

So a guy down at the Legion shrugged off questions about the monster fifty years later. That's not a name or memory anybody wants to carve in stone if they don't have to, he says. It's just easier to leave everything the way it is.

Why the hell does this damn thing keep coming up?

In his confession, Meirhofer had pointed cops to the rest of Susie Jaeger. Within hours, their search began.

With a backhoe, sheriff's deputies pushed over the weathered outhouse at the Lockhart Ranch, where David said he threw Susie's head and other butchered pieces of her. Deputy Don Houghton—the first lawman on the scene of Susie's abduction more than a year before and the guy who handcuffed the killer fourteen months later—drew the short straw. Protected only by his ordinary cowboy boots and leather gloves, he dropped three feet down into an ankle-deep layer of putrefied, lumpy shit mud and poked around with a stick until he hit something hard.

Fairly quickly, he lifted a foul wad of pages from one of the day's popular magazines—*Life* or *Look*—but it was heavier than a mere wad of paper. He plucked it out of the noxious muck and gingerly peeled back a soiled corner.

It was a small skull.

A child's cranium, to be precise, with its jawbone, clumps of hair, and five vertebrae still attached. No bullet holes, no obvious fractures, no charring.

Nobody ever found the rib cage that David said he tossed in a culvert. They tried not to imagine that a predator had dragged it away, but it was the most likely explanation.

The FBI's crime lab quickly matched the skull's intact teeth to

Susie Jaeger's dental records and determined that some matted hairs in the grisly package were microscopically the same as hairs from Susie's hairbrush.

While he stood in that poisonous hole, Houghton was pissed. Pissed that his boots might be ruined and he didn't earn enough money to buy new ones. Pissed that a seven-year-old child's parts had been casually tossed into human shit. Pissed that Meirhofer had robbed them all of justice by killing himself. Pissed that Andy had been so stupid as to let it happen.

Pissed that he even had to see a monstrosity such as this.

The only anger he could do anything about was his boots. He walked down to the creek and waded in the cold water for a long time to wash away all the foulness.

A CORONER'S INQUEST CONVENED in Bozeman two days after Meirhofer's suicide, not to rubber-stamp the coroner's ruling of suicide, but to examine circumstances that might have contributed to it.

FBI profilers Howard Teten and Pat Mullany had warned that the UnSub—now known to be David Meirhofer—might try to commit suicide when caught. SA Dunbar, defense attorney Doug Dasinger, and prosecutor Tom Olson took the profilers seriously and spoke with a single voice to Gallatin County Sheriff Andy Anderson: Don't take your eyes off of him.

So . . . why had a confessed mass killer and suicide risk gone unwatched?

Secrets.

The first was Meirhofer's insistence that details of his confession never be disclosed.

Next was the natural inclination of government officials to conceal some facts from the public. Gallatin County prosecutor Tom Olson didn't want the news of Meirhofer's confession to slam into Main Street before they could release it in his own carefully crafted words—so he demanded that only a few people be told.

And the last was deliberate miscommunication. Sheriff Andy Anderson thought about a 'round-the-clock guard at Meirhofer's cell, but he didn't have enough deputies. He informed the head jailer that Meirhofer had confessed to four murders, but ordered that the head jailer should *not* tell the morning jailer, because "he had a big mouth."

When that jailer came in the next morning, he assumed Meirhofer would be checked during the normal inspection rounds, every thirty or forty minutes. When two of the three jailers went out for coffee, then checked a false burglar alarm at a local school, the third deputy skipped his normal rounds. Jailhouse rules prohibited him from going into a cellblock if he was the only jailer in the place.

So the jailer who found Meirhofer's hanged corpse had no idea the accused killer had confessed or that he was deemed a suicide risk.

The nine-man coroner's jury unanimously censured Sheriff Anderson as "careless and negligent" about safeguarding Meirhofer; he'd failed to assign the necessary number of deputies to watch him and hadn't communicated with the men he had assigned. However, they stopped short of charging him with a crime.

When the whole grisly mess oozed out, folks whispered privately that Andy purposely let that scumbag Meirhofer hang himself. . . . Who needed justice delayed? But when other people might be listening, they took umbrage over justice denied. The unseemly gossip became local mythology, became vaguely credible conspiracy theories, became accepted history.

Like somebody said, elections around here were won and lost on back-fence gossip. A month after Meirhofer's suicide, after twenty-four years as sheriff, Andy Anderson decisively lost an election to one of his own deputies because nobody believed in him anymore.

He still lived in Bozeman, but nobody heard much from Andy Anderson after that.

A guy down at the Oasis Bar in Manhattan shrugged off questions fifty years later. Andy's been gone a long time, he says. Maybe he let it happen and maybe he didn't. Lots of folks think he did. Don't matter much now anyhow.

But why does this damn thing keep coming up?

IRONICALLY, AFTER ALL OF defense lawyer Doug Dasinger's desperate, last-minute bargaining to take the death penalty off the table, David Meirhofer might never have been executed anyway.

At the time of his arrest, Montana's new law required armed kidnappers and deliberate murderers to be executed if no mitigating circumstances existed. Meirhofer faced both charges in the death of Sandy Smallegan.

But outside of Montana, the rest of America wasn't so sure about capital punishment.

In the early 1970s, a moral, political, and legal maelstrom blew up. Debate raged over three words in the Eighth Amendment of the US Constitution: "cruel and unusual."

In 1972—a year before David Meirhofer snatched and killed Susie Jaeger—the US Supreme Court handed down a landmark ruling in the case of *Furman v. Georgia*. A divided US Supreme Court struck down most states' death penalty laws, declaring them "arbitrary and capricious." Existing death-penalty laws, the court decided, violated the "cruel and unusual punishment" intent of the Eighth Amendment and the due-process protections of the Fourteenth

Amendment. The justices didn't rule the death penalty itself to be unconstitutional, only the specific laws by which it was applied.

The five-to-four ruling effectively outlawed executions in forty states, including Montana. The Supreme Court said a death sentence must not be imposed unless the judge or jury finds at least one legally defined aggravating factor and then weighs it against any mitigating factors the defendant claims. To impose death, the court said, the judge and jury must weigh the circumstances of the crime and the character of the defendant—in other words, execution must not be the only possible outcome.

Americans' bloodlust had waned anyway. Public support for the death penalty reached its lowest point in 1966, when a Gallup poll showed only 42 percent of Americans approved of the practice. And at the time of *Furman*, nobody had been executed since 1967, as states had observed an unofficial voluntary moratorium on executions while the Supreme Court grappled with the issue.

Furman flung Death Row's doors open across the United States. More than six hundred condemned killers sentenced between 1967 and 1972 had their death sentences lifted.

But the law is a living, breathing creature, evolving to suit its environment.

After the Supreme Court had finally articulated its constitutional qualms, states like Montana began debating new laws to satisfy the court's uneasiness. Statutes in Georgia, Florida, and Texas became the new model, giving courts wider discretion in applying the death penalty for specific crimes, and providing for the current "bifurcated" trial system, in which guilt or innocence is determined in a first trial, then punishment in a second.

But Montana legislators, assuming they were complying with *Furman*, drafted tough new kidnapping and murder laws making death *mandatory* if a killing involved certain heinous circumstances, such as kidnapping with a weapon or killing someone to hide another crime or to obscure the killer's identity.

It was a fatal assumption.

In 1976, the US Supreme Court declared Montana's mandatory-execution law unconstitutional—the same law in effect at the time of Sandy Smallegan's murder and Meirhofer's arrest.

If David Meirhofer hadn't plea-bargained and instead had been convicted and sent to Death Row, his death sentences would have been tossed out anyway. They likely would have been commuted, or he might have been resentenced to multiple life terms in prison. Or less likely, he might have been sent back to Death Row under newer, constitutional laws.

No matter. His chances of eluding the hangman's noose were uncomfortably good.

And the good people of Gallatin County might still have been wondering who had killed Bernie Poelman and Michael Raney.

SANDRA MAE DYKMAN SMALLEGAN'S family waited 247 days to bury what was left of her. The undiscovered, imperceptible, obliterated rest of her remained scattered to the wind or on the haunted dirt-scape at the old Lockhart Ranch forever.

Earth to earth, ashes to ashes, dust to dust.

Two days after Meirhofer's suicide, SA Pete Dunbar urgently asked the Smithsonian Institution to return all the dismembered evidence the FBI no longer needed—in Sandra's case, a hand and two fingers, a piece of jawbone, some teeth, and a bucketful of bone shards, none bigger than a wild Montana bluebell blossom. Two plain cardboard boxes soon arrived at his Bozeman office and he delivered both to the local mortuary to prepare for two long-delayed funerals.

Sandy's graveside services were at Manhattan's Meadow View Cemetery on a Tuesday—October 15, 1974—for no other reason than it was about time they mourned. Family and a few friends attended. Her mechanic father paid fifty-five dollars for her plot in a couple of serene acres set out among the old Dutch farms south of town.

The pastor had ridden with the Dykmans to the cemetery. The air was frosty, and an early snow blanketed the ground everywhere but the gravedigger's black hole.

Most of a year had passed. Her family had long known she was gone. For self-preservation, they kept her ending abstract. It was a burden they all carried. The boys didn't go out as much as before because they felt people were always looking at them. Betty had struggled with bouts of depression and her hair had turned white almost overnight, but she kept putting one foot in front of the other for her sons and the rest of the little village that was, indeed, looking at her.

But she caught her breath at the first glimpse of that achingly small white casket—not much bigger than a shoebox, decorated with little lambs and shepherds. It hammered home a hideous reality.

Reverend Hill, who'd officiated at Sandy's memorial seven months before, spoke again.

This time, she was there.

"'*Out of the depths I cry to you,* Lord,'" he read from Psalm 130. "'*I wait for the Lord more than watchmen wait for the morning.*'

"As we gather today to commit Sandy's earthly body to the earth," he began, "we gather as a much closer group than normally gathers around an open grave. The events of the past eight months have brought us all closer than we normally would be."

He spoke to the family about God's plan, eternal life, resurrection, and the victory called death. There was little else he could summon at that moment.

"Out beyond is a life for each of us to live," the preacher promised them, and quoted Paul about faith, hope, and love. "Could there be anything greater to carry as we commit this body to the earth?"

He closed with the Lord's Prayer: *Thy will be done . . . as we forgive . . . deliver us from evil . . .*

When it was done, when Sandy was safe and warm again, Reverend Hill felt that he'd been granted magical strength and wisdom that he'd never had before. John Dykman knew how he felt.

"Roger, this isn't me, either," he told his friend and pastor when they were alone after the service. "I would be carrying on something awful. It is God."

Fifty years later, a guy who'd once loved Sandy and then hurt her shrugged off questions. He remembers crying when he heard what little they had found of her, but then he stopped because he didn't think he had the right to cry. If anything, he believed it was his fault because he'd screwed up big-time and wasn't there to protect her. It hurt too much to talk about now, even after so long. Please be kind to her family, he asks. They hurt more.

But why does this damn thing keep coming up?

EIGHT DAYS LATER—WEDNESDAY, OCTOBER 23, 1974—Susie Jaeger's meager remains were buried among the infants in the Catholic section of Bozeman's historic Sunset Hills Cemetery. Even in early afternoon, much like the day before and the day after, the sky was gray, and the air felt colder than autumn should have been. A stiff breeze from the southeast brought no warmth and made no sound in the graveyard's hundred-year-old trees.

Marietta and Bill Jaeger had decided that Susie should lie in

Montana, where she now also belonged to the kind people who'd fed and prayed for the family and who had looked for their little girl so long. They left Susie's siblings back home in Michigan because they didn't seem ready for this. They wanted only one other mourner there: SA Pete Dunbar.

Father Joseph Mavsar, whose own painful story of loss and grace had first inspired Marietta's forgiveness of the butcher David Meirhofer, spoke a few words over the grave.

Marietta had visited Susie at the funeral parlor earlier. When she saw the little white coffin—the same kind and same dreadful size as the one that contained the last traces of Sandra Smallegan— she wanted to run away. It didn't look like a proper coffin to her. She exhaled. She was grateful, at least, that her other kids would never see what had become of their sister. They were still too young. A time would come someday when they would know the abject horror of what happened, but not yet.

The undertaker approached Marietta and spoke, but she barely heard him. She was trying to hold it together outwardly, but inside she was a god-awful mess. Her face was blank. She willed herself to be composed, and she struggled to appear to be listening, but tears streamed out of her eyes. She couldn't stop them, but it seemed odd to her that she could be so otherwise collected and still have tears pour out of her.

After the funeral, Bill drove Marietta to Manhattan. As he drove slowly down Main Street, she looked for a sad little junk shop. When she spotted it, Marietta wasn't sure she should go in, but she did anyway. That was who she was.

While Bill stayed in the car, she went inside. It was everything she expected from a small-town "antiques" dealer: a cheap old building with dirty windows, cheap old lamps, cheap old glassware, cheap old farm and kitchen tools, all yard-sale rust and dust.

Marietta asked a girl at the counter if the proprietor was in. The girl said she was in the basement and pointed at the stairs. As Marietta took her first steps down, the owner appeared at the bottom and started up.

It was Eleanor Meirhofer, David's mother.

She was smaller, more compact, than Marietta imagined, like David.

"Hello, Eleanor. I'm Marietta Jaeger."

Eleanor probably already knew who she was, Marietta thought. Manhattan was small; everybody knew who belonged and who didn't, and her photograph had been in the paper a lot. She was no stranger.

Marietta continued down and Eleanor up, until they met halfway. The dead killer's mother and the dead child's mother both had tears in their eyes. Instinctively, Marietta embraced Eleanor, and both wept.

In that empty place between above and below, each supporting the weight of their separate sorrows, they didn't say anything for a minute or two. When they did, Marietta spoke first.

"I want you to know that I have forgiven David," she said, "and I know you're a Christian like me, so I hope my forgiveness and prayers for your son will help you."

They talked a few minutes. Eleanor thanked Marietta for coming and apologized for what had happened, but she never mentioned Susie. Maybe she was too ashamed. Marietta didn't press.

Then it was closing time, and the two heartbroken mothers had nothing more to give. Marietta had been in the store less than thirty minutes, just long enough to say what she had come to say. They said goodbye.

That night, Pete Dunbar and his wife, Margie, took the Jaegers to dinner at Bozeman's Elks Hall. Afterward, Marietta went back to the Dunbars' house, where they were staying. They had a few drinks before Marietta collapsed into bed. The day had drained her.

Bill and Pete, though, retired to the Dunbars' billiards room to play pool. Maybe Bill just wanted or needed to escape the sadness. But at this moment, just hours after he had put his little girl—or what was left of her—into the cold ground, he seemed dislocated from the grief. Throughout this ordeal, he'd been stoic and remote. He was a smart guy, but he tended to speak with his hands, obscuring his mouth, and he didn't like strangers anyway. That was who he was.

Marietta yearned for him to come to bed. To her. She wanted to be held, to share her anguish with him or for him to find comfort in her. But there's stoic and then there's deadened. She never knew which it was, really, but she remembered that he played pool that night.

The Jaegers soon returned home to their now-familiar routine of loss. Life resumed, still without Susie but with answers, however morbid.

At first, ghastly nightmares unreeled like movies in Marietta's sleep. In one, she was forced to watch her little girl's slaughter, and she couldn't wake. The phantasms eventually faded away, but not the memories of them.

Marietta has had only one dream about Susie since she buried her. In that dream, she is peacefully underwater when she sees three little girls swimming around her, their hair floating out behind them. The dark-haired girl in the middle turns slightly and sees her. She recognizes her as Susie, who smiles and swims straight toward Marietta. She comes close, kisses her mother on the mouth like she did that night, and then glides over her shoulder. And then she vanishes into the shadows of the sea.

Marietta took work as the assistant manager of a Christian bookstore, and she began to think about sharing her story. A few years after she lost Susie in the shadows, Marietta wrote a book about how she came to forgive David Meirhofer, even to love him spiritually as an unfinished, damaged soul. His arrest was a chance to treat the mental sickness that he never acknowledged; his suicide was sad, not satisfying.

It didn't happen overnight, but she came to believe that vengeance and hatred might keep her out of Heaven. Justice wasn't meted out on Earth, but in Heaven. She leaned heavily on the book of Isaiah, although she didn't know Reverend Roger Hill had quoted from it at Sandy Smallegan's memorial so many years before.

Marietta has lectured for decades against the death penalty. She's been interviewed by Vatican journalists and has testified before the UN's Commission on Human Rights in Geneva. People look at her and ask if they would be capable of such forgiveness. Capital punishment—even for David Meirhofer—wouldn't bring Susie back, but it would create another grieving family, she would say. To support revenge killing insulted Susie's sacred memory, she would say. Hanging David Meirhofer would kill something inside of us, too, she would say.

Maybe she's right.

Ever since the morning Susie vanished, Bill Jaeger had kept his torments secret. He developed bleeding ulcers and heart problems. In 1987, the day after his fifty-sixth birthday, he crumpled to the kitchen floor of the Farmington Hills house and died of a heart attack. Some said Bill was just another of David Meirhofer's victims.

Marietta eventually married again and lived for a time in Montana, not far from where it all started.

She's in her eighties now, living in a Florida retirement community. Reporters don't call much anymore. She tires quickly on her long tours from church to church, so she declines most invitations to talk about forgiveness and the death penalty. She knows that Susie's spirit is happy where she is, that she still knows and loves her mother, but we must all move on. Now she wants to live the life Susie might have lived—or maybe just the life she herself would have lived if Susie were here.

Either way, she is at peace.

Marietta's other daughter, Heidi, the sister who first discovered that Susie had disappeared, now a mother herself, enjoys a measure of peace, too. But it's not the same. She eventually learned the whole sordid story, and she knows what David Meirhofer was.

But to her, Susie exists as a kind of celestial insurance policy that no more evil can happen to anybody she loves.

She's also certain beyond a reasonable doubt that Meirhofer, the shadowman, was the wicked presence she sensed outside their tent that night. If she'd taken two more steps, she would have been the one he snatched and slaughtered.

Nevertheless, Heidi harbors no anger or bitterness. A long time ago, David was somebody's dark-haired, dark-eyed little boy—like her own dark-haired, dark-eyed boys.

She hasn't forgiven Meirhofer or resolved to be unforgiving, because he simply doesn't exist in her heart or mind. He's a shadow, a "being" that isn't real or tangible. She has no feeling for him, good or bad. He doesn't matter because he *isn't* matter.

So why does this thing keep coming up?

THE SHADOWMAN, DAVID MEIRHOFER, haunted many good men's dreams for a long time. Most are dead and gone, while some still dream.

Don Houghton—the young deputy who was there on the morning of Susie Jaeger's disappearance, who found her severed skull in the clotted shit of a tumbledown outhouse, and who arrested Meirhofer—still recalls every foul detail.

The college student who just wanted a side job ended up working for the Gallatin County Sheriff's Office for thirty-two years. As a captain, he supervised the patrol division, special ops, and the SWAT team.

Now in his seventies, he still rides his Harley-Davidson motorcycle to a part-time job at a Bozeman auto parts store. And he still thinks about washing Meirhofer's awfulness off his boots.

Howard Teten, one of the FBI's two original profilers who chased the shadow of a monster they understood intimately but never knew, is still alive, too. In his late eighties and still precise, he lives in a Virginia senior facility, where he reads prodigiously. He remembers everything but keeps his memories close. Teten never talks much anymore about the cases he worked after Meirhofer. People just want to hear dirty stories.

They want to hear about Ted Bundy, whose last arrest came shortly after Teten helped draw a psychological portrait of the killer, which was shared with police nationwide. Bundy hunted his victims where college kids flocked, places such as bars and ski resorts. He especially liked pretty girls who wore their hair long and parted in the middle. He also liked to move around, to mask his slaughter. Bundy was arrested in Florida soon after the Meirhofer case. (Interestingly, the Behavioral Science Unit's conversations with Bundy about the roots of his psychopathy helped later to unmask serial killer Gary Ridgway, the so-called Green River Killer.)

They want to hear about John Wayne Gacy, the killer clown who murdered at least thirty-three boys and buried them in the crawl space of his Chicagoland home. And Wayne Williams, the black psycho who challenged everything Teten's nascent BSU thought it knew about the race of typical serial killers.

They want to hear stories they never knew. Many years ago, Teten told a colleague in forensics a story about rape and murder in which a detective found a mirror lying beside a bed, out of place. That's not right, Teten thought. It meant something. To him, it meant the rapist-killer wasn't likely a typically enraged psycho, but probably a porn addict who liked watching himself reenacting his X-rated fixations. It turned out to be a significant clue.

Teten's vision coincided with the golden era of serial killers in the mid- to late seventies. He was fascinated by how effortlessly these monsters blended into the crowd, the same way David Meirhofer was always a part of life but mostly invisible. The misguided tendency to think they looked different or acted differently— as if we'd know them immediately by their wild eyes, helter-skelter hair, or bizarre way of talking—made them especially frightening, which made them especially spellbinding. No, they were us, ordinary and imperceptible. Our monsters were ethereal. Shadows.

Despite his role in one of criminology's most significant advances in the past fifty years—a period in which DNA profiling, immense computer databases, and the Internet became powerful tools in police work—Teten came to see profiling as a last resort. It could hamper an investigation more quickly than it could help. There could be no substitute for good detective work.

After twenty-four years at the Bureau, he retired. He monetized his skills as a private consultant to law enforcement agencies that needed the help of a profiler. In 1996, NBC launched a television series called *Profiler* and hired Teten as a technical adviser. But he soon learned that Hollywood's version of profiling diverged significantly from reality. The business of illusion rarely profits from facts.

Teten still teaches, although now it's helping his elderly friends learn basic computer skills. Meirhofer lurks someplace deep in his brain, but his partner, Pat Mullany, had done all the heavy lifting. What he truly doesn't remember, he simply chooses not to remember.

Pat Mullany, the monk turned mind hunter, is just one of the key players who is past caring about David Meirhofer. He died in a California assisted-living home in 2016. He was eighty-one.

Right at the end, his self-published book, *Matador of Murder: An FBI Agent's Journey in Understanding the Criminal Mind*, explored his role in the birth of the FBI's profiling unit. The first chapter? David Meirhofer.

What Mullany knew about the atrocities conceived in the human mind "could not be taken off like an old suit of clothes," he wrote.

"Has the profiler himself become victim to the darkest killers we produce?" he asked in *Matador of Murder*. "Has the profiler, like the media, become a spectator in the violence that surrounds us? . . . One can never run the risk of believing he possesses supernatural powers or some special gift."

It is not surprising that the onetime friar should turn to an inspirational passage for answers, and early on, he carved one on a plank of wood: *Faith is seeing the brilliant countenance of God shining up at us from every creature.* Even monsters had some good spark in them. He kept that faith—and that deteriorating piece of wood—until the end.

Lesley David William "Andy" Anderson retired from law enforcement when he lost the 1974 sheriff's election a few weeks after David Meirhofer's suicide. One of his own deputies defeated him at the polls, but Meirhofer's ghost finished Andy off. Checkmate.

Andy hid himself in plain sight after that. He and his wife remained in Bozeman, where he showed up at the Masonic Temple and Rotary occasionally, but otherwise kept a low profile. Public opinion lightened up to the point that when he died in 1986 of complications from a stroke at age seventy-four, his obituary in the Bozeman *Daily Chronicle* remembered him as "methodical and persistent" . . . "a terrific, dedicated law enforcement officer" . . . "never satisfied until he got answers."

Andy Anderson was buried in Sunset Hills Cemetery, not far from Susie Jaeger.

Doug Dasinger, the defense lawyer who'd believed in Meirhofer right up to the outer rings of Hell, decamped for Kalispell, Montana, soon after his client died. After that, he never talked about Meirhofer to anybody, although his kids heard much later about him puking after seeing Sandy Smallegan's frozen hand.

He'd wanted only to coach high school football, fish, eat anything he felt like, and read his John D. MacDonald novels. In the end, he became something he never wanted to be: He trusted an affable monster. A colleague remembered one of Montana's most promising young lawyers like "a saddle horse that wasn't broken right." Dasinger was already disappointed long before Meirhofer deceived him. It changed him, just not for the better.

One cold January afternoon in 1978, Dasinger lay down on his couch for a nap and died in his sleep from a widow-maker heart attack. He was only forty-three but his congested heart had been working overtime for years to pump blood through his neglected body. Maybe his many flaws made him real or maybe they just killed him. Whatever the case, David Meirhofer helped neither his literal nor figurative heart.

Prosecutor Tom Olson never stopped loving the law. It was life. Fresh out of the University of Montana's law school, he had clerked for a justice on the state's supreme court, joined the Marine Corps during the earliest days of Vietnam, then hung out a shingle as Gallatin County's first public defender. He knew both sides of the law, even if he never truly understood David Meirhofer.

In 1975, President Gerald Ford appointed Olson US attorney for Montana. When Olson came home to Bozeman in 1982, Gallatin County elected him by a resounding margin as the 18th Judicial District judge; there he wrote a guidebook to help courts deal sensitively and expeditiously with abused children. He retired from his stellar law career in 2000 . . . disappointed, regretful, and occasionally visited by the specter of one case.

The memory of David Meirhofer exhausted him. When a TV reporter came around, Olson talked about how the killer seemed to deflate before his eyes and how he regretted that he and Dunbar had saved questions about Meirhofer's motives for another day that never came.

In 2017, Tom Olson died from Parkinson's disease. He was seventy-eight. He'd been part of many criminal cases in his time, some more important to the law than Meirhofer's but none as haunting.

Byron Herbert Dunbar, whom his grandfather and everybody else called "Pete," retired from the FBI just five years after he brought down David Meirhofer. He took a new job as Gallatin County's assistant prosecutor, often trying cases before his old colleague-turned-judge, Tom Olson. A year later, President Ronald Reagan chose Dunbar to be US attorney for Montana, a job he held for ten years.

One of Dunbar's sons quarterbacked Montana State University's Bobcats football team, and later became an FBI agent, too. In retirement, Pete did chores at his family's ancestral ranch near Three Forks, traveled widely with his wife, and especially loved being near the ocean.

In April 2007, former FBI Special Agent Pete Dunbar died peacefully at home after an eight-year fight against metastatic colon cancer. He was seventy-nine.

The beginning of Pete's eternity had eerily ironic moments. First, his body was cremated. Then his memorial was scheduled a couple months after his death under the venerable cottonwoods of Headwaters State Park, near his birthplace in Three Forks, Montana. The park was not only once a part of his forefathers' vast ranchlands but a haunted place, where the most noteworthy case of his FBI career began. In a strange way, David Meirhofer was there.

So if they're all gone and nobody who's left cares that much, *why must this thing be brought up again?*

IN 2005, NEW OWNERS hired a laborer to renovate David Meirhofer's old Main Street warehouse, which had sat mostly unused for thirty years.

It occupied the lot adjacent to Manhattan's favorite 1960s diner, Cookie's Café, which once served tasty burgers for a quarter and where teenagers played the jukebox on Saturday nights. That's how the older townsfolk still describe its location, not by its address but "next door to the old Cookie's Café."

The derelict structure was more than a hundred years old and probably would have been condemned if it had remained vacant much longer. It was used for a while by a beekeeper who kept his honey and hives in it. Its bones were rough-hewn timbers, and its skin was rusting corrugated steel, peeling back at the edges. Inside, it was drafty and dark, more cave than garage, with a row of support posts down the middle, and a few little cubbies walled off with barnwood planks nailed to rough frames.

David Meirhofer came home to Manhattan from the Marines in 1971 and bought the place while it was still middle-aged. He needed a cheap place to store his carpentry tools, lumber, and other stuff he couldn't keep at home. His father staked David for a down payment and he rented out some space in the far back to a couple local guys.

After his suicide, evil tainted this place owned by a dead killer's heirs. It was neglected for a long time until a local family, the Fryes, bought it for next to nothing. They stashed a few things there, but it remained mostly vacant.

By 2005, one of the Frye kids inherited the slowly faltering building. Shoring up an exterior wall was the most urgent project. To get a good look at the timbers inside, a hired man had to demolish a dilapidated interior wall. As he started prying out dried-up wooden planks, he spotted something hidden down in the dark space between the studs.

It was a woman's leather wallet and a small address book. They were dusty but not as old as the wall itself.

The worker opened the pocketbook. It contained a couple photos, but no cash or anything else except a 1970s driver's license with the picture of a pretty, dark-haired girl. In the dimness, he held it close. That name was familiar. *Sandra Smallegan.*

He called his boss, who called Sheriff Jim Cashell, who showed up that afternoon. Cashell knew his local history. He knew immediately what he held and why the wallet and address book might have been hidden in David Meirhofer's wall. Back in Bozeman he closely examined the wallet and address book, which contained fewer than a dozen names and numbers, mostly those of girlfriends. Nothing spooky.

They had no evidentiary value. Meirhofer was dead. Sandy was dead. Almost everybody who had ever touched this case was dead or dying. These items didn't add to his understanding of this particular killer's mind because, like the profilers had told cops so long ago, he kept souvenirs. Justice might not have been served, but it didn't matter anymore. The case had been closed for thirty years.

Sheriff Cashell gave the things to Sandy's mom over in Harrison. Better for them to be in her dresser drawer than lost in an evidence box at the Gallatin County Sheriff's Office, as hidden as they'd been in David Meirhofer's hidey-hole.

They brought the darkness back, but Betty cherished them. She added them to her secret little shrines—bits of Sandy's jewelry and small things around the house, invisible to everyone but her. Not everything was invisible, though. Years before, she'd hung a big portrait of Sandy in her living room, and it never came down until she moved to the nursing home, where she put it up in her room.

When Betty died in 2019, after a long life that was mostly good except for the shadows that consumed her for a long time, her sons put Sandy's wallet and address book in her casket so Betty would have them forever.

Invisible to everyone but her.

But fourteen years before, when Sheriff Cashell returned Sandy's possessions to Betty, the Bozeman paper interviewed him for a news story about this spooky relic in the wall. The young reporter retold the harrowing saga of the paper's once-faithful but now-dead reader who clipped stories about Girl Scouts, David Meirhofer. The sheriff was anything but sanguine about the unexpected discovery. If nothing else, he had grown weary of the whole mess.

Why does this thing keep coming up?

IN THE EARLY 1980S, a serial child rapist terrorized Seattle and Bellingham, Washington.

In at least a dozen cases—probably many more—the so-called North End Rapist followed pubescent boys and girls to their homes, households usually headed by single moms. He lurked in the shadows nearby until night fell and the lights went out. When he was sure the family was asleep, he clipped the phone line and sneaked into the house. Wearing a mask and armed with a knife, he abducted those children from their beds. After binding and gagging them, he took them to a dark, hidden place not far away, and he sodomized them.

When he finished, he returned his weeping, traumatized, bloodied victims home with a frightening warning: *If you tell anyone, I'll kill you, and your whole family, and burn your house down.*

His known victims described their assailant only as being unshaven and reeking with body odor. Detectives surmised the kids were not smelling his sour sweat but the chemicals used to make meth.

As the North End Rapist's attacks escalated, he grew freakishly brazen. In one night, he snatched *three* thirteen-year-old children from their own bedrooms and raped them. The risk turned him on.

Six months later, he snatched a middle schooler from his bed and performed his same loathsome ritual. But this time, he dropped a glove and his car keys. When he was finally identified and arrested in 1987, he claimed to be a homeless day laborer. Police searched his car and found jewelry and photographs he'd swiped as souvenirs of his rapes.

Although prosecutors focused on only four cases they had a chance of winning, investigators believed the rapist had been far more active over the years. He later bragged to a state psychologist that he had attacked at least ten boys under the age of sixteen. The shrink reported to Washington State's corrections authorities that he was almost certain there were far more victims out there.

Cops hoped briefly that an emerging forensic tool called DNA profiling could prove the elusive rapist's guilt, but the results weren't as damning as they expected. Still, they had more than enough other evidence to nail him.

Surprisingly, the rapist's lawyer cut a sweet deal: Several serious felony charges would be dismissed in exchange for guilty pleas to aggravated first-degree rape and second-degree kidnapping. Prosecutors further agreed to recommend to the judge that he serve only nine years in Washington State Penitentiary in Walla Walla.

But at the end of his sentence in 1996, the prison psychologist said the North End Rapist remained an extremely dangerous sex predator who was likely to rape again. So he was committed to a special sex-offender rehabilitation unit within Washington's prison system. For more than twenty years, he played along with—then actively resisted—treatment, until the State couldn't legally hold him any longer.

In 2017, this knife-wielding serial child rapist was released back into society, as free as a bird. He's a registered Level III sex offender, the most dangerous and likely to reoffend (although the amputation of his left leg in prison likely increased the degree of difficulty). But he's not the only one in the rural area where he settled. He blends in.

Today, the North End Rapist is in his late sixties. He lives alone in a ramshackle trailer that's set back from a county road, in a secluded Skagit River bottomland that's less than an hour from his old hunting grounds. There's a little no-stoplight burg a half mile away, a lot like the little no-stoplight burg where he grew up, but he doesn't venture out too far anymore. He earns a little cash by selling junk, like his mother did. His world is mostly what he sees on social media. There, bald and one-legged "Big Al"—an ironic nickname, since he's barely five foot five and a hundred thirty pounds—has only a couple dozen friends on social media (including some who appear to be teenage boys). He lists his relationship status as "It's complicated."

But it's a small town. They think they know, but what goes on behind those doors, they say, goes on.

So why the hell bring this up?

Alan Meirhofer doesn't like to talk about it too much. Not his compulsions, not his cruelties, not his cryptic childhood in Manhattan, Montana. And certainly not his big brother, David.

What the hell happened behind those walls? Every terrible secret seems to fall into the spaces in between.

SIOBHAN MCGUINNESS, WHO FROZE to death even as she was already bleeding to death in 1974, was still a cold case up to late 2020.

Before that, nobody talked fervently about her case anymore, not even the carousel of cold-case detectives in Missoula who kept handing it off to the next and the next. Her folder sat figuratively on the edge of their desks, or in the back of their file cabinets, or in a box in the basement. It's not that they didn't care, but that they didn't have time.

Every decade or so, a local reporter would resuscitate her story. Cold-case mysteries sell papers. But whatever detective sat on the case at the moment would always say what the guy before him said the last time anybody asked—*We got nothing.*

Siobhan's mother and father refused to talk about it anymore, even to the Missoula Police Department. Other relatives eagerly described bumbling cops, family dysfunctions, political cover-ups, and vague conspiracy theories. And until a curious crime writer called, Missoula's investigators had never heard of David Meirhofer. It's obscenely tragic: A knife-wielding, child-snatching, sexually depraved serial killer who lived less than two hundred miles away had never been a person of interest in the sexual assault and stabbing of a five-year-old girl who was stuffed in a culvert and froze to death.

Back when it happened, Missoula detectives interviewed every nomadic hippie who strayed through Siobhan's home, every sex offender in town, and every random name that came over the transom. For decades, nobody panned out. Even after DNA profiling became a cop's most powerful forensic tool, no hits popped up in the national Combined DNA Index System (CODIS) database. For whatever reason, Siobhan's killer's DNA never got into the system. Maybe he got smarter about leaving victims or biological evidence. Maybe he committed only that one murder. Maybe his predatory career ended before the 1990s. Or maybe he was dead and buried before anybody ever imagined DNA profiling.

Yes, FBI Agent Pete Dunbar had asked Meirhofer, almost in passing, about Siobhan's killing way back in 1974. This killer who was so adept at deception denied knowing anything about it. Good enough. Nobody ever chased that particular ghost, and no file was ever opened on him.

Dunbar's perfunctory interrogation also touched on the murders of two little girls up near Kalispell when David was known to be there, as well as Donna Pounds in Missoula, Donna Lemon of Bozeman, and the Bernhardt couple slaughtered in their Billings home. Dunbar asked about the Girl Scouts attacked when Meirhofer was nearby for his truth serum testing. He asked about the newspaper clippings and pictures of girls the agents found.

Meirhofer denied knowing anything about any of them.

One possible reason for his denials: His loyal defender, Doug Dasinger, had negotiated only with Gallatin County prosecutor Tom Olson to have Meirhofer confess to four killings in a bid to avoid execution. No such deal existed anywhere outside of Gallatin, so confessing to murders elsewhere might land David on Death Row anyway.

Nevertheless, Meirhofer told Dunbar the truth about six of the seven Montana murder cases. They were later proven to have been committed by other killers, including a serial killer named Wayne Nance, who prowled Missoula at the same time Meirhofer was active.

But it was also proven that Nance definitely *hadn't* killed Siobhan McGuinness five days before Sandy Smallegan disappeared. Nor had he waylaid twenty-year-old nurse Donna Lemon on her way to a wedding, slit her throat, stabbed her several times, then dumped her body in Idaho—only two weeks after Susie Jaeger's abduction.

Meirhofer was never considered a suspect in Lemon's slaying. As with Siobhan McGuinness's case, his name wasn't known to cold-case detectives in Idaho for forty-five years.

Psychopaths aren't always as simple as Hollywood paints them in prime time. Meirhofer wasn't the only one to have disturbing differences in victimology. Individuality trumps formula. Circumstances, age, and developmental issues also play strong roles. Formulas can create tunnel vision.

Profilers at the time didn't consider the single significant commonality: a deep, invisible rage. They couldn't yet see how David Meirhofer's sadism was spiraling out of control, from a night-stalking kid who nailed stray cats to power poles to an affable neighbor who fed unwitting churchgoers tasty casseroles made with the meat of his victims. And until David Meirhofer's last few hours on earth, the profilers couldn't see how completely he'd conspired with shadows to take risks that aroused him more than sex.

One reason was that the term "serial killer" wasn't even coined inside Teten and Mullany's Behavioral Science Unit until after David Meirhofer killed himself. Until then psychopathic killers were labeled "chain killers" or "mass murderers," terms that emphasized their death tolls more than the mental demons that drove them. For a long time, Meirhofer was deemed to be merely a "local" murderer who employed different methods and weapons while killing four victims who shared almost nothing in common.

Two males and two females.

Three kids and one adult.

Two involving knives, one suffocation, and one shooting.

Two with chilling sexual overtones, two without.

Three random and one deliberate.

Two left to die and two taken away to be unspeakably butchered, cremated, and pulverized.

Of Meirhofer's four known victims, three were connected by his humiliation and rage. Susie Jaeger was the outlier.

Bottom line, one of the earliest known "serial killers" of the modern era literally didn't fit his seminal profile. As such, he wasn't a serious suspect in possibly related slayings.

And questions remain about whether David had an accomplice. Was it likely that he killed Sandy Smallegan, ditched her car at the Lockhart Ranch, and walked six miles home across rugged, snowy badlands in the dark middle of a subfreezing February night—or was there a second vehicle driven by a cohort? Could he possibly have made a quick getaway alone from Headwaters State Park with a frantic, screaming, unrestrained Susie Jaeger in the front seat? The suspicious loner David would never have partnered with an older accomplice . . . but did he team up with a younger, equally psychopathic killer? Whom could he possibly trust that much?

What was the genesis of David Meirhofer's psychopathy? Where did his rage come from? Was he ferociously confused about his sexuality? What about the Meirhofer family's dynamic—if anything—created two extraordinarily bad seeds?

Those questions have gone unanswered for almost fifty years. Maybe they're stillborn, or maybe no satisfying answers exist. The mystery keeps some of his family awake at night. Any chance to know for sure died with David Meirhofer.

Modern forensic psychologists and profilers are absolutely certain that Meirhofer killed others—maybe unknown children around Camp Pendleton or Disneyland in Southern California, in other Rocky Mountain states, in a Vietnamese orphanage, or who knows where else? The notion that he spontaneously suspended his psychotic compulsions for five years between Boy Scout Michael

Raney's 1968 stabbing and Susie Jaeger's 1973 kidnapping in the same campground is absurd.

Fact is, nobody was really looking any further after he hanged himself. And not to this day.

David Meirhofer remains a shadow.

Musty cold-case files at police departments and sheriffs' offices throughout Southern California are hit-and-miss. No obvious potential victims of Meirhofer pop out in the early 1970s, but nobody is quite sure what "obvious" is for Meirhofer. In 1974, DNA profiling was as yet unimagined, so the collection of biological material was haphazard; its being preserved for fifty years is improbable.

And Meirhofer's erratic choice of victims doesn't help to narrow the pool. He might have perpetrated almost any unsolved murder or abduction between 1970 and 1971 within a hundred-mile radius of Camp Pendleton.

Closer to home, was snatching little Siobhan McGuinness in broad daylight in her own neighborhood a thrill? Was it significant that the murder weapon was a knife? Did he consider roadside culverts to be good places to dump corpses?

No.

In late 2020, cutting-edge DNA technology turned the small spot of dried semen on Siobhan's body into a vast genealogical tree that ultimately pointed to a potential serial killer named Richard William Davis. In fact, familial DNA led the FBI directly to Siobhan's killer, but Davis had died in Cabot, Arkansas, in 2012 at age seventy, and his body had been cremated.

His obituary described Davis as "a loving husband, father, and grandfather" who loved animals. It went on to say, "Richard was a born-again Christian who believed in the word of faith and he was ready to be with Jesus. He worked many years in Arkansas as a truck driver."

Truck driving might have given Davis a frighteningly convenient means of finding and killing as-yet-unknown victims, but he wasn't a trucker when Siobhan was murdered. His family told FBI agents Davis occasionally "needed space" and would simply leave his family for weeks at a time. When he killed Siobhan, he told them he had been visiting a long-lost cousin in Portland.

That's just another sickening side of serial killings: They leave too many questions for too long.

And without answers, no unknown victim of David Meirhofer, Richard William Davis, or any other killer gets justice. And some of them might not even rest in peace.

And that's why this thing keeps coming up.

THAT WATERSHED MOMENT

MARK SAFARIK

SUPERVISORY SPECIAL AGENT, FBI (RET.)

In a thirty-year law enforcement career that he began as a beat cop, Mark Safarik became one of the most respected profilers in the Federal Bureau of Investigation's elite Behavioral Analysis Unit—only a generation removed from the BAU's original architects, Howard Teten and Pat Mullany.

In addition to being the author of several books and a consultant in high-profile murder cases, he is a lecturer at the University of Pennsylvania and the Armed Forces Institute of Pathology, and a board member at the Wecht Institute of Forensic Science and Law, Duquesne University. He's won the University of Virginia's prestigious Jefferson Medal and is a member of the highly respected Vidocq Society, a legendary collection of preeminent crime experts who donate their time and skills to solving cold-case homicides across America.

He produced the television series Killer Instinct, *and since 2008 he has been a consultant for popular television series such as* CSI: Vegas, Bones, *and* The Blacklist. *He is also familiar to true-crime viewers for his expert commentaries on* Dateline, Forensic Files, Court TV, *and the Discovery Channel.*

IN TODAY'S WORLD OF nonstop 24/7 news, we are inundated with crime events from around the world. Whether it is the mass murder of sixty-nine people on Norway's Utøya Island by Anders Breivik, or serial killer Robert Yates's twenty-three-year reign of terror, we are fascinated by crime. Serial killers, spree killers, and mass murderers commit high-profile, violent acts that capture our attention. In truth, any extraordinary crime fascinates us as we struggle to fathom the offender's motive against the backdrop of behavior that is so diametrically opposed to how humans should interact with, and treat, one another.

It is difficult to say whether our interest in the macabre has driven television programming or vice versa. Television is full of true-crime re-creations, documentaries, and docudramas, not to mention long-running shows like *Criminal Minds, The Blacklist, CSI, Luther, The Fall,* and myriad others that highlight various aspects of criminal behavior. As a former FBI criminal profiler who spent nearly thirteen years in the FBI's elite Behavioral Analysis Unit (BAU)—more colloquially called the profiling unit—I have hosted three cold-case homicide television series in the US and Europe and have been a consultant on fictional TV shows that purport to show the inner workings of behavioral and forensic units within police agencies. While they try to be accurate with the forensic science and behavioral analysis, the characters have only forty-three minutes to solve each case—while keeping the viewers entertained.

As you might suspect, they never get the facts quite right. Mark Twain once wrote, "Truth is stranger than fiction, but it is because fiction is obliged to stick to possibilities; truth isn't." Twain's quote rings true in the FBI world of criminal profiling. As we say, "You can't make this stuff up."

In my first few training days as a newly promoted supervisory special agent in the BAU, I and fifteen of my colleagues were introduced to the pioneering work of senior agents Howard Teten and Pat Mullany. Their legacy paved the way for me to become a profiler.

In addition to my years working in the BAU, I've traveled the world to help law enforcement agencies investigate complex and unusual multicides and reviewed and worked on thousands of homicide cases. I have testified in complex murder cases as to the dynamics of the crimes, what happened, how events unfolded, and why. Because of my background, I am uniquely qualified to provide context and perspective on the FBI's first use of criminal profiling, as a way to assist the investigation of the unsolved homicides in rural Montana. The David Meirhofer case turned out to be a watershed moment for the FBI and its fledgling Behavioral Science Unit.

The glut of fictional profiling television series makes it seem as if behavioral analysis has been around a long time. But it has not. In 1972, the Federal Bureau of Investigation Academy's fledgling Behavioral Science Unit (BSU) initiated criminal personality profiling on an informal basis; it was formalized in 1978. As you've just read in Ron Franscell's riveting narrative, Teten and Mullany were the heart and soul of the BSU. Both served as inspiration and mentors for my former partner Robert Ressler, who took up the mantle of chief profiler when Teten and Mullany retired. That we have come so far from our humble origins holed away in the underground bowels of the FBI Academy is a testament to the fortitude, tenacity, and outside-the-box thinking of those who went before me as they pushed the envelope of determining what we needed to learn—and then applying those lessons to understand the complexities of violent crime.

Today we speak of David Meirhofer as a serial killer, but when Teten and Mullany were working on the murders of Susan Jaeger and Sandra Smallegan, the term "serial killer" was not yet a part of the American lexicon. That designation did not exist until 1977, when Robert Ressler coined it to indicate three or more murders separated by a cooling-off period and driven by some internal need for power, dominance, and control. It was not until 1983 that profilers were specifically assigned the task of assisting law enforcement agencies in nonfederal investigations of violent crimes where all investigative leads were exhausted.

We have the luxury of hindsight in examining the four murders between 1968 and 1974 attributed to Meirhofer. The investigators at the time were looking only at two: Jaeger's and Smallegan's. Profilers today will tell you that it takes at least *five* victims to reliably link cases, by observing commonalities and/or differences in how the offender interacted with the victims.

That number also gives us the ability to observe what behaviors change—and which do not—over time. With only two cases to work from, it's very difficult to accurately determine a significant change in behavior. Teten and Mullany were faced with this problem when conducting their analysis. In addition, they had no crime scenes from which to make deductions. Jaeger's abduction scene yielded slightly more information than that of Smallegan, as there were discernible points of ingress and egress—but not much else. Both girls just disappeared. Here one moment, gone the next. No bodies to examine, no weapon, no scene to process, no evidence, and no witnesses.

Teten and Mullany were right about the sadistic nature of this killer. Abductors present a different kind of investigative puzzle than killers who murder their victims on the spot and flee. In 1999, I experienced that as I helped the FBI and the San Luis Obispo County Sheriff's Office with the abductions of college students Rachel Newhouse and Aundria Crawford. I was concerned when I examined the scene of Newhouse's abduction. A small blood trail that started on the top of a railroad crossing bridge and continued to where it disappeared in the railway parking lot suggested she was injured but alive when she was snatched by the offender. I became even more concerned when, four months later, Crawford, much like Smallegan, was assaulted as she slept in her home. She was taken alive from her house in a dense residential area. This was a very risky move for the offender, but one that I am sure he found exciting.

Like Meirhofer, that killer, Rex Krebs, had a remote barn location where he took these women to rape, torture, and kill them. And like Meirhofer, after Krebs killed them, he went to extraordinary lengths to make sure their bodies would not be found. Even though by 1999 the profiling unit had made great strides in developing the discipline of behavioral analysis, not having the victims' bodies, a weapon, evidence, or witnesses made my job—much like the one faced by Teten and Mullany—immeasurably more difficult.

The Meirhofer case was also unusually similar to another case I worked on. In late 2007, I was retained by the New Hampshire Department of Justice to conduct an assessment in the case of a man who had disappeared from a remote farmhouse owned by Sheila LaBarre. Other men previously seen with LaBarre had also gone missing, but when police investigated, LaBarre said the men were transients and had moved to another state.

In reality, LaBarre had been sexually and physically abusing them. She had poisoned and stabbed one to death, then burned his dismembered body in a burn barrel near her barn. It's actually quite rare for murderers to burn the bodies of their victims, which is done both to destroy evidence connecting them to the crimes and to conceal the crimes themselves.

Law enforcement investigators recovered small bone fragments of toes and fingers, as well as an intact unidentified digit from a human foot. In many ways, serial killer LaBarre utilized the same modus operandi as Meirhofer. Her remote farm allowed plenty of time to dispose of her victims by dismemberment and burning. And like Meirhofer using the outhouse to dispose of Susan Jaeger's head, LaBarre utilized her septic system to dispose of body parts.

Teten and Mullany were the pioneers and early adopters of integrating abnormal psychology with crime and crime-scene analysis. It is astonishing how much they got right by inference and deduction. However, Richard Walter, a well-known criminal psychologist and founding member of the Vidocq Society, and a colleague of mine, said that Teten and Mullany "overused psychology and underused investigation." Walter noted that it was too "speculative and projective," and I think he was correct. In fact, in the early eighties the BSU stopped referring to its approach as "psychological profiling." It was much more than that. It has since been described as criminal behavioral analysis or criminal profiling.

Today, one of the key attributes of any good profiler is a strong background in violent crime investigation. The experience gained by investigating and examining hundreds of such cases is essential in evaluating the range of cases the BAU handles. Profiling has been described by many as "part art and part science." I don't agree with that description. Describing the process as "art" suggests educated guessing. Guessing in this type of work is dangerous. A profiler's experience, education, and training provide the basis for making *rea-*

sonable inferences based on the physical, forensic, and behavioral evidence left at the crime scene. That information, combined with a strong working foundation of abnormal psychology, takes this discipline out of the part-art arena and into the realm of science and experience.

Teten and Mullany pushed the envelope, intrinsically understanding that in order to comprehend the thinking and decision-making processes of killers who commit serial, spree, and mass murder, as well as sexual homicide, we needed to study the canvas upon which these artists painted: their crime scenes. To develop a road map that could be applied to other killers, we needed to interview them about why they made the choices they did.

The Meirhofer case was the first true test of this process. It was a difficult pilot study that got some things right and some things wrong. But as noted previously, the profilers were working with minimal information. There was no historical component. They did not have the benefit of understanding the behavioral patterns derived from thousands of previously analyzed cases. There were no research interviews of the types of men they were trying to understand. Without research and an experiential history to backstop their observations, their resulting opinions blazed new trails.

It's worth noting that Teten and Mullany's profile played only an indirect role in solving the Meirhofer case. The Bureau was watching, however, and recognized that there was value in this new type of analysis. It demonstrated what was possible if we had thousands of cases, sufficient research, and multidisciplinary training in areas related to our analysis. It quickly became a new tool in the law enforcement toolbox.

Providing a behavioral profile to a law enforcement agency is not an end-all. It is not intended to solve cases on its own, but the

FBI saw its usefulness in certain types of crimes. It filled an investigative void. We came to understand that this type of analysis would be useful for the more difficult and complex cases—particularly where crimes and crime scenes provided significant psychopathology to analyze. Success, regardless of how major or minor, gave us a reason to push forward and refine the process. We recognized the potential. We just needed to refine the direction and scope of what we were trying to do.

Teten and Mullany served as mentors to the more well-known members of the profiling unit: Robert Ressler, John Douglas, and Roy Hazelwood. Teten and Mullany brought a young Ressler into the Meirhofer case as part of the tribal-wisdom approach to analyzing their cases. Having known Bob Ressler as my partner and mentor, I am sure he was champing at the bit to assist them. He always had that forward-thinking drive to understand what made some men kill so prolifically. It was this success that most likely spurred the need to understand these complex killers and helped Ressler and his colleagues develop the interview protocol and research project on the original thirty-six multicide killers that formed the basis for much of what was to come in criminal profiling.

Any good profiler will tell you that crimes are solved through the tremendous investigative efforts of detectives assigned to those cases. In this case, Special Agent Pete Dunbar and his local team did more to catch David Meirhofer than Teten and Mullany did. Most homicides just don't lend themselves to the unique dynamics of criminal profiling. But when investigators run out of leads and need additional investigative avenues to explore—as Dunbar did after hitting a brick wall in the Jaeger and Smallegan disappearances—a criminal profiler might be the thing that nudges a case toward resolution. Teten and Mullany gave the Susan Jaeger and Sandra Smallegan murders everything they had, such as it was in those days.

Their ultimate insistence that Meirhofer was the right guy paid off in the end.

As I look back on a long and rewarding career in the BAU, I recognize that, for so much of what I have been able to do, I am indebted to the efforts and forward thinking of visionaries Teten and Mullany, the FBI's profiling pioneers.

BIBLIOGRAPHY

In addition to more than thirteen thousand pages from the FBI's official case file on the Susan Jaeger and Sandra Smallegan investigations, obtained through Freedom of Information Act requests; court records; countless contemporaneous newspaper articles; and nearly two hundred personal interviews, the following books and papers were valuable resources:

Aggrawal, Anil. *Forensic and Medico-legal Aspects of Sexual Crimes and Unusual Sexual Practices.* Boca Raton, FL: CRC Press, 2009.

Brown, George R. "Sexual Sadism Disorder" in *The Merck Manual.* Kenilworth, NJ: Merck Publishing, 2015.

Campbell, John H., and Don DeNevi. *Into the Minds of Madmen: How the FBI's Behavioral Science Unit Revolutionized Crime Investigation.* Amherst, NY: Prometheus Books, 2004.

———, eds. *Profilers: Leading Investigators Take You Inside the Criminal Mind.* Amherst, NY: Prometheus Books, 2004.

Cannell, Michael. *Incendiary: The Psychiatrist, the Mad Bomber, and the Invention of Criminal Profiling.* New York: Minotaur Books, 2017.

BIBLIOGRAPHY

Chester, David S., C. Nathan DeWall, and Brian Enjaian. "Sadism and Aggressive Behavior: Inflicting Pain to Feel Pleasure." *Personality and Social Psychology Bulletin*. PsyArXiv. November 5. doi:10.31234/osf.io/cvgkb. Retrieved March 6, 2019.

Dietz, P. E., R. R. Hazelwood, and J. Warren. "The Sexually Sadistic Criminal and His Offenses." *Journal of the American Academy of Psychiatry and the Law* 18(2) (June 1990): 163–78. Retrieved December 10, 2018.

DiMaio, Vincent J., MD, and Dominick DiMaio, MD. *Forensic Pathology*. Boca Raton, Florida: CRC Press, 1993.

Gavin, Helen. *Criminological & Forensic Psychology*, 2nd ed. London: SAGE Publications Ltd., 2019.

Holmes, Krys, Susan C. Dailey, and Dave Walter. *Montana: Stories of the Land*. Helena, MT: Montana Historical Society Press, 2008.

Jaeger, Marietta. *The Lost Child*. Grand Rapids, MI: Zondervan Books, 1983.

Keppel, Robert D., and Richard Walter. "Profiling Killers: A Revised Classification Model for Understanding Sexual Murder." *International Journal of Offender Therapy and Comparative Criminology* 43(4) (December 1, 1999): 417–37. Retrieved January 30, 2019.

Kessler, Ronald. *The FBI: Inside the World's Most Powerful Law Enforcement Agency*. New York: Pocket Books, 1993.

MacDonald, John M., MD. *Rape: Controversial Issues*. Springfield, IL: Charles C. Thomas Publisher, 1995.

———. *Rape: Offenders and Their Victims*. Springfield, IL: Charles C. Thomas Publisher, 1971.

Memmler, Ruth Lundeen, MD, and Ruth Byers Rada. *Structure and Function of the Human Body*. Philadelphia: J. B. Lippincott Company, 1970.

Mayer, Adele. *Sexual Abuse: Causes, Consequences, and Treatment of Incestuous and Pedophilic Acts*. Holmes Beach, FL: Learning Publications Inc., 1985.

Mullany, Patrick J. *Matador of Murder: An FBI Agent's Journey in Understanding the Criminal Mind*. North Charleston, SC: CreateSpace, 2015.

Myre, Daniel C. *Death Investigation*. Alexandria, VA: International Association of Chiefs of Police, 1974.

Purcell, Catherine E., and Bruce A. Arrigo. *The Psychology of Lust Murder: Paraphilia, Sexual Killing, and Serial Homicide*. Amsterdam: Elsevier, 2006.

Ramsland, Katherine. "Howard Teten: An FBI Visionary." *The Forensic Examiner* 20(2) (Summer 2011): 22–27. Retrieved April 30, 2020.

———. *Inside the Minds of Serial Killers: Why They Kill*. Westport, CT: Praeger, 2006.

Ressler, Robert K., and Tom Shachtman. *Whoever Fights Monsters: My Twenty Years Tracking Serial Killers for the FBI*. New York: St. Martin's Press, 1992.

Weiner, Irving B., and Randy K. Otto, eds. *The Handbook of Forensic Psychology*, 4th ed. Hoboken, NJ: John Wiley & Sons, 2013.

Wilson, Colin, and Donald Seaman. *The Serial Killers: A Study in the Psychology of Violence*. London: Virgin Books Ltd., 2011.

Diagnostic and Statistical Manual of Mental Disorders: DSM-5. Arlington, VA: American Psychiatric Association Publishing, 2013.

ACKNOWLEDGMENTS

To perfectly reconstruct a history that everybody wants to forget is impossible. Thankfully, a few people generously shared time, thoughts, and more than a few meals with me. Their memories are the beating heart of this occasionally perverse story.

The pages you've just read contain the names of dozens of living people who helped me understand this bizarre true tale. I cannot repeat all of them here, but the reader should understand that almost all of them contributed crucial perspectives and unearthed memories that they'd just as soon have kept buried. When you read their names in this book, know that they were asked—and they usually answered—some very unsettling questions. And many of the real-life characters in this story passed long ago, but their ghosts allowed me to rummage around in the lives they once led. I am grateful to them all.

However, three of those people deserve special recognition. Pioneer profiler Howard Teten, now retired; retired Gallatin County Deputy Don Houghton; and Marietta Jaeger—all fundamental and meaningful heroes in this drama—were profoundly valuable. And a few more important players gave me all the time and memories I needed and were available every time I called: Heidi Jaeger, the

Dykman family, Jack Smallegan, Julia Williams, Ron Skinner, former Gallatin County Sheriff Bill Slaughter, and Reverend Roger Hill.

I logged thousands of miles, dialed hundreds of phone numbers, sent countless e-mails, hectored reluctant public officials, interviewed more than 150 people, and walked every key site in this extraordinary true story. The FBI shared its voluminous case file covering seventeen months of this grim but historic investigation. Along the way, I had many true guides whose names you *won't* see in this narrative, including Ann Dasinger Blair; Detectives Dean Chrestenson and Mark Blood of the Missoula (Montana) Police Department; Stuart Cooper; Victor K. Davis; Dr. Vincent DiMaio; Detective Mike Hammer of the Bonneville County (Idaho) Sheriff's Department; Daniel Hess; Dan Hodge; Captain Jason Jarrett, Gallatin County Detention Center; Roger Lincoln and John Lowe; Lorna McCormick; Scott McMillion; Brian Michaels; Dr. Katherine Ramsland; former FBI profiler Mark Safarik; Bruce Schendel of Fairview Cemetery in Three Forks, Montana; Traci Schumacher; Gallatin History Museum director Cindy Shearer and archivists Rachel Phillips and Kelly Hartman; former Gallatin County Sheriff Jim Cashell; former FBI Special Agent Michael Tabman; Gene Townsend; Richard Walter; Father Stephen Ziton; and a dozen of David Meirhofer's former high school classmates who shared their stories about his school days but only if their names were not used.

I wish to note, too, that dozens of law enforcement officers and federal agents played roles in bringing Meirhofer to justice. It was a vast team effort. Not all of them are named in the narrative—John Onstad, Jim Jordan, Doug Taylor, Bennie Davis, Steve Markle, Ron Greene, Hank Feddes, Carl Smith, Mike Hunter, Denny Thompson, and Jim Stanley chief among them—but they played essential law enforcement roles that weren't highlighted in the process of compressing several entangled lifetimes into three hundred pages. Justice, such as it was, could not have happened without them.

The dialogue in this book is not a figment of my fevered imagination. It is reproduced faithfully from thirteen thousand pages of FBI files and court and police transcripts; personal interviews by the author; contemporaneous media reports; and other official records in which one or more of the key participants detailed the conversations for investigative and research purposes. Where necessary, typographical errors and minor factual oversights (mispronounced or misunderstood names, for example) in the original, unedited transcriptions were corrected. Among the many organizations that gave me transcripts or recordings, or enabled interviews, are the Federal Bureau of Investigation; the National Archives and Records Administration; the Gallatin County (Montana) Clerk of the 18th Judicial District Court; the Montana Division of Criminal Investigation; the Boy Scouts of America; the Washington State Department of Corrections; the Washington State Office of the Attorney General; and the Headwaters Heritage Museum.

You wouldn't be holding this book if not for my literary agent, Linda Konner, and editor, Tracy Bernstein of Berkley. Then there's my ever-present support team, who always offered expert advice, a meal, a beer, a bed, a willing ear—and sometimes all of the above. I owe more than thanks to my indefatigable concierge archivist Leigh Hanlon, as well as Susan Scheuer, Vicki Burger, Dan Perala, and the late Bill Vandeventer.

And to my family, who understands that I occasionally drag this darkness behind me. To my wife, Mary; daughter, Ashley; son, Matt; and to Owen and Stella . . . my heart always belongs to you, even when it appears the occasional story has stolen it away.

ACKNOWLEDGMENTS

Finally, for those close readers who know where this all begins, snippets in Chapter One might sound familiar. They are my homage to Truman Capote's seminal true-crime work *In Cold Blood*. It should make us all feel smaller to know that these people and places— different but the same—run through it all.

—Ron Franscell

Bulldog Breeding Beginners and Beyond

By

Vicky Collins -Nattrass

Best wishes and Good luck

[signature]

Publisher Vicky Collins-Nattrass 2014

NEW ! revision 2019

Cover design by EPF Design

Professional services

Acknowledgements

I must thank several people for the help I have had with my bulldogs, namely the late Ellen and Les Cotton, who set me on the right track in the beginning, always being on hand for queries talking to me about the past in the breed. Norman Davis for my first bulldog bitch

My dad the late Robert Evans who bought me up on our Dairy farm able to do anything with animals, calves, chickens, rabbits, ducks, goats and horses you name it I've bred it. The best advice he gave me was buy the very best specimen you can afford to as foundation stock as it costs the same to feed an inferior animal as it does a good one!

My dear husband Dr John Nattrass in whose house the telephone never stops ringing when someone has a problem, who has had me asking endless questions about human health situations in the comparison to dogs , and listening patiently whilst I read and re read this book out loud to him .

However my real mentor, whose help with the breeding of dogs goes back to my Shih-tzu days, is Douglas Hodgkinson, sadly also no longer with us , we raised Brownhills Hobson's Choice, pet name Bing with a tube and teaching ourselves from a book, .This taught us a lot about hand rearing as the odds were stacked against his survival. He went on to be a happy healthy winning dog and has had a long normal life. Several shih-tzu litters and lots of different difficult situations later and I had a wealth of information , which formed the basis for my experience from day one when I started on my first bulldog litters.

Thanks also to Beth Handrick USA and Brenda Tuttle whose advice and support by e mail and telephone, on tubing and feeding, I had for five weeks with a nightmare bulldog litter which I eventually couldn't save any of them. I almost finished breeding.

I also must thank the young couple Vickie and Muzz whose constant questions on their first litter inspired me to start printing out a collection of articles on the subject leading to putting them into booklet form, now this is expanded into this book.

I wish to point out I am not Veterinary Surgeon, I have an NVQ in Animal care but I do not represent any official body you have just bought my opinion based on my own experiences.

Many thanks to Annick Sackx , Vicarage Vets,Saxilby for allowing me to photograph a C.section on Tracy Websters Spalfords Bulldogs bitch,special thanks to Betty Bloomfield whose excellent book on premature problem puppy rearing was invaluable to me in my early breeding days .

I wish to thank Alistair Mitchell **latterly** of Pilgrim Vets Boston who saved my Mavis and worked with me on Premature

/Reduction Surgery Ground breaking stuff in the UK I'm sure we will carry on working together on this problem .

Special vets Tom Bingham, Wolverhampton, Andy Trevan Redhill, Phil Shepherd Tranmere also go the extra mile for Bulldogs

I wish you the reader all the luck in the world and happy healthy bulldog litters!!

Many thanks to all who allowed me to use their photos, dogs whose photo's I have taken over the years; Tracey Webster, C section, Makeyia Dawn Spivey, Sadly lost Champion Girl with too many puppies girl, Jayne Emm-Hesmond Puppy on the back cover and many puppy rearing group members !

Introduction from the Author ….

It's now 14 years since I wrote Bulldog Breeding for Beginners, what began as a series of advice sheets for a young couple starting out turned into a popular book sold worldwide for people starting out in this fantastic breed.

This eagerly awaited new Edition has been 3 years in the making, with it ending as a parting of the ways with my publisher.

 I refused to release another edition without the volume of new knowledge added because my readers already had the first one, so here is my venture in self-publishing in softback.

I feel this is the most up to date work on Breeding Bulldogs I could do so now I await your interest

Enjoy! And hopefully learn some more tips that will save your puppies ……………..

From Original book

Now in 2019 many things have changed around the legal aspect of breeding so my latest revision I hope will make that clearer for all

Vicky

Contents

This is an exciting helpful chapter in case you are hoping to start showing your new puppy

This comes up by many prospective purchasers often the vets want to do this too early for this breed

Sample contracts on **page 200 201 203**

Subject index **page 204**

Introducing the Bulldog

Bulldogs are in the Kennel Clubs Utility group, basically the Companion dogs and dogs that don't fit into the other 6 groups, and that's what they excel at being your best friend. They are extremely loyal, protective if needs be, and really enjoy human company.

Before choosing the Bulldog as your pet ask yourself if your lifestyle would suit a bulldog, i.e. if you like trekking up hills for miles every day this breed is not for you...some bulldogs are extremely athletic but others just enjoy a regular walk around the park or down the road, make no mistake they do love and need regular exercise to tone them up they should be hard and muscular not flabby and fat, this will help insure your friend reaches an old age.....no over feeding! They don't like spending hours alone especially when young, chewing from boredom is the likely result of this, just like any other puppy. They don't enjoy going in Kennels and many are not keen on taking them so if you like going away a lot train your bulldog to sleep in a crate , mine have been welcome in many hotels , they are a great talking point and friend maker!

Because of the creases on the face in this breed these need daily care and can soon become sore if neglected, tails should be straight but are more often screwed and tight, these need cleaning and creaming to be comfortable, walking on the pavements keep the nails short without clipping but if walked on grass they can soon become long and splay the feet. When choosing your pup look at the nostrils ideally, they should be wide not pinched without too much overhanging nose roll this makes for unrestricted breathing.

Bulldogs belong to a group of dogs called Brachycephalic, i.e. short nosed, if this head shape appeals to you there are special needs to consider, these dogs may have problems in hot weather, as can others with this type of face. They are not a novice dog to breed, many problems and heartaches occur, and pedigrees should be studied to avoid problems caring breeders have been trying to eliminate.

 Living with a bulldog is like no other dog, once you have they are part of you, you can never go anywhere in a hurry with one, everyone likes to talk to us about our 'National Breed', however they are in danger of being over bred as a' designer dog' and this is reflected in the prices being sort. We have an active Bulldog Rescue/Rehoming service here www.bulldogrescue.org.uk yes, they do end up in rescue, surprisingly.

  If you were to ask me the worst personality trait of a Bulldog I would tell you Possessiveness, over toys food and definitely over their favourite person, especially in a multi bulldog home but they mix well with other breeds and adore children, the only reservation I have about that is that when young they are a' puppy dog' and can be extremely boisterous knocking toddlers flying! The couch potato image comes with maturity!! Bulldogs generally are not big on barking......but they do moult all year round in our centrally heated homes!! Very few Bulldogs do obedience as I would say they are rather stubborn and like to do things in their own time…...

There are many Bulldog Clubs all around the country where you can join and get advice.

Before even thinking of breeding you must evaluate the quality of your bitch. Look on the Kennel Club website and read the breed standard as this is the blueprint all serious breeders should be looking at before putting their bitch in whelp. She doesn't have to be perfect but should have a basic health check first, heart, breathing, eyes the Bulldog Breed Council have a new scheme and a comprehensive Health assessment which you can read about on www.bulldogbreedcouncil.co.uk.

There is just one DNA test for Bulldogs which is for Urate Stones, called an HUU test available, it's simple to test and should avoid affected puppies, using a carrier dog if you know your bitch's status should be ok, we must be very careful not to lose breed type in our efforts to avoid this condition. Read up how geneticists recommend you use the knowledge we have, too many people don't understand how we keep good traits and get rid of the bad ones and this is a whole book in itself. Visit a few dog shows you can find out when and where they are from the Breed Councils website nothing like comparing your bitch to good quality show bitches and also seeing the dogs that are at Stud. Using a good dog who has been health tested and has some wins in his name makes selling puppies much safer than using an unknown dog from down the road breeding bulldogs is so labour intensive you may as well rear quality and be able to ask the going rate rather than a dog who has no history .Even puppy buyers know that the best dogs are probably from show kennels and their owners are well aware of what faults their dogs have and avoid mating to a bitch who shares the same problem.

Do your research, you will be shocked how expensive and labour-intensive breeding bulldogs is so make sure you are taking every precaution to avoid trouble for yourself and later on for your puppy buyers.

If you are new to bulldogs I can't recommend highly enough **the Bulldog Bible by Tania Holmes** which you can buy from **Bulldog Rescue and Rehoming** main website it will explain a lot of peculiarities in bulldogs that are simple but don't need the vet to sort out .

My 'Living with Bulldogs' is also very useful to newcomers.

The breeding of nonstandard colours of the Bulldog is a concern of all serious Bulldog Breeders let me state here that in the breed throughout history Black and Tri colour bulldogs have turned up as flukes no one planned them, if they arrived the breeders didn't register them but found a pet home for them because essentially for the show world they **were rejects and the breeding of them on purpose was not encouraged .**

The main objection to these colours is the wonderful deep reds we have would probably be lost by the dominance of these dark shades, we are not being mean we are stating a fact.

Peculiar colours are now appearing and quite the most offensive colour I've seen was on the internet an apricot bulldog with blue merle and amber eyes it made me shudder. **The Kennel Club have now refused to register Merle Bulldogs at all because the genes involved bring many health problems to many breeds.**

Breeding for colour for money will always bring the wrath of Bulldog Breeders down on you we don't know if colour related problems will later emerge.

The colour issue is now quite serious in 2019 .

Recent figures released show that exactly 50% of all registered bulldogs in 2018 were CNR [colour not recognised] To explain why this sends pedigree bulldog breed enthusiasts into a rage you need to understand the following: colours other than standard colours were kept out of the gene pool for well over 100 years I have already mentioned the worry over pure deep reds well now there is another problem, in the litters of CNR puppies often several are standard colour , the KC is registering them as standard and people are buying them unaware they are siblings to CNR and carrying the genes to reproduce this by accident !All Stud dog owners are being advised to check using Mykc program before agreeing to let anyone use their dog it is from a standard colour line, otherwise we may find a puppy widely advertised as from your Stud and being a totally unwanted colour !

This is not raciest or snobbery!! its just we love the bulldog in the regular standard colours !

However if you choose to pay someone double or more than the going rate that would be for a top show puppy from a famous kennel puppy just because of its colour then remember you have been warned and you're going in with your eyes open .....

Standard Red and white Bulldog Puppies

Chapter 1

Welcome to Bulldog Breeding

After reading about the quality of your bitch and what you think you could offer the breed and you have made up your mind to ' have a go ' there are some essentials you need to think about, remember there is always a risk when you mate a bulldog bitch that you may lose her, it is up to you to find the best most knowledgeable vet who you trust before you actually get her into whelp, but even the best vet can't help if nature takes a hand .Following this advice may reduce some of the pitfalls that breeding bulldogs is renowned for

First of all you must make sure your bitch is healthy before you mate her, a vet check is important. Her heart must be sound and her breathing and palate suitable for an anaesthetic. All her vaccinations and worming should be up to date.

Choose a stud dog carefully, honestly assess your bitch and try to mate to some dog that excels in her weaknesses, try to make a friend of your stud dog owner as they can be a very good support and will be able to answer your questions as time goes on. Don't mate to your neighbour's dog just because he's a bulldog you could breed trouble without realizing it.

Try to talk to other people with bulldogs for advice, join your local bulldog club, visit your local breed clubs shows. You can find out about these from the website

www.bulldogbreedcouncil.co.uk or by getting the newspaper 'Our Dogs' which you would have to order as not many places have them for you to buy casually.

Pedigrees should be looked at, if the two dogs share ancestors and are closely related this can be called a line breed...it is important to have advice on line breeding as done with dogs that are already close bred you could find you are breeding health problems. Experienced breeders and reputable Stud owners should have a good knowledge as to what their dogs will produce, be guided by them If the dogs are not sharing the same ancestors it is known as an outcross, if you do an outcross mating you should look at the type and mate to type... and try not to double up on any obvious faults ...study the breed standard to discover this, evaluate your bitch honestly and try to mate to a better specimen.

The Kennel Club have a service **called Mate Select** it enables you to type in your bitches name and suggested stud and it gives you a number that tells you how closely bred the two dogs together will produce, breed average is 10 beware if a foreign dog is in the pedigree it gives a very low reading, if you see a lot of famous dogs their coefficient is high but the dogs are very like each other due to breeding for a line and a look, I would personally avoid mating's which produce a number over 20 as this indicates very close mating's have been done. The Kc are likely to refuse registrations in this case

Breeding out Faults

This is a simple attempt to explain to you without getting lost in a sea of technical terms how one should approach breeding to rid a 'fault'

You have a bulldog called Freda who has very good breed type, has straight stifles and some movement in one knee she has no other major standard faults that you know of but this is a health issue. She has really wide healthy nostrils and breathes exceptionally well in the heat, she has good clear eyes with no tear staining. She is line bred on one side of her pedigree but the other has no common ancestors and could be classed as 'OPEN' pedigree. Her line bred side [sires] has very famous dogs, well photographed and her father is still being shown, a close examination of him would show that he has excellent bend of stifle, and research shows several relatives on that side of the pedigree also have very sound rears, you now look for a male sharing some of those ancestors on the sires side , who has a sound rear .Also looking to make sure the rest of the points your Freda excels in are not compromised , you find a young male who is out of the grandfather ,this mating is done , a litter of 6 puppies all but 1 have good stifles , you keep a bitch puppy and mate in to that line again.

Creating a line

This is using a kennel name, an Affix[which has to be bought and approved by the Kennel club and yearly subscription keeps it for your exclusive use see Kennel Club Website]

The kennel name identifies for the registered life of all puppies that they were bred by you and you can add it at the end of any dogs you buy in. By breeding to sound foundation stock you can slowly build your own 'line' however this will take years before it becomes a recognisable look as being from your kennel and you could really do with finding an experienced bulldogger who will act as your mentor ,because their experience could save you making mistakes that they already have learnt by !

One major reason for improving on what your bitch is like is the breeding of Bulldogs **is such a labour of love it's a shame to raise   puppies that will have problems and health issues,** for yourself and for any future owners.

Give Time for Attention

The time you are going to have to spend with your bitch and the puppies has to be taken seriously into account, there is no way you can do other outside work at the same time, unless you have help. The first three weeks you will have to be on constant watch and unless you can work out some shifts with the family you could find yourself in deep trouble, if you have work commitments as well.

Mating the bitch

When your bitch comes in season note carefully the first day, use a good quality wormer like **Drontal** on her. There are several methods of deciding if she is ready to ovulate.

The bitches vulva [genital organ] will be very swollen and hard described quite accurately in some books as turgid, as the time for mating approaches you will see it start to look less swollen and if you feel her it is getting softer ….No she has not gone off ! She is softening to allow for mating. Just touch her around her back end near the tail, as she reaches ovulation and the correct time for mating you will see her lift her vulva up. It is quite marked when she does and there can be no mistake. I would say 85% of bitches act in this way It is a good indication that the time is right. To be more certain, and because bulldog bitches can be hard to get into whelp, most breeders use other methods to take the chance out of it. Some people use an instrument called a **Draminski,**it is quite expensive but said to be quite accurate. I tried one out from the USA before they were available here, but my bitches hated it. There are smear tests which I do myself watching the progression of the cells from the vagina.

You could take advantage of the progesterone testing undertaken by private companies. Just have a blood test at the vets and send away or i-dex Progesterone test, these often need more repeated to pin point ovulation which will make it more expensive although this can be worthwhile. One of these methods will tell you when the correct mating day is likely to fall.

Booking the Stud Dog

Prior to this make arrangements with the stud dog owner and be on standby if the vet tells you your bitch has ovulated.

Most Bulldogs are quite capable of mating naturally and like countries abroad the use of Artificial Insemination is now allowed by the UK Kennel Club, a new form is required to be filled in. The up to date situation you will find on the www.Kennel Club UK. Org

AI has its uses, the transmission of infections and disease from use of a very popular stud dog is avoided, stressful mating's requiring many handlers for assistance all make breeders want to take advantage of a more modern and scientific approach.

Most bulldogs are mated twice on alternate days, and usually, if the stud fee is paid up front the stud owners give a free mating if the bitch misses but having a blood test will help avoid the missing! Give the bitch 1 folic acid tablet a day from the start of her season until at least 6 weeks in whelp.

If you go to work and need to plan your time off to look after her ,I recommend you take her for an ultrasound scan [vets can do this or sometimes there are local scan owners or mobile ones] , between 28 to 35 days is ideal, this is the optimum time they can see and count the puppies ,after 35 days they go up in the ribs , although they can be counted at this stage it's no guarantee that she will give birth to that many , some get reabsorbed and sometimes there are more puppies than were seen but it gives you an idea and confirms she's in whelp .

Looking after your 'in whelp' Bulldog Bitch

Now you have mated your bitch it is important that you look after her correctly. I always worm my bitch prior to mating and do not do it again during pregnancy, although many vets recommend you do and will advise a safe wormer.

After mating treat your bitch as normal, just start giving her one folic acid tablet [from chemists] a day from when she comes into her season and until she is six weeks into her pregnancy. You may notice she is sleepier than usual. After about 14 to 21 days you may find she goes off her food. I haven't found many bitches that actually vomit but think the canine equivalent of morning sickness is at this time. Some bitches may bring up yellow frothy bile when hungry so regular feeding times will help her avoid this.

Do not treat her any differently food wise until the 5th week has passed, she can then have slightly increased amounts, at 6 weeks she needs a good puppy growth food as in whelp bitches should have this, no calcium supplements before the whelping but as soon as the puppies are born supplement the bitch with calcium to avoid her getting eclampsia.

Try to avoid stress in these latter days, short regular walks in cool weather, or early evening, watch her carefully a good indication things are well is the colour of her mouth membranes, a nice pink colour shows her circulation is working well if these go pale and look a bit yellow [more later on this] see the veterinary surgeon as soon as possible especially if she has a large litter on board, if she doesn't want her walk just let her out in the garden instead.

How will you know she is in whelp?

Some vets are good at palpating and feeling the nodules said to feel like a string of pearls... which are puppies around the 23/28-day mark, but I do not advise this. To be certain an Ultra sound scan will be more accurate, done between 28 and 35 days is the optimum time, before that is too soon and after that time the puppies move up into the ribs.

 This may cause them to be hidden, so counting the puppies on a scan will be are no guarantee that the number seen will be born. Re-absorption is common in bitches. It was, before the days of scans hard to diagnose and maybe owners thought it was a phantom pregnancy when no puppies arrived on the due date but there is much more evidence now about Reabsorption.

Myself I have owned a bitch who carried puppies till the 42nd day mark [seen on a scan] and then on day 63 .... nothing.

Sometimes nothing is seen, in our case twice I saw nothing at the final third attempt she lost a small amount of tissue. I took her for a course of antibiotics, she never did produce puppies.

By 5 weeks even a maiden bitch shows some thickening of her breast tissue, and after this if she is carrying a reasonable amount of puppies for the breed she will start to look thicker in the girth, often as puppies are carried in the two uterine horns she may look uneven if you look down on her one side more protruding more than the other.

At this time, you may see some stringy discharge a creamy white with some clear mucus mixed in it which always confirms to me that all is well, and the bitch is definitely in whelp. If any discharge is smelly, greenish or bloody take her to the vet for a check-up as soon as possible.

Feeding of the bitch

There is a special food made by Royal Canin HT42, I have had success using this from the time of mating up till day 42 when it should be changed to puppy growth as below.

Now this is the time to increase her food gradually and change her onto some high-quality food, I always feed the puppy growing food at this time as it has all the additives to take in to help her grow the puppies, POSITIVELY NO SUPPLEMENTS especially of calcium.

If you are feeding a puppy complete food all she needs is added in balance. There is much debate about the problems caused by giving bitches extra calcium before the birth, it is thought it can actually cause pre-eclampsia so the rule of thumb must be to administer after the birth only calcium supplements .Some people give Raspberry leaf tablets which are a herbal remedy supposed to aid birth I have tried these but saw no difference in the birth with or without the tablets! Except I felt whelps had quite a greasy feeling after mum had been fed the additive.

I do feed my bitches extra chicken, and grate cheese over the food to encourage her to keep eating. Try feeding her jars of baby food from your fingers if she stops eating as this will provide fluid and nutrition.

As her increasing girth presses on her organs you may decide to divide the meals into several smaller ones as towards the due date, she may just not have much room for a large meal. Her appetite might be erratic, sometimes eating ravenously other times being 'picky, coax her and be kind, even hand feed her as she is probably feeling quite stressed, tired and uncomfortable as a full load of puppies can affect how she can lie comfortably to sleep. This will affect her breathing as when she does try to get some rest, she may not be able to fully expand her lungs.

I have found bean bag cushions or an old duvet very good for the expectant bitch at this time. If she hasn't changed much and is a first-time mum don't be surprised if she has a few puppies hidden away, sometimes maiden bitches really keep their muscular shape till quite near the end.

Watch out for

This is now a time when you should keep careful watch on her mouth membranes; this is such an easy but informative method of telling you if she is suffering from any circulation problems.

The colour of her gums and inner lips should be a nice warm pink, if she is that and bright eyed one can assume things are progressing well. However, if she looks pale or bluish it's a very urgent trip to the vet to assess her ability to cope. If you press on the flesh inside the flews [inside sides of mouth] it should refill back to pink in a few seconds if it doesn't, this is a warning thing are not going to plan.

It is worth mentioning here that the amount of eggs that are fertilized is huge but the number which can implant is smaller and influenced by natures ability and the size of the bitch and her resources [Hence the stud dog, if he's fertile really doesn't have an influence on the size of the litter].

Sometimes nature makes a mistake, the average number of bulldog puppies born is four or five but there are large variations as to what is normal. Extra-large litters in bulldogs 10+ are a serious risk to your bitch's life.

A situation can occur when a small bitch can conceive too many puppies for her system. The first sign of which would be pale mouth, she is acting really uncomfortable, not resting or sleeping, refusing to eat or vomiting regularly. Rapid weight loss of the fat cells around her face and neck, legs etc. But a very large still expanding girth should alert you to a potential life-threatening situation. An X-ray or ultra sound could shed a bit of light on   her quantity of puppies but sometimes you must make a terrible decision to bring the puppies early.

Depending on how early it might not be possible for them to survive but if you wish to save your bitch at all costs, do not take chances if you are in this situation. [*See later chapter on Too Many Puppies*]

I had a small bitch Carmen conceive and carry 13 all were born alive but hairless in places at 14 days before their due date, their mother collapsed and couldn't breathe we thought she had gone but as soon as the vet removed the uterus and the pressure on her vital organs she started breathing again. Unfortunately, all the puppies died within 3 days as they were much too immature to survive but the bitch lived on to be 10 years old at least but was never mated again.

 My own experience of this is not unusual, several bitches I have known of have died for this very reason so keep a watchful eye on the very large bitch, and if you see her struggling consider the above and discuss with your vet.

If it is only a few days early the bitch could have a steroid injection to help the puppy's lungs a short while before beginning a C section, however this may not help as time needs to elapse before it makes it through to the puppies possibly as long as 24 hours but worth a try. Some Vets are reluctant to do this as there is a risk it may trigger labour

Whelping area

When we think about mating our dog, we must take into consideration the needs of the bitch to rear her puppies in a safe situation. Bitches that rear their own puppies that can be left with them all the time need a quiet corner away from other dogs, pets, visitors, and small children. Everyone's household situation is different and ideally a separate room is the best place, many people utilise their dining room, conservatory or kitchen obviously ground floor is best   so you can let the bitch outside easily, but I have known people use the spare bedroom with success. The early days are most critical while the bitch learns her job and gets to know her puppies after 3 weeks you will find she might be quite happy to be around people   and not mind you bringing the puppies into a more public position. Every bitch is different so you need to observe how comfortable she is, many family pets who are bred would hate to be away from the hub of the household so think hard about your individual situation and be flexible and innovative with how your bitch is acting.

Special needs for rearing bulldogs must be planned ,these puppies are not left in the whelping box with the mother due to danger of crushing , that is unless you have a good family rota for 24 hour watching, most breeders of bulldogs for instance put the puppies on the bitch then put them safely in a box with heating like *a make shift incubator* , until the next feed .The room used then should have plenty of comforts for the breeder, a bed[put-u- up] or a sofa bed ,TV , computer etc. Alarm to set, a lot of breeders use the corner of their lounge which has the added advantage of rearing well socialised puppies

My own experience with Bulldogs

When you do not keep the puppies on the bitch except for feeding you may in the early days not need to have a box.....I have found some bitches become very territorial in their whelping box at feeding times and when you need to remove the puppies after they stop feeding she will try to bite you .In fact even the mildest bitches can act this way their protective instinct being very strong. It is after all not natural for the puppies to not be constantly with their mother. *I will discuss this in pros and cons later.*

I have got over this by having a nice blanket which I lay down in the warmest draught proof place and then bring the puppies' box down and lay my bitch down and put the puppies on her. This works well until they start crawling around when you need to put them into the whelping box, the bitch may have got over her fierce protective phase and be much more relaxed after the first 10 days .The bitch soon learns the routine and will come as soon as she hears my alarm go off and waits for her puppies.

Practical items needed

If you are using a room with a carpet down you do not want ruined I recommend you get a few big plastic tarpaulins and using the thick brown tape you stick parcels with , fix it completely over the room area you are using to the skirting board . I scatter a few washable; cotton rugs over it so it's absorbent and not so slippery or you can put newspaper down.

Whelping boxes

For the whelping box you can use a traditional wooden box with or without the pig rail [to help avoid crushing, however as puppies grow, they can be dangerous in themselves. I have seen a puppy get behind and in between bitch and she's sat back crushing the puppy by the neck against the rails, so I think they have limited value. You cannot beat watching and keeping count of where all the puppies are]

The' Rolls Royce 'of whelping boxes are called Snowsilk , they are beautifully made with white PVC coated surfaces and are easily washed down, which is not easy on wooden boxes. They have various additions to be purchased to extend the run area as the puppies grow.

If this is your first attempt at breeding and you are not sure if you will do it again I recommend the following: there are disposable whelping boxes which are great for today's houses as storage can be a problem, you buy a cardboard one, they are strong and clean and afterwards you just burn them.

No risk of cross infection from litter to litter which can be a problem sometimes. I recommend you buy a powerful sanitizer cleaner that kills all known strains of canine disease like Trigene.

A good idea to utilize as a whelping pen is the metal one that slots easily together from Croft manufacturer called the Freedom Pen ,if you put blankets or cardboard around the outside you can create a nice cosy whelping box as the puppies grow it becomes a pen suitable to house them until they leave you, and is big enough to house an adult as a sleeping area .You can buy extra panels to extend the area. I just have two complete pens and make various areas to suit all situations. For tiny puppies a strong cardboard box at one end can be their sleeping area and the mother can be in there with room to get away from them if she wants to. We use different size plastic beds as they grow, even quite small puppies learn to go into their bed area and cuddle up together .This pen has a plastic tray which is removable so you can actually use the pen as a playpen outside on the grass or patio if the weather is clement .Well worth the investment of £110 * [Croft or others from eBay]

Due to puppies biting the bars it's wise to block the lower area around [sort of like a baby cot bumper, but not fabric due to strangulation risk] puppies often get their jaws caught in the cage bars and lock their jaw and scream as they can't free themselves so it's a must to do this.

Heating

We use and recommend underneath Heat Pads and have a heat lamp only for really cold weather as Heat lamps tend to be uncomfortable for the mother, and you do have to watch for overheating the puppies.

When the mother is with the puppies and if the room is draught free little in the way of heat is needed, her body warmth should be enough to keep the puppies at the correct temperature. However we do keep our room extremely warm 70 to 75 degrees Fahrenheit almost tropical. New born puppies have to be kept at 80+ degrees for the first seven days when not feeding.

We put our puppies in a box to keep from being crushed, a cardboard box or ideally a plastic clear stacker box that we can see through and watch the puppies , we do not close the lid ever but have it covered over partially or a towel over to cut out the down draughts . I replace a hot water bottle at each feed giving a hot one, an unheated area in the middle and a cooler one at the end giving the whelps a choice of where to lie comfortably. It is possible to use a heat pad thermostatically controlled, special ones are sold with wire protected by a sheath of metal to avoid electrocution when puppies start chewing.

Collect newspapers because you can never have enough of them for using as litter bedding. Make sure your family and friends save them for you too.

Take a deep breath, stock up on quick meals and chocolate for you to boost your own energy.

Traditional whelping box

Chapter 2

The Birth

Onset of Labour

About a week prior to the due day , make sure you have everything ready so there is no last minute panic .Do have the bitch checked at the vets for any problems that could be occurring, this is the time to discuss the possibility of a C section some vets will only do them if the dog is actually struggling in labour where others will say bring her in as soon as you are certain she is in labour, as they do not want to risk her and the puppies by letting them get in distress first , discuss the possibility of her self-whelping or at least trying, however some bitches are not a good prospect to self-whelp so consult the vet as to how he feels she will be best cared for.

If it is decided to do a C section discuss the fact you want to be at the surgery and help with the puppies, this should not be a problem with most vets .Do not hand your bitch over and leave, puppies need constant stimulation to get them going, I have heard many bad reports about puppy mortality through going home and leaving the bitch in just the vets nurses care. If this is a problem seriously consider finding a more accommodating veterinary surgeon.

Bulldogs can self-whelp there is no denying this, there are many factors to take into account that will influence whether your bitch of any breed will need a C section. If she has a small litter the puppies are likely to be bigger and sometimes there is no release of the hormone to start the labour also if she has a large litter, she is likely to get tired out before she passes them all. Each situation should be assessed on its own situation.

It is a common misapprehension that **the bulldog puppies' heads are the problem when in actual fact it's the shoulders** that are the widest point. The most common cause of distress in self whelping is the problem of a dystocia, a bad presentation, if they are in the birth canal puppies get caught up behind.

 The incidence of water puppies is a deciding factor in some breeders plans .If you have experience of breeding puppies before you can try to self-whelp her or if you have someone who has self-whelped any breed around it is possible to try but be aware that it can be dangerous to her and the puppies, if things go wrong or if she gets inertia and then just stops in the middle, you may have to take her to the vets anyway. So be prepared!

You will need to make sure that your car is ready, with a full tank of petrol at all times for emergencies.

You should also put a strong collar and lead on the bitch when she needs to relieve herself as it is not a good idea to allow her outside at night in early labour, in case she finds a hidey hole to give birth in, so always go with her.

Natural birth

Expected Date of Delivery

Because most Pedigree breeders do two mating's and fresh semen lives72 hours up to 5 days on average, the date of the arrival of the puppies could vary considerably, most deliver on 63 days but many at 61 or some even much later than 65. If your bitch passes her due date, I would recommend her being checked by the vet as there is a common condition called Inertia. Bitches in some breeds are prone to it, **[bulldogs particularly suffer from this]** .The vet will feel inside your bitch to see if the cervix is opening and   if it is not it is probably not ready .Bulldogs are known to have a high incidence of   C sections ,I would definitely advise no such operation unless the cervix is open and the bitch is in some sort of distress, immature puppies die due to lung immaturity ,every day inside the uterus is needed ...on a scale of 9 weeks , 2 or 3 days early is a lot of time .

Getting the timing right

Whilst mostly there is no hurry, remember that the puppy's placentas are only meant to support life for the norm and after this passes you may find that some puppies aren't getting the proper supplies through from the mother. It is important to be aware of this and to have a good comfortable relationship with the vet and share your worries.

Only you know your bitches' habits and demeanour so your vet may not realise how out of character she is acting or even assess how ill she is becoming. Remember she is relying on you to keep her safe, report if you think she is not herself and is ill, dullness in attitude when she is normally perky and bright should be watched for.

There is an optimum time for bitches to have litters some say from the second season, but I find that the third one is a good productive one and certainly a first litter should be had before the bitch is 5 years old. [*I don't think most bitches of any breed are mature enough to make good mothers at the first season and to register puppies with the Kennel Club the bitch must be over twelve months.*]

It is worth asking someone in your breed with experience what they recommend. It is true that there are many champion bitches who after being campaigned in the show ring at their most fertile and productive time never have any puppies or die having a litter much too late for that particular bitch. It is possible to breed your bitch then put her back in the ring. Many experienced breeders completely recommend this as they claim a litter helps' spring of rib' mostly after just one litter the bitches undercarriage returns almost to her previous tight look .It is subsequent litters that make them rather saggy and puts them at a disadvantage to the young bitches with tight undercarriage Most bitches lose a vast amount of coat at around the weaning time which probably delays the return to the show ring.

Prelude to the birth

Well, we have our healthy bitch that will be due within the week, so we have to now start watching her closely. **Do not leave her alone for long periods and start sleeping nearby** her whelping quarters   which she should be introduced to about 14 days before the due date so she feels safe in there. In the last few nights you could put the alarm on every two or three hours, so you wake up and check on her.

At about 5 days to go, you could start taking her temperature. The normal temperature of a bitch is 101 degrees Fahrenheit or 37 centigrade, any fall in this could herald the start of labour, but there is a small early false drop which you may just catch and be confused by. Generally, the proper temperature drop is down for a few hours, but minor dips can be ignored. When the temperature drops to average of 98.F or 36.7 C she will almost certainly be going into labour within the next 12 to 24 hours.

Usually bitches refuse to eat when labour starts which is another good clue. *[There are the exceptions to this!]* She may start to act excited or nervous and be restless, she may start digging in her bed area and some bitches like newspaper to shred at this time.

 If you let her outside in the garden to relieve herself go with her as some bitches like to choose their own whelping area , under a shed or bush so don't lose her !Just keep a watchful eye on her but don't interfere too much natural whelping is a private occasion for most bitches and too much human intervention can cause problems , it is not the time for visitors either ,only let her close family come around and keep any other dogs out of the way .Most whelping's take place at night which I think its nature's way of keeping the process quiet and secretive and this is what you should be promoting if you want your bitch to safely and happily deliver her puppies naturally .

Make sure you have the following items listed below ready

Clean towels; cut up pieces of rag to rub puppies; Spare newspapers, bin bags

Disinfectant Hibi scrub /Dettol or Savlon and a bowl to wash your hands in, or you could use that antibacterial gel that is now available everywhere as used in hospitals to control infection.

Cotton wool or lint [good if you need to hold the puppy to help ease its way as they are quite slippery] kitchen towel, tissues

KY Jelly as a lubricant a little just around the vulva may help a stuck puppy

Warmed [heat pad or hot water bottle] cardboard box/ or stacker box, to place already born puppies in whilst next one is passed ,several blankets to cover for draughts and to snuggle the puppies ,**Make sure the pad is well covered to avoid overheating**

Pieces of strong thread or catgut to tie the cords, blunt ended scissors,

Cord clamps are a good idea if you see any but not essential [plastic ones are very good for this mainly because they are not heavy and do not pull on the cord you can then tie it off above and take the clips off]

Pen and paper to record the progress, clock,

Phone number of vet and an experienced person used to whelping if you just need reassurance.

Flask of coffee/sandwiches /chocolate [it can be a long job]/book, radio or TV

Room temperature must be draught free and 80 F or 26.7 C

Imminent Whelping

Your bitch may start shivering or panting , acting anxious, this first stage may last 6 to 20 hours, no contractions are visible at this stage , but the behaviour of your bitch should make you aware that something is happening , however if she settles down and sleeps and doesn't progress this may mean she has inertia, watch her carefully.

When they move into the second stage some bitches are made of stern stuff and without any warning a big push towards her rear and the first puppy may appear, normally though you can see the bitch strain, sometimes they go down on their front legs and push backwards into the corner of the whelping area, if you see your bitch doing this is safe to assume the first whelp is on its way in the birth canal. You should note the time you see the first strain, the next time maybe another fifteen minutes, and gradually the contractions get closer together, do not let your bitch strain hard after the first contractions for more than an hour, inform your veterinary surgeon of the timing and if you can see the puppy and it is not progressing delivery. *[This may be the time that a C section is decided upon]*

Each puppy is born in its own sac containing fluid and you may be able to see it in the vulva, like a big bubble, you can sometimes see the puppies nose or feet squashed against the surface, as the bag emerges with the puppy inside most bitches know to tear it open but bulldog bitches may not do this easily.

I usually grasp the puppy and burst the bag and clear its nose, putting it where the bitch can help licking it, the placenta sometimes comes out with the puppy and the water bag but sometimes it takes a while to be expelled, if it is still attached inside **DO NOT PULL IT** you may cause a haemorrhage when the arteries are closed off on the side of the uterus the bitch expels it.

Do not rush to cut the cord, it may be better to tear it rather than cut it to emulate the bitches method of detaching it , but tie it off a good distance from the puppy first , and then about 3 inches from the puppies navel and tear in between take extra care not to pull at the cord at the puppies navel as umbilical hernias can be caused *[these can also be hereditary and well as environmental but if the puppy develops one you know you haven't caused it if you are careful]*Some bitches break the cord themselves but bulldogs being Brachephelic due to position of teeth may need help .

A problem occurs in some whelping's when the puppy has a short cord and is only just outside the bitches body and attached still , in which case you must tie two places tightly and cut between so the puppy nor bitch bleed from the cut ends .The placenta may take at least 15 minutes to detach from the wall of the uterus so don't be in a hurry, the bitch may pass another puppy in its water sac in between and then both placentas may arrive together, each bitch is different and each whelping goes differently .If the cord tie comes off retie it I have seen a whelp with a pump fountaining blood on each heartbeat .

Puppies come at intervals of anything from 10 minutes up to 1 to 3 hours , the same applies to all subsequent puppies , if the bitch is just resting in between not over straining all is ok but if she starts to strain vigorously do not let her go for

more than an hour actually pushing. If she just lays there with her head in between her front paws it is likely she is getting ready to push again, putting the puppies already born to her nipples may stimulate the next delivery as it is a natural release of hormones when the puppies suckle this may help keep the whelping going.

When the puppies are placed in their stacker/ incubator box try to take care she doesn't get too agitated hearing them cry, bitches having their second litter are very maternal and protective.

You can look at the bitch to see if you can see the puppy, ideally puppies come nose first but a high percentage come backwards with no trouble , if your bitch has been straining for an hour and you can see nothing at her vulva I think you should assume you have a problem probably caused by mal presentation or dystocia [lack of contractions or inertia] certainly if the puppy has a tail and you see it presenting first you probably have the puppies rear legs folded and it will be impossible to pass a puppy in that manner.**[Vet help needed]**

The experienced breeders knowing what they are feeling for scrub up or put on a latex glove use some KY jelly as a lubricant and gently insert a finger to see if the puppy is in the birth canal.

Unless you are experienced this is best left for the vet to do as you should tell him your bitch is having problems and not managed to give birth after an hour of productive straining. He may give a shot of Oxytocin and wait to see if that starts things moving, he may be able to move the puppy with his fingers and free its passage out but it may be necessary for him to do a c section at this point. In the past vets made home visits now this is extremely rare he will ask you to take her to the surgery, leave the existing puppies in their warm box at home, they should go to sleep until you can bring her home. But if your vet is some distance away you should take the homemade incubator box with you so as the bitch gives birth to the other puppies they can be warm and afterwards you can put all of them on her for the vital colostrum in the early hours .To my surprise it's not the mums levels that drop it's the puppies own ability to absorb the antibodies.

 Dark greenish discharge before the birth of any of the puppies is a danger sign that requires veterinary help, it simply means one placenta has detached, after the birth of one it is not any indication of problems but normal.

Puppies that fail to breathe and get going after the birth need urgent attention , wrapping them in a warm towel or cloth you need to hold them downwards to allow fluids to drain from it , you need to rub vigorously, and if you need to you swing the puppy to shake out fluids its best to get the vets nurse to show you how, you need to support the puppy but to elevate it and then lower it to free the lungs and allow drainage .Mouth to Mouth resuscitation would be far too much for the puppies , a tiny spot of brandy has been known to shock the puppy into breathing ,and smelling salts can help but caution needed as puppies have very fragile breathing systems .

Several methods which work like artificial respiration are recommended, if you hold the puppy upside down then gently the other way up you force the organs to be stretched and compressed which can start them breathing .Another method is to hold the puppy at both ends and gently compress the puppy inwards, then stretch outwards, in a concertina motion, try both ways anything to get the puppy going.

At the vets he has a product called Dopram which can be bought on the internet it's a heart stimulant and a little drop is placed on the puppies' tongue, this can work miracles in kick starting them   but all drugs should be used with caution and on veterinary advice only.

In nature the bitch will eat her placentas and I have no objection to allowing her to eat a couple but if its large litter it will probably make her very loose motions if she eats a lot! I think its original purpose was meant to hide the evidence of new-borns from predators but also it may provide extra nutrients needed for those first days for her. It is a good idea to count them there should be one for each puppy; the vet can inject oxytocin to expel any retained ones. If your bitch becomes lethargic and has a foul smelling discharge after birth suspect a retained placenta and seek urgent veterinary advice as it can develop into quite a life threatening situation as it decomposes inside your bitch .

As the whelping is completed your bitch should be sleepy and lying down with her puppies, they should all be placed on the bitch's teats and observed to see they are actually obtaining the colostrum, she needs a good drink and time to recover. If there is any danger she is not accepting the puppies please put them in the box whilst you leave the room and sit with her all the time they are with her, most bitches quickly realise the puppies are theirs and will take them away from you and try to bury them in the bedding .Do not allow this as many puppies have been crushed because the mother hides them and forgets and sits down on them .Offer the bitch a drink, water or milk feeding is thirsty work. If you feed and water your bitch and see to her needs, she will reward you by taking care of the puppies, a content bitch is a good natural mother.

You need to examine each puppy if they are marked differently give each one an identifying name e.g. spot or white head, weigh them, open their mouths and check for a cleft palate .This looks like a dark line and is the roof of the mouth not sealed, its more common in bracheaphelic breeds but is not unknown in any breed. Harelips are where the nose is not properly closed in the top of the lip sometimes both sides are affected and its accompanied by a cleft it is very unwise to try to rear such puppies as they would need surgery to close both palate and lip and there may be other related conditions hand in hand with these abnormalities so the kindest sensible thing is to let the vet euthanize the affected   puppies. Hare lips only can be raised

Sometimes an extra-large puppy is born, also common in bracheaphelic breeds, these puppies are usually water logged, mildly affected ones can be treated by very small vets injection of Lasik's but really swollen distorted puppies usually die within a very short while after birth naturally.

The causes of this type of problem are widely debated but recent research seems to compare this condition with the human one Hydrops fetalis caused by incompatibility in the parental blood groups, some people site diet as a cause, I think whole litters so affected are incompatibility but odd puppies affected are probably caused by the individual puppies faulty lymphatic system .If any puppies survive with this before you sell them make sure they have a thorough testing of their hearts.

To summarize when to call in your veterinary surgeon

If you see a green Verdi discharge before the first puppy is born, [after one is born the discharge is normal]

If she strains hard for an hour with no progress

Goes more than 3 hours in between puppies but you are convinced she has more to come

If the puppy is showing and stuck do not wait for more than 10 minutes before calling for help

Inertia is described as two conditions, primary and secondary, **Primary** when the bitch never gets going at all and **Secondary** inertia after much straining maybe weakness of muscle tone, so she has given up. Caesarean Section maybe the only way forward if these conditions occur.

After a C section very careful introduction of the puppies is necessary as the act of birth prepares the bitch for the feeding and acceptance of the puppies, once she is fully around from the anaesthetic she should progress and take over feeding the babies but give her time to realise they are hers.

If your bitch refuses to lie down and nurse the puppies, I am afraid you must make her. The puppies' need that vital colostrum for the protection from diseases this is at its strongest 6 hours from the birth but is probably gone by 24 hours, so timing is important. However stubborn she must feed even if you have to hold her down, it is rare that a bitch never feeds her puppies, but I have experienced extremely spoilt bitches that are treated like the owner's child and just have no inclination or instinct to rear her own babies.

If you suspect your bitch is like this **DO NOT MATE** her and if she acts this way certainly do not try to breed her again hoping she will improve, she won't and puppies survival is much more likely with natures intended food than if you try hand rearing.

Finally

Examine each puppy carefully firstly for cleft palates secondly that check they have an anus, check the legs etc. any that are worrying you let the vet decide the viability [however some breeds especially bulldogs sometimes have turned backwards legs , so do not let the vet put these to sleep as it will right itself in a short time].

The following describes a C section and the discussions and points raised about it

Caesarean Section

Primarily in dogs the C section is an emergency method of delivery, for Dystocia, and inertia, however there are some breeds that are routinely delivered this way to avoid complications; namely Bulldogs and Boston terriers.

This does not mean that these breeds cannot self-whelp but due to a high risk incidence they are, more often than not, when it's established they are in labour, delivered at the vets by C section, often just the vets availability decides when and if they are sectioned.

The rights and wrongs of this can be argued for both natural and human intervention, I have known some very healthy bulldogs deliver their pups, even huge litters naturally whereas some with small litters often suffer inertia, start in labour and then stop, no amounts of inject able oxytocin will restart these bitches, and there are very real dangers of a large puppy due to water retention blocking the birth canal and putting the others at risk behind.

It is important that bitches, with a history of C sections in the breed, are taken to the vet about a week before delivery date and the situation fully discussed with your vet. You should have a birth plan agreed with him in good time as when the bitch is in labour and is giving you concern it is not fair to expect the vet to make instant decisions over the telephone.

I have a pictorial delivery of bulldog puppies by C section for you to see the photos may be self-explanatory, but I am going to write the stages and procedure also.

On arrival at the vets the bitch is weighed so the correct amount of anaesthesia is used, some vets use a sedative first but mine does not. The vet injects into the dogs vein and administers the anaesthetic Propofol

Fig 1 Queenie

Propofol is a short-acting intravenous anaesthetic agent used for the induction of general anaesthesia, maintenance of general anaesthesia in human medicine and sedation in medical contexts, such as intensive care unit (ICU) sedation for intubated, mechanically ventilated adults, It provides no analgesia.[1]

Propofol is approved for the induction and maintenance of anaesthesia in more than 50 countries.

It is also commonly used in veterinary medicine and many veterinary anaesthetists' regard it as the induction agent of choice for small animals (dogs, cats etc) as it can be administered to effect, reducing the risk of accidental overdose.

As soon as she goes drowsy which is usually very quickly a tube is inserted into the trachea and fluothane/ oxygen started. The propofol only puts her to sleep the fluothane maintains her under anaesthetic and acts as painkiller and is left on until the operation is complete.

Inhalant anaesthetic used Fluothane [Halothane] or Isoflurane 1%-3%

The bitch is then placed on her back and they usually use a special plastic cradle to support her, the under belly is shaved along the central line and disinfectant wash is used to cleanse the area.

Fig 2

The vet makes her incision through the outer wall and the inner layers exposing the uterus which in the bitch is y shaped

Fig 3

Fig 4

The uterus is opened close to the horn and the first puppy in its sack is seen and taken out , the bag is broken the cord is clamped, cut and the vets nurse takes the puppy and begins to immediately clear the nose and probably uses the sweep method of shaking out fluids .

Fig 5

The placenta for that puppy may come away at this point ,if not it has to be eased away very carefully avoiding pulling as this may cause haemorrhage .The vet carries on getting each puppy out, first all the puppies from one horn then the other side working the puppies down and out rather like a milking action .She tries not to burst the water sack until each puppy is being lifted out. Speed is important. The vets nurse deals with them as they are handed to her, they need a very warm area to place the puppies and as they sometimes are sluggish if the anaesthetic has been taken on board they need rubbing vigorously. If the owner is around many vets hand the puppies after the initial throat and nose clearing to the owner especially if there is a large litter to be delivered.

Sometimes Dopram is given to the pups on their tongue it's a respiratory stimulant and assists breathing, vigorous rubbing will get the circulation going, the puppy turning a nice healthy pink colour instead of a greyish blue colour on its feet pads and nose, if the puppy has no congenital problems this is what should happen.

Dopram-V is a potent medicine and not a dietary supplement. Dopram-V stimulates breathing within a few seconds of use.

After the last pup is born and a thorough check for any puppies tucked up in the horns, the vet starts to close the bitch , there are at least three layers of uterus ,muscle and skin and they use dissolving stitches internally and the outside ones are usually removed after 10 or 12 days .

Fig 6

The bitch is washed with antiseptic and patted dry , given a long acting antibiotic injection .The oxygen/ gas is turned off and the bitch is placed on her front and head in a recovery position, unless the room is really warm it's a **wise precaution to cover her with a heat retaining blanket as this will help to avoid shock .**She must not be left unattended as she may come around really quickly and injure herself falling from the table ,some vets place the bitch on the floor at this point to avoid this .

Fig 7

The Puppies: now the vet turns her attention to checking the puppies, firstly for cleft palates and harelips possible in any breed [but more common in bracheaphelic heads] and any other abnormalities, hernias, absent anus

Fig 8: Sometimes a vet will find a puppy with its stomach open besides the cord an attempt to close this with a stitch is often made.

Myself I have rarely reared a puppy that has had any new-born surgery, but it is worth a chance to try. I have all my puppies injected with Vitamin K this has been recommended to me by breeders in the USA and although vets sometimes say they don't know what good it will do , it is cheap can cause no harm and is routinely given to all human new-born's

Fig 9 purple tummy

my experience is most vets will give it a try . In Human Babies it cuts down on internal bleeding this is the definition of its use in humans. This condition can be prevented by the Vit K injection 0.1ml at birth.

Haemorrhagic disease of the new-born (HDNB) was first identified over 100 years ago by Townsend (1); it presents as unexpected bleeding, often with gastrointestinal haemorrhage and ecchymosis, and, in many cases, intracranial haemorrhage. In 1961, the Committee on Nutrition of the American Academy of Pediatrics (AAP) recommended that vitamin K1 (hereafter referred to as vitamin K, the only form of vitamin K1 used in neonates) 0.5 to 1.0 mg be administered intramuscularly to all newborns shortly after birth to prevent this problem (2).

References

1. Townsend CW. The haemorrhagic disease of the newborn. Arch Pediatr 1894;11:559-65.

2. Committee on Nutrition, American Academy of Pediatrics. Vitamin K compounds and the water-soluble analogues: Use

in therapy and prophylaxis in pediatrics. Pediatrics 1961;28:501-7

After Examination

The puppies should be taken home immediately in a warm box and then put on the mum as soon as she is comfortable to receive the **vital antibody rich colostrum**, if there is a reason mum is not ready to go home attempts should be made to get all the pups to feed on her as soon as possible .After the feed they should all be encouraged to sleep.

Keep bitch very warm whilst she recovers and also place the puppies in a warm box [stacker box will do] whilst she recovers and is fully awake.

 NOTE Very Important. The bitch should have pain killers for the first two days as sometimes they are extremely stressed with pain causing excessive panting and salivating, the pain killing injection given at the birth will only last about 20 hours effectively on a bulldog bitch.

Disadvantages of C section

> Several situations are a disadvantage to bitch and puppies to have the C section

• Puppies may take on some anaesthetic making them sluggish to feed. As the essential antibodies contained in the colostrum are only able to be absorbed in the puppies' gut for the first hours it is very important that all puppies receive their share of colostrum.

- Usually in a normal whelping, ill or weak puppies do not survive the trauma of a natural birth However all puppies get taken home and you may be very upset to find one or more die quite suddenly with no apparent cause.

- The newly delivered bitch may take time to understand that the puppies are hers, cleaning and feeding will probably be much slower to establish, and many c sections delivered bitches never attempt to clean their puppies [in which case you must be very diligent and see that they eliminate urine and faeces by stimulating them yourself.]

- Bitches are recommended to have a maximum of 2 C sections [a Welfare initiative from the BVA , RCVS leading to the Kennel Club now refuse to register puppies from a 3rd litter   ] where as a normal delivered litters 4 if the bitch is fit and well with no problems can be registered

- **As most breeders do two mating's at two or three day intervals and the semen can live up to 5 days inside the bitch ,one must be very careful not to take the puppies out too early .Their lungs are immature and dying is a real possibility most experienced vets require the bitch to actually be in labour before they consider doing an operation** .In this situation to decide if she is ready one can run the pre mate blood test and it will show that the bitches hormone levels indicate that labour is imminent ,the exception to this is when your bitch is struggling [*please read and discuss with your vet Too Many Puppies chapter*].

Contra indications specifically for the bitch

- She may die under the anaesthetic

- She may get an infection in the incision

  She may go into shock from the operation

- The incision may open up or she may bleed internally without giving any indication until it is too late, can cause death

- She may rupture the uterus in subsequent labours due to scar tissue being weak; it is wise to not leave the bitch straining too vigorously in a self-whelp after having had a previous c section always remember this.

- Bitch sometimes become disorientated after the C Section and may harm the puppies if she is not watched carefully, the motherly instinct may take a while to kick in

- If the bitch bleeds and pools under the skin she may develop a Haematoma, it is a pocket of blood, some vets try to drain it but it usually refills , sometimes it will disperse naturally after a time .however some bitches find it develops into a hard fatty lump of fibrous tissue unsightly but not life threatening .

- Sometimes the bitch may react to the internal stitches and there have been occasions where in time a small swelling may occur and it is actually a stitch working its way out to the surface, which after it's cleared the body causes no problems. Obviously, any lumps which appear should be checked out by your vet.

Most vets will expect her to be awake enough to walk to the car before releasing her to go home, you will be amazed how brave she is, and bulldogs are made of stout stuff!

Make sure you are careful not to allow strangers near her and protect young children as whilst the effects of the anaesthetic are still there, you must not trust her to behave as she normally does. Calm behaviour from you will be what she needs to cope with the shock of the operation and to find she has little ones to care for.

Your bitch will have a clean wound from her operation .Just wipe it if it looks sticky in a day or so I use salty water, pat dry and dust with antiseptic wound powder if it's a hot time of the year and it is sweaty .Generally keeping it dry will mean it needs little or no attention, it heals quickly with few problems .The stitches are removed at about 10 days unless the vet used dissolving ones.

Chapter 3

The Puppies and getting her settled

Getting her home

If the birth has taken place at the vets, take your bitch and puppies home as quickly as possible, get her settled down and then put the puppies on for their first feed.

It is very important that they get the first thick yellowish looking milk called colostrum as this contains the antibodies the puppies will need in their first few weeks to fight infections.

Put the weaker puppies on the teats towards the rear and the stronger puppies on the forward ones you will have to keep constantly putting the puppies on the teats in the first days as they fall off before they get good at feeding!

Watch and listen for a 'ting' sound that means they are actually suckling and swallowing, and check they are all on a nipple as they suck at the skin sometimes and are not on a teat at all!

After about 10 minutes of suckling, rub them to get them to eliminate and put them in their box for a rest, offer your bitch a drink water at first but later on she may enjoy puppy milk .[This is the only time I feed adult dogs milk as it gives them the runs normally]

Your bitch may be panting alarmingly at this point and she may act strangely, she must take plenty of fluids drinking is vital do not worry too much about eating in the first hours, you can give puppy milk it's the only time I give adult dogs milk but it's feeding as well as fluid. You can tempt her to eat with anything if she won't eat her normal food, I have been known to open a tin of salmon in desperation to get them eating but usually some fresh cooked chicken will get them eating again, add some of the dry food to it and by 2 weeks she will be eating 3 or 4 times her normal food. The use of jars of chicken baby food licked off your fingers is recommended to get her going at this stage if she doesn't want solid food. Watch her if she starts to show her spine she is not eating enough, at this point she may start to lose her coat and you should commence weaning the puppies at 2 to 3 weeks to help her cope.

It is a good idea to start her on calcium tablets to help ward off eclampsia. This is rarely seen just after birth but more common when the puppies are feeding strongly and taking a vast amount of milk. Watch her discharge it is normal to be greenish/bright red just after birth going to normal red blood, then gradually turning brown. If it becomes profusely red oxygenated blood she may be haemorrhaging, but if it has dark lumps like liver in it is probably just afterbirth placenta particles. If It smells foul there is a problem Vets ASAP Check her teats regularly for hot spots and soreness [see Mastitis]. Feed her naturel yogurt to help her and the puppies with the flora in the gut that will be destroyed with the necessary antibiotics she will be taking; puppies can have a small amount each day too from a finger.

The puppy's first hours

Your new normal healthy bulldog puppies should be looking rather like little guinea pigs/or jacket potatoes they are firm and wriggly and should be a nice pink colour in their faces and on their pads.
They twitch as they are sleeping; this is a good healthy sign.

Make sure she is in an area without any other animals. Keep people and children well away from her as she comes around, she may be aggressive towards you but be firm with her as its imperative she allows you to touch her puppies to help her, so don't let her think she's in charge but be kind as she is probably feeling bewildered and sore.

When you get her home she will be very sleepy after the op, and cannot be trusted not to overlay the pups by mistake especially if she is a first time mother, so place the puppies in a warm box and her in the whelping box and let them sleep….In the first day I usually put the puppies on the bitch to suckle hourly, and then put them to sleep until an hour has passed since they went into the box, Watch for the puppies to get rounded bellies and listen to each one suckling, if they swallow it makes a 'ting' noise if they are just sucking without getting anything you will have to help them, massage the bitch and paddle down towards the teat… especially for the small weaker ones .

Please note in the early hours you may not see much milk at all but keep suckling the puppies on the mum **DO NOT BE IN A RUSH TO TOP UP, THIS CAN BE LETHAL IN BULLDOGS ASPIRATION PNEUMONIA IS EASY TO START BY INHALING MILK**

You may have to buy some substitute milk formula, the kit I recommend is Royal Canin first stage milk [includes a feeding bottle teats etc] to top up any weaklings, but first of all try very hard to get them suckling from mum it's the best way and as bulldogs are very bad at inhaling milk from bottles only top up if they are struggling to feed [if bulldogs inhale milk it sets up a respiratory infection and causes pneumonia fatal in a tiny puppy]Increase the times of suckling because they don't need much to keep going but the bitches supply is helped by frequent feeding ,try sponge feeding if you really think they are getting nothing .

For the first 3 to 5 days one has to hope that everything is working correctly in the puppy internally, unfortunately some perfectly normal looking puppies pass away with no warning. I always think that it is something we cannot see; however, this is very upsetting but concentrate on the healthy ones as if you neglect them to nurse the weakling you may lose them all. First 3 days I never get too upset over losing the pups with no apparent reason, this is nature, maybe the puppy has an internal problem you can't see, check to see it has an anus as this can be the cause of early neonatal deaths, if these puppies had had a normal birth they maybe wouldn't have survived the birth which is a test for the viability of new-borns in itself.

 Look after the strong ones and do not blame yourself, if you lose some.

After each feed you need to take a piece of cotton wool and wipe each puppy to stimulate it to urinate and to pass motions. If you neglect this puppy will become ill so it is very important to do it each time, however they may not pass anything but urine at every feed. The first motions are blackish but soon become the normal yellow. The urine is quite a bright yellow too. If they get sore with rubbing, you may use Sudocreme Nappy rash cream on the anus. Hopefully the mother will take over this job, but some mothers do not like to do it, others are fanatical, and you never see any mess in the nest at all and they continue to clean up the pups well into the weaning period. **Try to rub only on the area around the anus where there is fur to protect it.**

Frequency of feeds is also something I am asked about a lot. In the first few days before the milk has come through properly any feeding is stimulation to bring the real milk through ,so I usually put my puppies on the bitch , pee/poop them and put them into their box and I then time an hour, for me to rest up and after that it starts again, **I continue hourly till the milk changes consistency and becomes whiter and watery looking** then if the puppies are sleeping satisfied I extend the time to 1 and ½ hours after last one goes in the box ,I then let the puppies and nature guide me sometimes due to growth spurts it will seem as though they are ravenous before they are due and other times are really sleepy, as a rule of thumb I put them on the bitch more during the day , and satisfy the growth spurt and let them go a little longer if they are sleepy during the hours of darkness therefore establishing a pattern which through to weaning you can carry on so that they sleep longer at night by 12 days or so this should have developed and you can leave the puppies 2 to 3 hours according to how they are sleeping and gaining weight . I never go 4 hours with my puppies in the day but I try to get them to do so at night, when the three week mark and solids have been introduced I let the puppies wake me, and find they do get into a routine of doing big sleeps whilst its night time.

Pro's and Cons of Keeping the Bitch and Puppies separately

This is to help you decide how you will manage those vital first three weeks

 Make no mistake puppies get squashed by Bulldogs not intentionally, they just are clumsy, they also like to cover them with their bedding and then as they can't see them, they forget where they are and sit on them!

Most bitches are actually very good mothers, but **the risk of crushing is a major one.**

Practicalities must come into this, if you have a big family who will watch over these more difficult breeds whilst you get some rest then they could stay with the bitch but if you are alone or intend to go to work for short periods you really cannot contemplate leaving the puppies with the mother unattended.

 For the first 3 weeks its safer to put them on the bitch, watch over them then take them off her and put them safely in their draught free " incubator "[a cardboard box or a plastic stacker box which could be quite a big one] bitches who have previously had a litter left with them all the time will not accept the puppies going away and she may try to bite you in her efforts to keep them with her .I found that first time mums accept this method with no trouble, so start as you mean to go on.

If you leave the puppies with the mother you will have to take the bitch out with you anytime you need to go away to do something, make a drink etc., some breeders sleep with their head in the whelping box, spread newspaper around so that the bitch wakes them up if they fall asleep on 'duty'.

If you keep the puppies separately you will find they soon get into a routine. I have a clock radio that I set every 2 hours or my phone, my bitches learn when the alarm goes off the puppies are coming out, it's quite sweet how they are keen to see them, and wait by the box for them. I put two hot water bottles in my stacker box; I change one at each feed therefore giving a choice of temperature for the puppies to wriggle onto...

Please avoid using coloured collars to identify them they are a strangulation risk

Disadvantages of separating from the bitch

A definite disadvantage of removing the puppies after being fed to timetable is that when puppies are left with their mother they feed on and off all the time. I have found by enforcing the time break in-between feeds the puppies become very ravenous and I have had trouble with them drinking and gorging so fast they get chronic gas and pain, I keep Infacol baby drops for treatment as it is very distressing for you and the puppy if it starts screaming with pain.

In an emergency you can give a spoonful of fizzy lemonade that will work nearly as well, if you gently rub the puppy's tummy you can ease the tautness...however should the puppy's stomach start to bloat seek urgent Veterinary treatment immediately. This happened once to me with a Shih-Tzu puppy, so it is not always large breeds that bloat up.

After about 3 weeks the bitch can be allowed to spend more time in with the puppies, it's vital they get socialised and the interaction between the canines in the house is important, don't be alarmed they do play really rough...but it is part of the learning pattern as to how quickly they learn their place. This makes for harmony in the house and is important.

Weighing the puppies

Weigh the puppies at birth, record each one's weight and expect them to lose weight in the first few days, at about 4 days they mostly will have regained their birth weight. A rule of thumb is most breeds double their birth weight in the first 7 to 10 days but often with bulldogs it takes longer due to most puppies have water loss while mums milk comes through .Puppy's vary but most put on at least an ounce a day and sometimes more, as long as they are appearing healthy lively and feel vigorous that is the best indication that all is well. I still use ounces mainly because people panic about losing 5 grams which can be the difference of a poop or empty bladder! Do not become obsessed by weight gain once a day is enough

However a **normal** puppy after mums milk has come in on day 3 that doesn't put on weight or loses has a problem do not let it go on for more than a day or so before you have it checked at the vet, that is why as a beginner watching and charting their weight is essential .I make a little chart for each puppy and at each feed I note if they pee or poo, and if they feed well , I look at their markings and name each one by that i.e. Spot on head ,white head , etc. if they are identical I put nail varnish on the foot and mark which puppy has which leg painted that way you can see straightaway if there is one with a problem .**30% of puppies born die in the first 3 weeks,** but these chances decrease with each passing day. If your puppies are being fed and looked after completely by the bitch do still weigh as this would be your first indication something was amiss. *For early puppies I think differently about weighing see later chapter.*

Milk ……………. Bitches is best, but sometimes you need to help out

The worst happens and your bitch dies, either on the table at the vets or soon after birth. The first thing you could try to find out if there is anyone with a newly whelped bitch who could act as foster mum /wet nurse to the orphans, it does not have to a bulldog it can be any breed, but their best chance of survival is feeding from a bitch not bottle. However unless the bitch is at the same stage her milk may not be good enough if her own puppies are say 5 weeks old as the levels change as the puppies needs require , Also unless the bitches owner has bred bulldogs I'm afraid it is probably better for them to stay with you .Feeding Goats milk although it works is not ideal as the proteins and fats are not anything like a bitches so I highly recommend you use a good quality puppy milk substitute i.e. .Royal Canin's Puppy milk ,[or Whelpi]if not able to get the first choice .

Substitute Milk

	Dog	Cow	Goat
% fat	8.3	4-5	3.5
% protein	9.5	3.8	3.1
% Lactose	3.7	5.0	4.6
% Ash	1.2	0.7	0.79
% total solids	20.7	14-15	12.0

I strongly advise against using Carnation Milk ,this was ok to use when there was nothing else made and can still be

used in an emergency but only as a stop gap the ingredients of these mixes do not compare with the milks we can buy now .

There is some debate as to the quality of bitches milk, this is because the bitch in nature makes her milk just the correct strength for her puppies and as time passes it changes constituents and suits the age of puppy. Some bitches are blessed with real quality milk and others not so good I once had two bitches whelp within a day of each other one had 5 puppies the other had 4, the one with five was acting really strange and I feared she was going to kill a couple who she obviously didn't like!! I took them from her and put them with the 4, dear Dora accepted them as her own and reared 6 'fat as butter 'puppies as her previous litter had been but the one with three reared three scrawny puppies who only began to thrive on weaning, this experience taught me that there can be a vast difference between bitches milk quality.

This aside most bitches milk will be preferable to any supplement .Bottle feeding a bulldog is a very risky thing to try ,if they are strong sucker's this may be the best but if they are at all weak and likely to fill their mouths up with milk and inhale it the preference would be to tube feed them. Certainly if you have any quantity you will need to consider this as trying to bottle feed a large litter of 7 or more could be almost continuous as when you have fed the last it will be time to start again with the first one .[*See tube feeding section*]There is a newest method of feeding which if they can suckle is excellent its using the little wedges of sponge that are used for women's make up , you trim them to fit a puppy mouth dip them in a pool of milk , then as the puppy starts to suckle you drip feed by syringe into the back of the sponge, its time consuming but it is safer if you just need to top up a few times or have a small litter obviously it doesn't work for weak puppies where your only hope is tube feeding . You can google this method on You Tube.

Topping up puppies should only be done if you are really quite sure they are not getting enough, I just put them on the bitch more frequently first to see if that improves the milk flow, if I find one is still looking thin and hasn't got a little round tum after a feed I may try to top up, **but this I would do for an odd feed as if the puppy gets stronger it will not need topping up at each feed, maybe just once or twice in a 24 hour period ,** you must be flexible and very observant and trust your instincts.

It's essential that your bitch drinks, I'm not too worried about food at this early stage if she eats all well and good but she may not want much, my method I've had much success with is 'treat your bitch like a princess and she will look after those puppies', give her little snacks of cheese chicken etc. when she's fed, so it becomes a lovely time not an ordeal try to be calm around her. She can have Fengreek herbal remedy milk supplement

Things to watch for in the bitch

Later on the bitch may start to show her spine if she is not eating enough as she is losing her own body weight. Her coat may become patchy as she loses condition for such is a bitch that they give their all to their offspring to the detriment of themselves. If she does this I would wean puppies from 14 days instead of 3 weeks to help her cope.

Head shaking

A peculiar phenomenon in bulldogs is head shaking, it appears to be bought on by stress or hormones and can affect either dogs or bitches. It happens to some bitches after giving birth, the treatment is to give icing sugar or glucose as it is thought to be related to low blood sugar. The bitch starts shaking her head and it becomes violent shaking her flews flying and she looks very disturbed. Normally after a few minutes she would stop when she has swallowed the sugar. This is not epileptic nor is it eclampsia, which also can be shaking but is also accompanied by staggering like a drunk. It is alarming but should not last for long it may happen on and off for a couple of days and probably will never happen again. Obviously if it keeps happening consult the vet and if there is any suspicion that it could be eclampsia do not delay.

Danger signs in the bitch

If she starts to act like she is drunk staggering she may have eclampsia, urgent veterinary attention is needed, do not wait its life threatening.

Smelly discharge from her vagina [*some brownish losses is normal but not foul smelling*]

Nail Clipping

New-born puppy's nails grow very fast every few days cut off the bit that grows over the end of the quick, besides scratching and possibly causing infection on the bitch, they will not walk well if their nails are long and it will cause the feet to splay.

Moving around

They should be able to crawl and motor around their bed from the early days but by 3 weeks they start pulling themselves up on the front legs and very soon wobble up on their back ones, walking quite bandily and like a toddler, very heavy puppies sometimes do not get up on their back legs until 6 weeks this is not unusual. Puppies should be chunky but excessive, big puppies may have trouble with their bone growth and mobility and this should be watched and advice sought from the stud dog owner if you don't know any other breeders.

Don't be afraid to seek advice we all started somewhere and I myself had the very best tutors from old respected breeders who gave their help at all hours for which I am eternally grateful.

I did breed other breeds and animals prior to bulldogs, but there is always something to learn with each litter one breeds. No one knows everything!

contentment

Paddy saved by tube feeding after the vet gave up on him

Chapter 4

Development of Puppies

It helps when you are rearing puppies if you know a little about what they can do, should do or are capable of.

I have several things I watch for and timescales I work to assess if things are progressing normally,

9 to 14 days the eyes and ears open[while watching for nice pink noses after a few days you may be alarmed to see purplish shadow ,Don't panic it's not heart problem but the pigment starting to come through early]

14 to 21 days Sometimes an apparently normal puppy will die without warning ,sometimes 'fading puppy' [the cause of this is unknown and of great controversy amongst vets] develops at this time , give the puppies a rehydration solution instead of milk when they are weak as milk supplement given at this time can kill as they don't digest it, feeding the fluids can gradually build up   energy before putting them on the bitch again , use top up as a last resort , along with tube feeding . Bulldog puppies are vulnerable at being bottle fed their squashed up faces mean it's very easy to inhale milk into the lungs setting up pneumonia, so only top up if you can see that they are not getting enough from mum. Check they have little fat tummies after they have nursed and always   listen for **the 'ting' of the swallow**. 2 weeks +start weaning [*see my weaning chapter*]

My confidence grows with each passing day after this point, start them on 6 feeds a day weaning them off their mum, completely by about 5 weeks, I find my puppies just tend to lose interest in the milk as they get a new diet and I don't compulsorily remove the bitch from them I always let her back in with them whenever she wants to go with them.Observing what they do and comparing to this list can give you a guide as to how you are doing but remember **every puppy and every litter is different nothing tears up the rule book like a litter of Bulldog puppies!**

Week 1

They sleep 90% of the time and the rest of the time is spent feeding,

They are very vulnerable for hot and cold; they can seek out their mother's milk bar, and will cuddle up to heat, they cannot control their own body temperature.

They cannot eliminate themselves either their mother must lick them or you must stimulate them

A healthy puppy's temperature is 96 to 97 degrees F, 35.5-36degrees C, taken rectally.

Pups lose weight for the first 48 hours, after weighing them at birth I do not weigh them if they are thriving until the 3rd day as I tend to worry when I see that initial loss.

The test I find to check all is well is to look at their feet pads if they are rounded and pink .,if so they are doing ok, if they are pale and flat there is something wrong, they are dehydrated. I always take great store by the colour of their mouth membranes; they should be a nice pink not deep red, not blue tinged or yellowish.

Keep the whelping box temperature around 85 F for the first week, chilling brings on hyperthermia but too hot brings hypothermia both are killers you must get it right and the settled nature of the puppies will tell you, if they are heaped together they may be cool if they are spread around laying on their backs and panting they are definitely too hot.

Observe your puppies when asleep, healthy puppies twitch and jump, they are peaceful and are not crying. When you pick them out to put them on their mum, they should become wriggly and 'vital' floppy puppies are not healthy.

Puppies move around the whelping box very fast be careful they do not burrow under the bedding as this can get them squashed if their mother is around.

Week 2

Eyes open 9 to 14 days ears which are sealed at birth open around the same time.

Their body temperature rises slightly to 97-99 degrees F

The whelping / puppy box temperature can drop a little to 80 degrees

Check and trim nails

To avoid puppies lying flat on their chest bones put lumps of padding under the base sheet so they are not permanently lying flat on them, it helps exercise them ready for walking too.

VERY CAREFUL OBSERVATION IS NEEDED BETWEEN THIS WEEK 2 AND 3 I KNOW IT AS MY 'IFFY WEEK' just when I thought I could relax sometimes a seemingly healthy puppy dies, don't be too complacent sometimes puppies with a heavy worm burden fail to thrive [discuss this with your vet]I recommend Drontal Puppy Suspension .

Week 3

Puppies start to try to stand up , lighter ones do this earlier but do not worry if heavy big puppies are slow ,some perfectly normal bulldog puppies are still are not up on their back legs until 5 or 6 weeks .Some puppies can be 'swimmers' but most recover with no treatment.

They can eliminate without help, weaning can start ,they start playing with litter mates, they can smell things and they will crawl to newspaper and relieve themselves so this is early training time.

Handle each puppy; a soft baby brush will get them used to handling for the future and make human contact enjoyable.

They should be moved into the bigger whelping box now, with maybe a small padded area, I put a small cloth washable dog bed in one corner. Do not use old carpet this soaks and creates fumes of urine

Week 4

Puppies eat food, bark, play bite, growl and chase each other, they still sleep a lot. They need their mother to teach them canine manners you should not worry too much if she is rough with them.

Always feed them before you let mum in with them at this stage a child's t shirt snug fitted will stop puppies feeding and biting her.

Puppies naturally find an area to eliminate in, I put newspaper in the corner of their run and usually as they are basically clean they don't mess in their beds but seek out this area

Week 5

Rapid growth, they start to develop personalities and the order of dominance starts to show. Introduce them to noises, there is a tape made of household noises and fireworks, car engines etc. available from the Blue Cross Charity or you could make your own,

Week 6

They should be completely weaned now

Try to spend a little time each day with each puppy individually away from the litter.

There are some interesting plans to socialize your puppies on the web worth having a look at.

Start weighing weekly now but don't get paranoid about weight as long as puppies are growing and feel solid you are doing ok

Week 7

Puppies are inquisitive can get into trouble biting things and even hurt themselves by getting caught up somewhere and twisting, if they are out of their comfort area please don't leave them alone .

Week 8 and 9

Fear period begins, learns his name, can start house training by kind attention

They start to enjoy individual attention they start to interact with humans more than each other.

It's time to go to their new homes, first vaccine and Vet Health Check. Always wait 48 hours after their vaccine before you let them go to their new homes I have had some puppies react very badly to their injections so as a precaution keep them with you. **DO NOT** sell puppies without your own vet checking them, and tell all new owners to take them to their own vet within 7 days for a health evaluation.

Any problems at this stage it is wise to take the pup back, refund the full purchase money, sort the problem if possible and then resell the pup or place as a pet with a knowledgeable bulldog person if there is a permanent problem or contact Bulldog Rescue and Rehoming for further advice.

Feeding the puppy's best quality puppy food is the best start you can give them see my weaning page

To Summarize development milestones

Eyes open at 10 to 14 days, ears also are opened then as prior to these puppies are born deaf and blind.

They should be able to crawl and motor around their bed from the early days but by 3 weeks they start pulling themselves up on the front legs and very soon wobble up on their back ones, walking quite bandy and like a toddler, very heavy puppies sometimes do not get up on their back legs until 6 weeks this is not unusual.   Puppies should be chunky but excessive, big puppies may have trouble with their bone growth and mobility and this should be watched and advice sought from the stud dog owner if you don't know any other breeders.

Don't be afraid to seek advice we all started somewhere and I myself had the very best tutors from old respected breeders, Cottons [Aldridge]and Norman[Ocobo] who gave their help at all hours for which I am eternally grateful.

I did breed other breeds and animals prior to bulldogs, but there is always something to learn with each litter one breeds. No one knows everything!

I feel very strongly that the puppies should be allowed to play freely with their mother until they leave the nest as she teaches them good manners, puppies deprived of mothering are not well adjusted when they go to their new homes, mother dog can be really rough teaching them to behave, but this is her way of toughening them up. When playing bulldog puppies bite each other and make blood curdling screams, it is not the same as other breeds that usually let go the instant a litter mate cries out.....not bulldogs they hang on harder! They also bite our ankles and really hurt. It's a wise precaution to not let tiny children near the pups when they are being playful as the teeth are like needles and their bite is very hard, they are unaware of their own strength.

Puppies should have their first injection and vet check at 8 weeks keep them for a few days afterwards as reactions sometimes occur , make sure they have this protection before they leave you.

Insure them with Kennel Club as they leave you [this comes free with registration documents] covers those vital 5 weeks, when purchased you activate this before they leave you.

Do not be in a hurry to register the puppies at first, as red and fawn look very similar and mistakes can be made, register them at about 4 weeks and the documentation will be through in time to sell at 9 weeks

Do not let anyone with dogs touch the puppies till they are at least up on their legs and preferably not until they are vaccinated which can now be done at 6 weeks by some vets but this is not every vets view

Microchip all the puppies before they leave you as puppies get stolen often this is compulsory from 2016 and it is safe to do it after 6 weeks of age

Find an experienced breeder or stud dog owner who you can **RING ANYTIME FOR ADVICE**

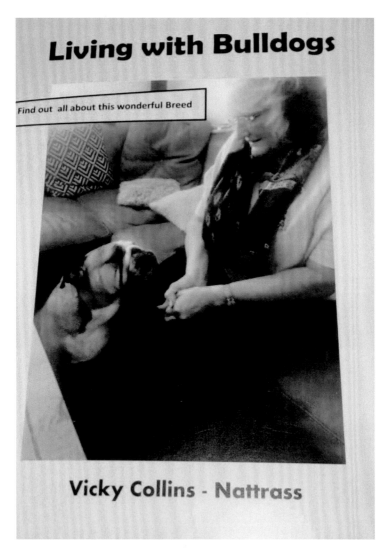

Living with Bulldogs

Find out all about this wonderful Breed

Vicky Collins - Nattrass

This is my latest book designed to help new owners to the breed a good addition to puppy packs

Chapter 5

Problems Abnormalities or Not?

Bulldog puppies have a few conditions that are unusual and peculiar to the breed

Cleft Palates

Cleft palate/hare lip puppies are common in all Brachycephalic faced dogs, so the vet usually checks for this as soon as they are born.   Unfortunately it is best to have any of these put to sleep immediately as they cannot feed normally, they become distressed and the mother will get very upset and maybe hurt the others in her confusion .The only way they could survive is if they were tube fed until they were strong enough for an operation but usually they die and fade crying a pathetic cry [like a seagull] so do leave them at the vets.

The following is very important:

Eyes

 please note before their eyes open sometimes they swell and need careful bathing, use Fucithalmic cream there is an infection in the sealed eye, it will squeeze out through the side and should cause no long term damage ,vets is needed though to get the medicine .

Feet on Backwards?

IF any puppies look to have their feet twisted round DO NOT WORRY DO NOT ALLOW THEM TO BE PUT TO SLEEP this will become normal over a few days it is common and although looks scary I never have heard of any not going normal after a matter of days or weeks...

Fig 12/ 13

fig 14

Hernias and Open Stomachs

Hernias, some lines have hernias commonly, they can be small and are ok to be left but sometimes they need repairs, [dogs cannot be shown if they have a repaired hernia] sometimes the vet will close the belly with a stitch but many do not survive with this condition due to infection .

Water Puppies/Walrus Puppies

Fig 15

Water puppies, this is another strange abnormality that sometimes affects bulldogs, if the puppy is just bloated with water the vet can administer Lasik's /frusemide   and the puppy will urinate out the excess fluid, and can be saved.

 There is some doubt as to whether the mother's retention of fluid is a diet related cause, too much salt [unproven]but it can be a faulty lymphatic system and heart related in the puppy so they should be kept an eye on, advice must be discussed with your vet. I have seen a puppy which is referred to as a Walrus puppy these cannot be saved they are gross and are not properly formed ,leave these at the vets, remember that nature doesn't let its imperfections live in most cases and try not to get too upset if the worst happens .fig15

Cherry Eye. fig 16

 A common Problem in the breed is Cherry eye, which could develop anytime from 5 weeks onward it must be removed or tucked. We favour removal as there are vets who will do this under local anaesthetic. **We do not agree with any anaesthesia in any puppy unless its life threatening before they are 1 year old.** There is a list of vets who are known to understand our breed if you ask from the breed club the secretaries should know ones used by their members also on the www.bulldogbreedcouncil.co.uk and www.bulldogrescue.org.uk .

Entropian and Ectropian

These are conditions of the eyelids turning in and turning out, they do not always show in small puppies but as the dog grows, they irritate the eye and can cause ulcers. Extra eyelashes and in growing hairs also can occur in this breed, there is laser treatment available which can remove these hair follicles ,permanently if the dog is troubled with these. The Animal Health Trust has a machine.

Cheyletiellosis[walking dandruff]

Sometimes puppies get a mite infection. This is transferred to us and it's an incredible itchy rash they find their way onto us and we get red trace rash. Sometimes, mistakenly diagnosed as Scabies in humans. Treat the puppies with a safe veterinary recommended shampoo or Frontline spray on veterinary advice only.

Fleas

Ask your vet for a recommended spray if you are unlucky enough to get fleas on your puppies, if they are scratching its usually fleas.

Vitamin Supplementation

With today's excellent balanced dry complete diets, the need for extra vitamins is ruled out. In fact, it's positively dangerous to supplement with calcium this breed's bones as they are growing. There is much evidence on the internet about this, I have personally looked after a puppy whose legs were bowing due to the diet it had, being too overweight causing him to walk on the outside edge of his feet. It's a common statement by many breeders that you can't get a puppy too fat, I beg to differ I have seen a gross puppy with health issues due to a too rich supplemented diet, try to look at your puppies and just get them **chunky not too fat.**

Spines

As the puppy grows you may observe in the short-backed ones particularly, a dip occurs in the spine, this may indicate Spina bifida. Abnormal spine formations called Hemi vertebrae may also be present at birth. An indication of this that breeder can watch for is if the puppy urinates and poops without stooping and appears to have little control. A roach back at 5 weeks is not good and standing on their heels at the back also indicates this may have a problem a Veterinary Check-up is urgently required if you suspect this.

It's not a good idea to sell a puppy with this condition, I recommend you look for a pet home aware of this problem as the lifespan can be severely reduced by this condition; litigation is becoming   common with problem puppies due to the prices being paid.

Fig 17

Tails correct or not?

The correct tail of a bulldog and the most desirable one to strive for as a breeder is a short straight one, low set and carried straight down, this however was in a minority. A survey showed 75% of bulldogs in the UK had screw or curled tails in 2008, this % is much improved now in 2019.

This is an area that breeders have been working hard on to produce a 'mobile tail ' preferably straight but as long as it is able to be lifted it should not cause an issue .These are fine if not too tight but some puppies have tails so tight they are inverted and cause a lot of pain to the dog. If the owner creams and cleans them daily they can be ok but at around 5 months they commonly go tighter and get infected in the teething stage. Some vets are in a hurry to remove the tail; in some cases, it may be for the best, I would hesitate to have an operation on a bulldog for anything except life threatening conditions before 1 year old due to possible bad anaesthetic reactions. If you do need an op on a puppy please stress that it's important to watch the puppy in case it chokes on its vomit in the recovery period. **Many dogs come around but are lost in the aftercare.**

Heart murmurs

Many bulldog puppies appear to suffer from minor heart murmurs that will disappear by the time they are leaving the nest, however it's always best to check more thoroughly before one lets a puppy go if one is heard by your vet. Having the first inoculation at 8 weeks gives you the opportunity to find this out. It is very unwise to sell a puppy without this first jab as the health check is for   everyone's future benefit and if you are using the puppy contract from the Breed Council it must be done.

I learned from my own experience that human babies often have small murmurs after c sections especially if premature, this is because **when born naturally they do a big breath which closes the valves in the heart however by c section it often closes slowly over a short time** this I believe is the case with bulldog puppies too . **Grade 3** in heart noise must be taken seriously and it can seriously affect their life span dying at 3 years or even earlier, don't put others in the position without them being fully aware of such a problem when time to sell arrives

Cause for concern?

With the best will in the world and taking every precaution to breed a healthy litter one may run into difficulties, in recent years I have been asked the following questions by new breeders.

Birth Defects

Puppies with cleft palates should not be attempted to be reared, so be advised by the vet and do not take them home. Harelip puppies if not severe can survive, but only if it doesn't affect the ability to get suction on the mothers teat, I saw a bad one where it was a double harelip a flap was not joined at all and it had a cleft so I advised euthanasia and was annoyed that the vet had sent it home with a first time breeder as he had no chance. It is much kinder all round as it's distressing for you and the poor puppy, to leave it at the vets, also I've known healthy puppies go downhill because the breeder struggles with a hopeless case   .

fig 18   Cleft Palate

Water puppies

 A puppy with only slight water retention can survive if the vet gives a tiny but regular over about 24 hours furosemide injection and it will pass the water urinating, however severe water and hideous bloating should also be left at the vets.

This condition can be linked to lymphatic problems, heart conditions any puppies reared that took on water must be especially checked out for heart problems before you sell.

Care must be taken when the water is conning out of the puppy, I've seen bad scalds where it has heated between the puppy and the heat pad

fig 19

Mavis 's lost puppies you can see the water on the ones in the fronts faces

Puppies born with a hernia or their stomach wall open could be saved by the vet stitching straightaway however I have rarely reared a puppy that has had any operation, as it's a shock to their system.

When you stimulate the puppy to urinate and eliminate check that its anus is open particularly on bitches, it's quite easy to be mistaken and the puppy passes faeces from the vagina, so check for this carefully, this is also a need for euthanasia if it happens as there is nothing the vet can do in such a small puppy.

Bottle feeding [not really recommended tubing /sponge feeding in preference]   fig 20

I only do this if I have to, I do not rush to top up a bulldog puppy, in the early hours I just keep putting them on the mum, more suckling, more milk produced just the same as in humans, the watch word being, feed and water the bitch well and she will provide all that's needed for her babies. In the situation where the bitch has no milk or the puppy seems to be struggling to get milk from her [its hard work to draw milk from mum]. I would probably use a 1ml syringe if the puppy was small and be extremely careful; if the puppy is a few days old I would tube feed.

Only if I had to would use a bottle, with a soft teat [Royal Canin do a pack of 1st Stage milk with bottles, in this the large teat was perfect to feed my last problem puppy on.] I face the puppy away from me into the room and hold the bottle and the puppies head in one hand, create a seal around the puppies lips and the bottle by curving your finger around it [a friend taught me this way recently and I had the best success with this method after using different positions and various bottles for years.]

If you don't have a Royal Canine Representative nearby most vets and pet shops can order these milk packs, they are brilliant, you mix up the feed as you need it and it's not lumpy and is creamy looking. Amazon supplies it and mousse.

It's essential if you hand feed to wind the puppy just like a baby, if you don't you will find you have a restless puppy who cries in pain, frightening both of you Infacol is able to be given at each feed for windy puppies with no harm about 1/3rd of the dropper before or after the feed .

Constipation

Hand feeding brings further problems and you may find your hand fed puppy has poop like little pellets, I use Lactulose syrup, just 0.2ml every feed till the motions become soft again, and then only if the puppy starts to get hard again, dosing every couple of days, I have never needed to do this very often and advise going to vets if the puppy is struggling continuously with constipation.

Consequences of Hand rearing

Puppies never look the same as their litter mates reared on the bitch, they tend to be potbellied,[reminiscent of starving African children] this is due to the high volume of waste that they take in from artificial feed compared to the bitches rich milk ,they need more volume of artificial milk to get the values of protein and fat their mother would have provided. Do not worry too much about this as soon as they start to be weaned, they catch up and become the same as a natural reared puppies.

Weaning early

If you are hand feeding due to the high risk of milk inhalation [setting up pneumonia] it's advisable to start to wean at 12 days onwards, you can use Royal Canin mousse in tins its great like a pate I add water, if I use starter I soak and then add a little milk and feed like a soup at first from a syringe rapidly going onto a saucer once the puppy gets a taste for the new food.

I have found that they love the RC Starter which soaks down really quickly and I have recently not needed to feed scraped beef as they have eaten the starter and I have progressed them onto Medium Junior which they have eaten with great relish .Eukanuba, Hills or Pro plan are all good quality foods all can be used in this way but take much longer to soak down, you need it to be completely soft and fully absorbed in fluid as feeding any dry to tiny puppies could cause bad problems as the food would expand inside the gut causing painful distension. Highly recommended is Nuriment paste for weaning to as another alternative.

After the feed of solid food you may notice the puppy shaking, this is due to the food being cool and the digestive system working hard the core temperature is lowered so after each feed put the puppy in the warm area of its box, it is nothing to worry over but looks alarming, it can continue up to 6 weeks old, some puppies never do it, some do.

Danger signals

Rapid breathing, chesty sounds, purple bluish tinge to the mouth all are signs that pneumonia may have set in, rapid veterinary treatment is needed, do not delay as its fatal if the puppy becomes too weak, treatment is usually antibiotic injection, drops to take home and you have to pray hard .

Do not confuse the change in skin colour of the mouth area as when the pigment starts to come through it does make the muzzle look purplish. Look at the pads on the feet if these are rounded and nicely pink it's a good sign.

Fading Puppies

For this condition **read 'don't know what's wrong with them'** if you and the vet can't find anything wrong then you will be told you have a fading puppy, apparently normal healthy, probably the biggest, strongest suddenly stops feeding and becomes weak and probably dies before you have time to realise it is even ill. I recommend you weigh **your normal puppies** once aday; they should put on ½ oz to 1 and ½ oz a day. No weight gain or a loss at over a week old would make me suspect something was wrong, they sometimes start to go downhill at around 2 to 3 weeks just when you thought you could relax, check they are getting a full tummy from nursing on the bitch, if not top them up after nursing on her, if they are refusing food use the rehydration mixture and take them to the vets ASAP. *[special needs for prem puppies discussed later in Premature puppies]*

I have asked for a vitamin K injection, routinely given to human babies, a vet once gave one of my puppies this and it recovered and was reared. Most vets doubt the good, but it won't harm, its cheap, in the USA they use it on their puppies as a matter of course. Usually the vet would give a broad-spectrum antibiotic and you must take the puppy home keep it very warm and hope...use the rehydration fluid for the first few hours then if the puppy has perked up get it back on the bitch ASAP. Very weak puppies of good colour could probably be helped by tube feeding at this point but unless you can be shown how, it's not an easy thing to do. As soon as the puppy responds get it back on the bitch as the gag reflex in a healthy puppy makes feeding by the tube difficult and risky.

This is also a time when a prayer wouldn't go amiss......

Heavy Puppies

Bulldog Puppies who have a hearty appetite can become very heavy and this can cause them to be flat and be swimmers. If you can make the bedding mountainous and lumpy so they don't lie on their sternum all the time it can really help to avoid this condition. Putting them down propped up, giving them a good gripping surface can all help them get up on first their front legs then their back ones, which if they are heavy it can be unnervingly late nearer 6 weeks than 3 which normal to try to stand up, a trick I have learnt is slow puppies can be helped by placing them on a blanket in a wash basket , for a few minutes several times a day , the puppy wants to get out so pushes up on its legs and strengthens them .A few days of this can have a puppy up and walking in no time !

Puppies with flat or inverted chests sometimes do not grow out of it this means heart and lung room is compromised take veterinary advice if this condition does not improve as these puppies are prone to early death as little can be done about a skeletal defect.

Puppy Strangles

Juvenile Pyoderma also known as Puppy Strangles

Another alarming and not very common occurrence in your puppies which needs swift diagnosis if to be effective is puppy strangles. It materialises at between 4 weeks and 4 months of age, it first swells around the lips, eyelids, chin and muzzle, developing into pustular spots.

First giving the breeder the thought, it is an allergy, but the lymph nodes around the neck may then swell which is probably where the name puppy strangles arises from. Most puppies become lethargic, some have a fever, loss of appetite and appear to develop joint pain.

The cause of this condition is thought to be immune system related, because of this aggressive urgent treatment with corticosteroids is indicated combined with powerful antibiotics to avoid scaring. The death of the puppy could occur if the treatment is not started early enough so any pustular spots on a young puppy need to be considered as puppy strangles, some vets do not think of this disease so mention the possibility to them, mild beginning symptoms might be put down as milk spots, it can affect just one puppy or the whole litter. Look out for it in litters that have had bad start for various reasons.

Fig22

These photos illustrate this stressful condition which is

PuppyStrangles.

Suggested treatment tested with success

Puppy should be put onto a course of Prednisolone 5mg half tablet daily and Cephalexin 250mg half tablet twice daily. If the problem does not rapidly respond to treatment or is a severe case, then Antirobe 75mg one tablet twice daily and Cephalexin 250mg half tablet twice daily. If the problem is severe around the eyes Fulcithalmic cream can help soothe the eyes. Good hygiene methods are essential and it soon clears up and does not usually re-occur however as the condition has not really got a known hereditary factor it's considered unwise to breed with a puppy who has been affected as it is immune related

PS. Wilfred, my puppy I had this problem with is now 8 years old and as fit as a flea, has never had any issues with skin breathing etc. so, I think if cured this doesn't re occur or affect them long term. He is not sterile either but has not been used at stud.

Canine Herpes Virus CHV

Having never experienced this myself, I had no opinions on it until recently when I came across a litter which had this, I was at the birth and quickly realised this was not normal.

The puppies despite looking perfect no clefts, no water and no hernias they were very 'flat' out of 8 we couldn't get 4 of them going they just didn't respond and I knew they had no will to try I began to think none of them would leave the vets, they had been taken out of the bitch by C section because she was really struggling a small short backed girl who had lost condition they were only 3 days early.

On returning home I looked up what could be the problem and the symptoms seemed to be likely to be this virus researched it, this is what I've learnt

Canine Herpes Virus can be known as fading puppy syndrome it is a viral infection which infects the reproduction organs of male and female dogs. The infected dogs themselves show no outward symptoms however this is considered one of the most virulent in canines and the death of many new-born puppies, causing one or whole litters to die rapidly. Chances of survival if contracted after 3 weeks are higher but new-borns have little hope.

Symptoms in Adults are not seen but are thought to be the cause of abortion, still born, sometimes genital sores and it has been be linked to Kennel Cough *although the research isn't conclusive in that.*

Symptoms in Puppies are:

Sudden Death of New-borns

Weakness and failure to breathe when born

Weakness and Lethargy

Persistent crying

No suck reflex or appetite

Bloating and bruised abdomen

Soft white, pale yellow or green faeces

Chilled, unable to get warm

Haemorrhages from the nose

Please note: **HUMANS CANNOT CATCH THIS VIRUS**

If your puppies are still born or die suddenly you need the vet to draw blood and identify if this could be the reason, you need to know because if it is all the dogs in your kennel could be carrying this so you needed to know if a full vaccination programme throughout your breeding dogs will be needed before you can breed again, please take Veterinary advice on this.

Early warning signs

Any puppy that seems to be fading should begin antiviral medication be placed in very hot temperature approx. 90 to 95 degrees f. Because it is **known that the virus** cannot survive high temperatures. Vitamin K injection may help and can't do any harm.

I strongly recommend that you consider and discuss with your vet if you should vaccinate approx. 7 days after mating and again 14 days before delivery, this is an option that you have, I think it must be worth doing however the availability of the vaccine is not always good.

The litter I saw of 8 had only 2 survivors, they had a serum spun of their mother's blood and very expensive care.

They remained looking new-born into the second week they had 'staring coats '[**a very strong sign puppies are ill is if their coat doesn't lie smoothly but sort of looks like its standing on end, this is a good visual sign that all is not well with any puppy .**] They were really knocked back but gradually they have begun to thrive.

Staring coats?

What is this, very observant breeder's will, know the instant their puppies are not doing so good because their coats become standing up and not normal, they look almost like they are greasy and it is a very indicative sign all is not well.

They often hunch up their shoulders and back, watching puppies' body language can alert you early if you see them acting abnormally.

Chapter 6

Rearing on

Pro's and Cons of Keeping the Bitch and Puppies separately

Make no mistake puppies get squashed by bulldog bitches, not intentionally, they just are clumsy, they also like to cover them with their bedding and then as they can't see them, they forget where they are and sit on them! They are actually very good mothers, but the risk of crushing is a major one.

Practicalities must come into this, if you have a big family who will watch over them whilst you get some rest then they could stay with the bitch but if you are alone or intend to go to work for short periods you really cannot contemplate leaving the puppies with the mother.

For the first 3 weeks its safer to put them on the bitch, watch over them then take them off her and put them safely in their draught free " incubator "[a cardboard box or a plastic stacker box which could be quite a big one] bitches who have previously had a litter left with them all the time will not accept the puppies going away and she may try to bite you in her efforts to keep them with her .I found that first time mums accept this method with no trouble, so start as you mean to go on.

If you leave the puppies with the mother you will have to take the bitch out with you anytime you need to go away to do something make a drink etc., Some breeders sleep with their head in the whelping box, spread newspaper around so that the bitch wakes them up if they fall asleep on 'duty'.

If you keep the puppies separately you will find they soon get into a routine. I have a clock radio that I set every 2 hours and my bitches learn when the alarm goes off the puppies are coming out, it's quite sweet how they are keen to see them, and wait by the box for them. I put two hot water bottles in my incubator; I change one at each feed therefore giving a choice of temperature for the puppies to wriggle onto...

A definite disadvantage of removing the puppies is that when puppies are left with their mother they feed on and off all the time. I have found by enforcing the time break in-between feeds the puppies become very ravenous and I have had trouble with them drinking and gorging so fast they get chronic gas and pain, I keep Infacol baby drops for treatment as its very distressing for you and the puppy if it starts screaming with pain. In an emergency you can give a spoonful of fizzy lemonade that will work nearly as well, if you gently rub the puppy's tummy you can ease the tautness...however should the puppy's stomach start to bloat seek urgent Veterinary treatment immediately. After about 3 weeks the bitch can be allowed to spend more time in with the puppies, it's vital they get socialised and the interaction between the canines in the house is important, don't be alarmed they do play really rough...but it's part of the learning pattern as to how quickly they learn their place. This makes for harmony in the house and is important.

Artificial Feeding and Desperate Measures

Just as in humans' mothers milk is best but sometimes nature lets us down, the bitch occasionally has no milk or worse still she may die, either on the operating table or a few days later, not an uncommon occurrence unfortunately so you are left with needing to hand rear the litter. If the puppies are lucky, they will have had the vital colostrum which will set them up to protect from various diseases till they are old enough to have a vaccine for themselves. In all the years of rearing I thought it was the mother's milk that changed so colostrum wasn't absorbed but it's not it's the puppy's own gut that can only absorb the immunity for the first few hours.

Only in an emergency would I attempt to tube feed, I have done it with good results, but such care has to be taken it is not a novice experience, and you really need someone to show you how to do it.

Puppies without a sucking reflex can be saved if one tubes them until they are strong enough to suckle a sponge. but you need to be aware that when the gag reflex comes in its not safe to be tubing a strong puppy, weak ones yes but not one that's thriving.

Hand reared puppy lived to be 11 years old

Chapter 7

Tube feeding Puppies

Tube feeding puppies at all can be extremely dangerous, so I strongly advise only doing it as a last resort. If you can get an experienced person to show you how to do its much safer, however as sometimes this technique is needed in an emergency, I am going to attempt to describe the method I use. This differs from written advice I have seen in other books as I learnt my technique from the Neonatal unit of my local hospital on the premature birth of my twin granddaughters.

Firstly it is IMPERATIVE that we do not get milk into the puppies lungs as this will almost certainly result in aspiration setting up infection in the lungs leading to death, care should be taken at all costs to avoid this.

Tiny puppies have tiny tummies. feed very small amounts as distension of the stomach can cause pain and also death. Remember a bottle feed can be refused when the pup is full …err on the 'too little side'

Begin by measuring the tube along the outside of the puppy, place the tube beside the last rib and hold there and extend the tube along the body to the nostrils, mark the tube so it is just about ¾ of the length of this measurement. Putting a small piece of medical tape around this mark means you have not to re measure every time you use it [however puppies grow fast so regularly check and adjust the mark as the puppy grows]

Next gently insert the tube into the puppies mouth, young pups have no gag reflex so this is easy to do holding the pup in an upright position, stop at your mark, puppies will sometimes cough if you have not got it in the right location, [until you are practiced at this to ensure it is not in the lungs a .02ml syringe of sterile water can be injected down the tube before milk is used, if the puppy coughs remove the tube and start again]when puppies mouth opens they often curl their tongue giving you a good guide to insert into the middle space .

Now put the already prepared warmed milk into the 5 ml syringe now attached to the tube without the plunger [DO NOT USE THE PLUNGER] all other books say to press it, however if you just elevate the syringe this will allow a slow and safe gravity method to feed the puppy, no pressure is needed at all as it empties at a safe speed and cannot hurt the puppies stomach as using the plunge can, if it slows tap or blow in the top.

This is a very rapid feeding method compared to bottle feeding pups which are healthy and have a strong sucking reflex, which is more time consuming but if the puppy is weak it can save lives…..however **Never feed a chilled puppy ,this causes death as hypothermia stops the digestive system functioning.** Should your pup be chilled and weak use a rehydration fluid in tiny amounts until the puppy seems stronger and is able to digest again, this can be fed to tiny puppies from a finger or a dropper at 30/60-minute intervals?

Feeding amounts the capacity of a puppies stomach is very small which is why naturally pups feed little and often, as a guide an 8 oz puppy can hold a maximum if 8mls this is slightly less than a tablespoon, a 24 oz puppy could hold 24 mls, rule of thumb 1ml per oz of body weight .Give 2 hourly or if the puppy seems hungry adjust the times never the amount. If the puppy develops diarrhoea it is being overfed, little mustard like seeds in the poop are also over feeding but I tend to ignore those as its quite common when hand feeding. If the puppy cries it may have wind, Infacol can be given from a dropper and a warm tummy massage can help.

Rehydration Fluid [*recipe later*] is worth using the extra fluid causes no problems but weak puppies can be turned around with this

Try to bottle feed if the pup is strong enough to suckle, especially if the need to hand feed has not been from newborn as the pup approaches the 2/3 week mark the gag reflex starts to apply and they fight the tube insertion and efforts to wean the pup should commence early, just before or around 12 days.

Keep the tube spotlessly clean and sterilise it by rinsing very well in hot water not boiling as it will harden the tube. Flush it out very well after each feed as residue milk can stay in it.

Never use MILTON I'm sure I killed my early puppies with the steriliser as it kills the natural essential flora in the gut.

And finally, Good Luck   if you succeed it is a very rewarding feeling, looking at your hand reared baby but remember MUM is best

Fig25

 Please take note I do not use the plunger to force milk into the puppy I let gravity take it down. If it stops I blow in the top to restart it .

insert the tube into the little v that forms on the middle of
the tongue when mouth is opened

Fig27
Elevate the syringe, pour in the measured amount of milk

Fig 28

Do not use the plunger allow gravity to let the milk go down
do not force feed

Fig 2   Pinch
the tube to hold in any milk so none escapes and withdraw it
slowly

Bulldog Puppies Growing on

Weaning   for normal thriving on mum can commence on day 16 you can give them Royal Canin mousse mixed into a soup with Starter milk or if needs must from 12 days

Older methods used and favoured by a lot of old breeders are: The method of using scraped beef, [Best beef joint raw, sharp knife slide it over the meat and it brings the meat off like a pulp a bit like pate, it doesn't have fat in it] it can't choke them, you roll it into fingernail size balls and feed it individually to them 1x a day for 5 days

 I have not needed to feed by this method for several years I favour using Royal Canin Mousse or Starter as previously described

Give a Lactol or Whelpi drink from a saucer

Buy Eukanuba /Royal Canin or good quality puppy food, soak it in water until soft then mix with Royal Canin First stage milk or Whelpi to make a sort of soup give this to the puppies once a day too. Do not introduce more than one new food on the same day as this could be too much for them; after they have accepted one add the other. I don't recommend but if you want to feed raw mince from 3 weeks you can but, only buy the best human quality from reliable clean sources. I have found that supermarkets pre-packed seems more consistent as small butchers may not sell enough to be as fresh.Freeze the mince completely before using it this kills bacteria. I consider feeding raw meet at this stage a definite risk for getting e-coli or some such bug so I don't feed it anymore, my puppies are chunky heavy well reared, modern puppy foods in my opinion far superior to how they used to be creating a need for bulldog breeders to feed the mixes described above so I don't use them

Continue with allowing them to feed off the mum till at least 5 weeks but feed them the solids first. You can let the pups with the mum after the first 3 and a half weeks if you see how she is with them but I still would let them sleep separately at night.

Gradually decrease the milk from the Royal Canin Starter and by the time they are 6 weeks they should be on 5 meals a day well spread throughout the day, eating it dryer with only water in it.

They should put on roughly 1lb a week and at this stage they should look chunky. At around 6/7 weeks they all look perfect bulldogs, all little champions and are adorable, after this time they start to grow lanky towards 12 weeks by the time they are 16weeks they can look 'pin headed and tall' but usually they pass through this stage and become chunky as they pass the 6/7 month time.

Do not feed extra milk once they get into their Royal Canin , water is all they will require, and milk in puppies over about 7 to 8 weeks can make their stools too loose

Worming

We strongly recommend you use Drontal worming suspension you can give it from 2 weeks old every 2 weeks,the vet will supply this we do not like Panacur as some puppies we know have reacted badly to it .Do not neglect the worming ,it usually sets them back a day or so but afterwards they make great growth spurts...worms can take all the goodness from the pups food and most puppies are born with them as they cross the placenta from the mother .

Do not think if you can't see any worms that they don't have them, modern wormers dissolve the worms to make them environmentally friendly. So there will be no signs of them in their faeces.

Check the mum's teats when weaning begins to make sure she has no congestion or inflammation as the pups take less from her.

Nail clipping

Nails grow surprisingly fast on new born puppies by 2 weeks you need to cut the sharp little points off them as they scratch the bitch when they are paddling her to obtain the milk. Thereafter every few days they need trimming to keep the bitch comfortable.

Fig 30

Chapter 8

Medicines for Emergencies

There are a few items you may like to have on hand to use if it's an emergency.

INFACOL this is for wind sometimes you get a really windy puppy who screams with wind, a dropper of this can bring immediate relief. Buy from supermarkets

NUTRI_DROPS these are for giving an energy boost to ailing pups and also the bitch can turn around what's happening and brighten them up enough to feed. From Vets or mail order

CALCIUM TABLETS for the bitch a supplement that best started just after birth. Chemist

Another useful product to keep in the fridge is a **Jiff Lemon** to break up the phlegm in the throat of a stressed-up bitch after her milk is coming in and she excessively pants.

LECT-ADE or life aid vets Electrolyte mixture like Dyrolite for humans. Very ill puppies require injections of fluids subcutaneously by the Veterinary Surgeon.

Or try making the

Rehydration Fluid

My emergency homemade Rehydration fluid has saved many puppies for me and for friends. It was recommended by Betty Bloomfield, a famous Problem Puppy Rearer and it works like magic. It is made from household ingredients so you should always make sure you have these in stock

1 pint of cooled boiled water

2 ½ teaspoons of glucose powder

¼ teaspoon of salt

pinch of bicarbonate of soda

Mix this thoroughly and you can keep it refrigerated for 24 hours when it must be changed.

It needs to be fed warm and in tiny puppies dripping it off my finger every 20 minutes then letting them rest and starting over again. They can feed on just this for up to 48 hours, but the point is to get them back on mum as soon as possible. If they can't take milk you can make a 50 /50 strength with this mix to gradually get the puppy eating again .Larger puppies with a tummy upset can be helped by this and also I buy Bio Natural Yogurt which I always keep in the fridge as the bitch can eat it too. It sometimes will tempt a difficult eater and it will settle a stomach upset quite quickly too.

Chapter 9

Contracts and Legal things!!

Whenever you do any dealings with dogs even with best friends and family, have all the details written down, you may not be surprised to know that the end of many lifelong friendships has happened due to mating or breeding agreements, word of mouth and trusted ones is a recipe for problems. The main types of contracts are :

Stud

What are the terms? A fee payable upfront, a fee payable on the birth of puppies live ones] a puppy back, which pick of the litter 1st 2nd or 3rd pick ,who gets a pup if there is just one, what if there is just 1 dog and 1 bitch and the breeder wants to keep a bitch ? But the stud owner wants it….

All these things must be written down and signed by both parties then all eventualities are covered.

Puppy sales

Selling a puppy today is a minefield the high cost seems to make people think their puppy will never have anything wrong with it due to cost !The Bulldog Breed Council has an excellent puppy contract for sale which costs only £2.80 but if filled in correctly protects the buyer and the seller, I highly recommend it.

Obtainable from www.bulldogbreedcouncil.co.uk .

You can make your own if you do include a clause that the puppy must come back to you if it needs rehoming as this is a way that you can be responsible for what you are bringing into the world by your breeding activities, and you will be respected by your buyers and other breeders if you are seen to care for the future of your 'offspring '

Kennel Club Paperwork

You can obtain registration forms from the Kennel club for each litter or if you pay 'upfront' the stud owner will give you a signed one at the time of mating ,most stud owners hold back the paperwork until you have paid for the stud so you need this document signed by both parties to register the litter , most litters are now registered online .The time it takes to come through now is much quicker than in the past so if you wait until the puppies are 4 weeks old ,they have a good grip on life , they are showing the colour they are likely to end up as and you can think up names suitable to their characters .

If you are a regular breeder or would just like to put your mark on the puppies, you can register an affix at the Kennel Club. Most proper names are gone so many people make up names from combinations of letters that mean something. It takes about 7 weeks to get an 'affix' and I think costs £70 initially with a £20 a year maintenance fee .Then every puppy you breed bares this name, ie.Kezias Just Joshua is my stud dog's name .If you buy a dog in, you can register it with your affix at the end of it, i.e. Bonifacio's Sorciere at Kezia my Kennel name

The Kennel Club has brought in the Assured Breeder scheme, the breeder has special registration documents and has puppy sales wallets with terms that the breeder must abide by, and a questionnaire the buyer fills in as to the level of care and service they received, the breeder agrees to abide by certain criteria as to the way he breeds his dogs which in actual fact most reputable people would do anyway. The puppies from these breeders are going to be listed specially as such so that could be a good selling point if bulldogs ever reach a point that they are taking a while to sell.

As this scheme has been adopted by UCAS most breeders now will be inspected and have their records checked every three years whilst actively breeding

Endorsements

If selling a puppy using the Kennel Club endorsements, you must have a separate contract that the buyer signs recognising they understand what the endorsement means.

Insurance

Pet plan do Instant Puppy Insurance one registers with them and then phones at the point of sale and the puppy leaves with 4 weeks free insurance to cover those early days...vital I wouldn't let one go without it....however be aware that Bulldogs exceed the maximum purchase replacement on death price which is sometimes limited to £750 so please point this out to the buyer , when they transfer the puppy into their name at the Kennel Club they get free insurance there for 5 weeks too so they have time to search around for a policy to suit them, always tell every puppy buyer to keep their single bulldog insured, I have not been able to find a breeder insurance that is affordable so my own are not now insured.

Micro chipping

I believe it to be a safe and essential part of owning a bulldog; all my puppies leave here micro chipped. It is now made compulsory 2016 to be done by the breeder.

A small illustration of how a bulldog puppy turns out when mature, would you recognise him?

Chapter 9

Advice for breeders and owners with some important behaviour matters discussed

Beginning to train your puppies in the nest

Early on puppies soon learn to wriggle along to a news papered area and will use it, the bitch usually stops cleaning up faeces [if she ever did] when the pups are being weaned, make sure you clean up the run regularly as this is a cause of dogs learning to eat their own faces[called coprophagic and revolts people]I sometimes think they learn it from the way nature has made the bitch clean up after them ,but it is a good idea to try to stop this bad habit developing .

If you have Summer puppies after about 4 to 5 weeks they can go out in a playpen on the grass or yard which gives them an idea what to do outside! I feel the more we can do as breeders to train our puppies before they leave us the better balanced and happy pets they will make.

You can print off advice to give to your new puppy owners from this chapter:

House training the single puppy advice

Keep a close eye on your puppy when house training the more attention it gets whilst learning the quicker it will respond, please remember that you have a baby just like a human and while small they cannot physically control their bladder or bowels, they are not being Naughty or Dirty

Ways to avoid   accidents in the wrong place

Do not let your puppy wander around without supervision.

Keep it in view or attached to a lead

Always take puppy outside on waking or after eating, playing, and after being confined in the crate When you observe it sniffing and circling take it out side immediately

Five to 30 minutes after any of these events   follow the steps

take the puppy to the chosen toilet area

say words to encourage the behaviour 'be quick' or' go potty'

when puppy starts to eliminate praise it quietly

after the puppy finishes, praise enthusiastically, pet it and reward it with a small titbit

Reward each time with praise but as your Puppy learns give food treats intermittently.

Paper training

Spread newspaper liberally on the kitchen floor, and whenever you see the pup about to squat, pick it up and place on the paper, does this even if it's too late!

Gently reminding that this is the place to eliminate.

NEVER hit the pup if it has had an accident

Soon the pup will look for the newspaper . Praise it and reward it with a titbit.

Gradually reduce the amount of newspaper until there is just one sheet ...by the back door

When the pup has learned to head for the door, encourage it to go outside and praise it enthusiastically. Once the pup is old enough [around 20 weeks +] it can control its bladder for several hours but before this mistake will occur. Ignore accidents but praise good behaviour and the pup ever eager to please will quickly learn

An observant patient owner can be quickly successful in housetraining but ignoring the dog can lead to long term problems.

Use of a crate is highly recommended however the owner must be there to observe waking and to allow the pup free range to the elimination area.

Author Vicky Collins-Nattrass @2007

A further advice Sheet for your new owners:

Ok !   You bought your puppy but now you're learning really starts ……

Tips for looking after your new Bullie baby….and keeping him safe

Remember that your puppy   will turn out just how you treat him in these early days, my main thought you should apply is ask yourself when he's big will I want him to do this ?if the answers no you have to work at instilling kindly the behaviour you want

The first few nights he will probably miss his litter mates or his mum a cuddly teddy bear [with its eyes removed] and the radio playing softly will help him not be so lonesome, in a safe area in your kitchen or under stair area make him his bed, or buy a crate as his indoor kennel ,when he's settled they rarely soil their bed so this will also help house training after the first night if he cries ,after one check up to make sure nothing's wrong ,you have to ignore his cries. If you bring him to bed or run to his cries, he will learn a powerful lesson that you come at noise and demand.

Other than safety issues its best to generally ignore bad behaviour and reward good.

Make a good check around to make sure wires plugs and small things that could be choked on are well out of a little puppies' way even if you are in the same room you will be surprised at the speed and the damage a pup can do in minutes

Your breeder should have given you a care sheet specifically on the diet and a routine that your new puppy is used too… even if you don't like the food the pup has been reared on follow it to the letter for at least a week whilst the puppy gets used to its new environment, then you can try by adding one thing new in small quantities to the existing diet .Never add more than 1 new food in 48 hours or you will not know what upset his tummy,

Don't give a bulldog puppy the hide chews they go slimy and if left alone I have heard of and had experience of a bulldog choking on one [these are the stuff that those mock shoes are made of]

Put a collar on the pup only when you are with him it's easy for an inquisitive puppy to hang itself, but let him wear it a few hours a day before you try out walking

If your puppy hasn't had his final Parvo shot do take him around in your arms and in your car before he has completed his jabs. Experiencing many sounds sights and noises is imperative to be in place before 16 weeks when a natural shy and spooky attitude develops, this will help him develop into a well-balanced and well-behaved dog.

Remember it's at least 16 weeks before the bladder is under full control [like babies who are not able to be potty trained till their bodies are capable of control] if you train your pup before this, it's you who is trained!! :-)) Scolding and shouting can create fear issues with puppies. It may start them eating their own faeces as an attempt to hide the evidence that gets the anger directed at them or make them sneaky and hiding where they are defecating.

All puppies now are compulsorily micro chipped, pedigree dogs get stolen everyday here in the UK , a chip may alert a suspicious vet to check for the number enabling you to make a positive identification ,it's a wise precaution. Do check for any escape routes out of your garden and if it's overlooked by a public pathway NEVER leave him outside alone whilst tiny.

Care should be taken that if he corners any cats his eyes may get scratched, causing ulcers, if cherry eye develops seek help from your breeder as to which vet to go to correct this, do not let your tiny puppy have a general anaesthetic unless its life threatening not to...6 months is safer and make sure your veterinary surgeon is bulldog knowledgeable.

Worm the puppy according to the instructions from   the breeder it should be 2 weekly till 12 weeks then 3 monthly for 1st year then every 6 months for life, especially if you are letting the dog /puppy play with children, modern wormers dissolve worms are environmentally friendly so if you don't see any don't assume there are none, the puppy will thrive after a worm burden has been removed.

Take the puppy to training classes or to vets puppy parties to socialise him , this early meeting with other dogs may help avoid dog aggression coming into play as he matures .barking at noises can be kept to a minimum by praising the puppy for letting you know about the 'nasty' intruder but you will now deal with it.... Taking away the pressure to protect will relieve the puppy of the burden of being a protector.... become your dogs 'alpha person' pack leader and you will have a happy harmonious home for him.

Do not let your bulldog puppy go up and down stairs, not only is it easy for them to throw out their joints but it's a real danger that as they come down, they gather speed and momentum causing a broken neck or spinal injury I have heard of both of these injuries happening.

Keep in touch with your puppy's breeder, or if this fails join your local bulldog club where you should be able to meet someone to help and be your mentor as you discover the personality of our wonderful breed.

Good luck e mail any questions to me
vicky@keziabulldogs.co.uk hugs to your Bulldog puppy x

The following article written by myself has been published in a club magazine, but I hope you may find them useful in understanding the needs of a well-adjusted puppy, for your potential buyers its important they assess if a Bulldog is the breed for them

Socialising Puppies

The needs of my lifestyle and requirements from a dog are different in some ways to the average pet owner; I usually breed my own show prospect, so I start my socialising from birth.

Early days already covered previously

3 weeks

5 weeks   lots of handling

8 weeks   handling

 Early vaccination can play a big part in getting puppies to be well adjusted, Nobivac can be given from 6/7 weeks which gives a little protection to start the process of introducing puppies to the world.

I introduce the pup to my extended family, parents, grandchildren; my cats play the sounds familiar tape, so they adjust to household noises and situations /thunder etc... and I vacuum up around them daily.

CAR

When I get a new puppy at this age I take it everywhere in the car with me, it has always meant that every dog I have loves the car and has no fear and are never car sick, important for showing as many miles will be covered by a show puppy .Also it gets used to being away from the other dogs, it's too expensive to have to enter 2 dogs as they are afraid alone at a show so this starts young the separation issues …

Some dogs become Vet phobic as it's the only time they go in the car mine just go everywhere.

HANDLING & GROOMING

I put on a soft collar and leave it on for a while in the house, I then attach the lead and usually a walk along with an older dog, pup gets the idea of walking on a lead ,if the puppy is resistant to the lead I found its easier to get them to walk back to the safety of home rather than away ..so a few yards outside the property and coming back in can work wonders. If this fails I go to a completely new area with the favourite older dog and get someone to walk it away from me and the pup.

Its equally important that I can do anything to the puppy, grooming, nail clipping, all are practised at this age, I do all treatments i.e. ear cleaning with little fuss and never expect a problem and usually this works very effectively, I find if I anticipate a problem dogs pick up on this ….I just do everything matter of fact.

CAGE

I always use a cage not as a restriction but as a security measure, after a short while they always retire to the cage

as a place of safety never punishment, none of my older dogs ever have the doors shut but go in of their own accord, the use of a cage really helps with toilet training as they don't like to mess in their beds.

Careful observation of the pup can get a routine going, outside to eliminate as soon as pup is fed or wakes up and as soon as the door can be left open the pup soon gets the message the correct place to eliminate. I also like the pup to be able to have its sleep out, I NEVER wake a pup to play, and I always remove over excited puppies from playing too rough with my grandchildren or my other animals, too much rough housing can hype a dog up into an absolutely uncontrollable dog who everyone hates....I treat them to a calming 'bolt hole' and no one is allowed to intrude on them there.

10 weeks

Ring craft and Dog training

I take the pup to Ring craft as soon as the vaccines are effective contact with other dogs and breeds at this age are very important , and I ask as many people as possible to touch and pet the dog I don't insist they do anything except sit around the room and watch at this stage, I stand the dog everyday a couple of times on table, I used to let them down as soon as they struggled but I now wait till they stand still and calm and then let them down with lots of praise and a titbit , the theory being when they are 'good' they get rewarded doesn't always work some dogs hate showing and never perform for you]

12 weeks +

Traffic and Noise

Now gentle introduction to other dogs and to traffic should begin, I tend to walk my older dogs early and they do tend to fear the traffic but the pups who are taken on roads in traffic at this stage never seem fazed by it, allow limited contact with dogs outside the family, and I let them play freely with my own dogs who are mostly very tolerant of puppy loutish behaviour but check any way 'over the top' behaviour and learn their place in the Hierarchy by an angry growl or nip ...

Separation anxiety

I try to leave the pup alone for short periods if only while I go upstairs....if the pup barks I try to ignore so I go in after the barking stops[bulldogs are not yappy, this doesn't work as well with Shih-tzus] this in theory teaches the pup the barking doesn't bring my immediate attention.

Boredom

I try to leave harmless dog toys with pups to play with while they are alone, I cannot allow toys in the adult dogs area as they cause fights, possessive behaviour is very strong in bulldogs ,I never ever give them things I will not want them to chew in future as they don't know that the new shoes or slippers are new…..if I have a very bad chewing puppy in the teething stage I use a run to restrict where they can go while I am not able to watch them.

Work

I always used take my pups to work with me, I used a play pen system whilst they are not toilet trained, and the cage but they quickly become very sociable as the customers pet and greet them, they are were all taught not to JUMP up at all at this stage and I can honestly say this worked with them all.

Playing

I don't play that much with my dogs

I think as they are part of a group, I have not had the need to play, they play with each other mostly, I never play TUG games. I never tease as I think a lot of dog problems come from teasing [I am particularly referring to Bulldogs here] I am aware however that a single pet dog would need some time set aside to play, as play can be learning I just don't find it appropriate in my situation as the group of dogs play together constantly .I require calmness from my dogs in the show ring

16 weeks +

At this age the pups are being trained on the mat to stand walk and to allow complete strangers to open and check their teeth, their own 'best pace is decided, and training continues ready for the first Show around6/7/8 months depending on the maturity of the pup.

10 months+

Around the 10-month stage skin problems can occur and I find this is linked to bitches having a season and to dogs suddenly realising what mating's about...... I feel this is a particularly stressful time and careful handling/ and the correct understanding can help them through this stage and then they can develop into well balanced dog.

When looking for the ideal owners of your puppies consider the reasons people buy a puppy

Human expectations of Dog Ownership

People expect the following from their dogs:

For them to act as Surrogate Children

Companionship and affection

Loyalty

Protection .early warning

To vent feelings on good or bad

Obedience...indoors and out

Hobby and leisure activities

Status symbol [being seen with pedigree dog]

 P.a.t. dogs as therapy,

Working dogs ......protection, guide, sniffing,
sheepdogs.....herding, guarding, gundogs

Breed or stud work to make money....

Understand English language!

We expect them to mix and socialise, adjust to all situations
fit into our lives, come ready trained

Forget they are essentially dogs and place human
expectations on their behaviour

 Situations/experiences we require dogs to accept ...

Lifestyle changes

Children
Old people
Pets
Places
 Noises
Transport modes
Livestock
Visitors
Different types of clothing and hats visitors may appear in
Water, bathing and grooming
Different floor surfaces
Solitude
Crowds
Kennel situation
Vets

Bear these situations in mind when you are placing your puppies in their new homes and try to breed the very best dogs with the most excellent temperament because we as breeders hold the future of any breed in our hands!

Good luck!

Vicky Collins-Nattrass @2007

Kezia and Bonifacio Puppies in 2011, we are trying to breed much smaller nose rolls now ,and seem to be gaining ground, also trying to lose exaggeration, necks without so much flesh, pet owners love overdone but to take our bred onto the future we much watch out for becoming overdone , for healthy active lives .

Chapter 10

Facts and Figures

As a general rule the recommended temperature to keep the puppies

Environment, in the box at are:

30 degrees C [86 degrees F] First Two weeks

26.5 …… C [80………..F] Third week

22-24……….C [70-75   F] Fourth Week

22………….C [70………. F] Fifth week and after

Normal Temperature of a Dog is

38.2 C to 38.7 C   100.90F to 101.70F

Puppies are lower at birth 36 C   96.5 F

1-2 weeks old rising to 37 C   98.5 F

4 weeks old rising to   37.8 C   100 F

After which they will be average normal dog temperature.

When puppies are born, they have a very poor control of their own body

Temperature, which is why you must be vigilant and do this for them, too hot is as bad as too cold.

Colour of the mucus membranes [mouth and tongue]

Deep Cherry Red ...... indicates systemic infection

Bright Red ....too hot

Pale membranes .... Circulation is poor

Bluish grey colour ...... breathing problems

Dark Blue or Mauve indicates complete collapse of breathing/circulation this

Is extremely serious and the damage it does usually results in puppy's death, this can be caused by being too cold or too hot!! Get the environment temperature correct

Because we rarely leave puppies to nurse spontaneously, we need to work out an average feeding timetable, I feed as below

Home from vets........ an hour after I put the puppies back to sleep, I feed again I continue this till the milk is through at 3 days when I then start to spread it to 1 and a half hours.

Week 2 every 2 -3 hours

Week 3 every 3 -4 hours introducing solid feed 1x for 2 days then 2x for 3 days Eventually feeding at 6am   10 am 2 pm 6pm 10pm 2pm[4 to 5 weeks]

Spacing them out to 6am 11pm 3pm 7pm   11pm leading to at 8 weeks 4 feeds breakfast, lunch tea and supper time.

I allow the puppies appetite to guide me if they start messing about with a meal, I cut out 1 and re-space them, it would be helpful that you inform the new owners that this is what will happen, by the time they are

4 months on 3 feeds a day

6/7 months 2 feeds a day

I feed top quality puppy food until 10 months to 1 year old when I change to a less high protein diet, it is a false economy to feed poor quality food to growing puppies but when they have finished growing they do better on a lower protein food, less coat problems and bone deformities.

NEVER EVER ADD CALCIUM TO A PUPPY ON A GOOD DRY DIET THIS CAN AND WILL CAUSE GROWTH PROBLEMS ON THE JOINTS.

Fig 32

Experienced puppy socializers

Vixen

Chapter 11

More information on Weaning

Weaning using modern feeding methods

There is no hard and fast rule with me as to the right time to start weaning, the reasons vary with each litter a hand reared one could start at 12 days with the weaning porridge, if they are thriving .If I feel the bitch is really starting to show she's pulled down[spine being raised] by the feeding a large litter I would introduce solids at 16 days but in most cases in my breed [Bulldogs] I would start their first tastes at 21 days .Toy breeds and small breeds much later, nearer 5 weeks.

I recommend mousse if the puppies are young. This is an excellent product especially useful if you have had to hand rear its makes a good stepping stone from just milk towards solids as it can be fed from just 2 weeks.

Royal Canin's mousse is highly thought of for early weaning and now Nutriment paste also has a huge number of breeders using it.

Another excellent product I have had much success with is Royal Canin's Starter soaking down in about 15 minutes this is easy to make in a very liquid consistency for very young puppies mixed with the 1st stage start milk substitute as a kind of soup ,this is my rearing milk for emergencies for new-borns too .

When the puppies are coming up to 3 weeks old you can use these products, it also works quite well to use a blender and grind up a proprietary good quality puppy food if you want to feed a quick soaking version for early tasting. After a short while puppies prefer the taste made up with just water and they quickly progress onto dry food , some people soak the food for most of the dog's life however dry dog food is meant to be fed dry , its ok to dampen or soak briefly but do not soak for hours as the food quickly goes sour.

Therefore, I particularly like the Royal Canin Starter as it doesn't have to be soaked for hours on end prior to feeding.

The above recommendations are the modern way of feeding puppies; however, I am aware many people have traditional tried and tested own methods. The main advantage to feeding a proprietary puppy food is it has all they need in vitamins and minerals in a balance in fact you must not feed any extra vitamins as this could cause   problems. You can add a small amount of tinned puppy food, cooked mince, or cheese on top of the dry food to encourage eating if they become bored with it ,not too much as it will alter the balance of protein .

Feeding raw scraped beef is a traditional way of introducing solids to many heavy breed puppies and moving onto raw minced steak.

Some use baby rice and milk [strong disadvantage to this is that it goes sticky and reminds me of wallpaper paste horrible to clean off the puppies after they have almost bathed in it on the first tasting sessions !]custard, scrambled egg, Farex Rusks ,rice pudding all are traditional puppy feeds, chopped chicken, grated cheese added to the soaked dried mix is commonly used .Sometimes Chicken and Rice Baby food in a jar can be used to feed to particularly problematic puppies especially if they have been ill or slow feeders ,**however this must be temporary and they need to go on a food made for dogs as soon as possible.**

Remember that you must introduce only one new food at a time as if you get loose bowels you will not know what caused it. Organic yogurt is my standby if any tummy upsets start and the re-hydration mixture .see *[emergency medicines]*

I start on giving 1 meal a day before the bitch feeds at lunchtime for two days if all is well and no tummy problems I then move on and feed a second meal at about 8 pm, gradually I get onto a time table of 5 meals a day at 5 weeks at roughly

6am,10am,2pm,6pm,11pm when I go to bed, I give them milk to drink only in the first weeks of solid food, usually the bitch tends to not want to feed them by 4 weeks and I take this as the natural time for coming off milk feeds altogether.

Some Toy breeds and smaller breed puppies don't require such early weaning the bitches seem to produce enough for them till nearer 5 weeks, ask advice from someone who has been breeding your breed what the normal weaning time is, when I bred Shih-tzu I used to wean at 5 weeks , Bulldogs I wean at 3 weeks or earlier if needs be.

Having fed Royal Canin Starter I aim to be putting the puppies on Royal Canin Medium Junior at about 7 weeks, so they are well   used to their diet that they leave me and go to their new homes and are completely used to the food I send them with.

Any of the good quality food Hills, Proplan Purina Eukanuba are suitable but beware of using the cheaper puppy food it has not got the quality you need in those early days, it is quite noticeable the difference in a puppy reared on quality food and one that isn't, they may look the same size but when you pick them up you will feel the solidness of a well fed puppy...it feels heavier than it looks.

 If you choose not to feed a dry puppy food, you will need to add some vitamins ABEDC drops is a favourite from the chemist it's meant for human babies.

Calcium must be used with caution, it's been found by extensive research by most puppy food manufacturers that too much calcium on growing bones can cause problems, heavy breeds particularly can develop problems with rapid growth in the joints, consult your vet before thinking of adding any extra calcium or minerals taking with you the contents list from your puppy food bag.

Some people feed their puppies ad lib [*food down all the time*] this I have found not to be successful, you are not able to see what each puppy is getting, and they get into a habit of snacking and don't eat a proper amount. They also seem to lose their appetite, so I feed and then remove any leftover food and throw it away. If they regularly clear their bowl I add a little more if I have to throw some out each time I reduce it till they clear the bowl and then start adding a little more as their appetite grows .As they grow and are on 5 feeds a day they start to mess around with a couple of feeds, this I note and rearrange the feeds reducing them to 4 and later again I take the messing around instead of eating time to reduce the feeds to 3, I increase the amount fed at the new feed and space out the timings between.

 When they are older with their new families, I explain about this not eating the three meals and it helps the new owners to know when to drop their feed to twice a day. I continue to up about 9 months or a year to feed night and morning after which I feed my adult dogs only once a day.

Practical guide to feeding bowls and methods

First tastes I usually give off a saucer, graduating to a plate but the very best dish I have found was a heavy white ceramic dish meant for serving party nibbles on, its sectioned and is too heavy to tip up, it is easy for them to reach and the sections mean you can put one at each .I usually move the food around as the puppies cram it into the edges and can't get it so when they slow down I move it into the middle with my finger or a spoon. At first I also offer a drink of milk [Royal Canin's 1st Stage or Whelpi /Lactol] after each solid food meal , I give up doing this at about 5/6 weeks or when I see they are drinking water regularly .

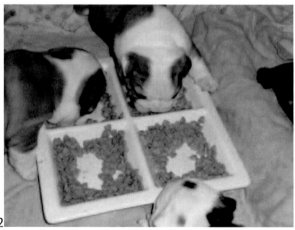

Fig 32

As the puppies get bigger, I use none stick Victoria sandwich tins, they are shallow and cheap to buy, you need to supervise the feeding as a greedy one will knock the others off the food. There is a multi-feeder purchasable which seems a practical way to feed a large litter Visit http://www.weanafeeda.com/html/weana.html, where you can buy online in different sizes suitable for your breed.

Another idea is to use a shallow tray [baking dish or a stainless steel one] and put an upturned basin in the middle to keep them from climbing in the food,

Always use Stainless Steel or porcelain for your adult dogs as bacteria grows in plastic feed and water bowls, only use plastic for a short while, as it soon becomes smelly and hard to clean.

Do not put a deep water bowl in with young puppies I find that they sleep with their heads propped on the edges I worry that they could drown easily, so I usually pick up the water bowl or have it very shallow for the night time period, watching them whilst I am around .Once the puppies have gone on to dry food you need to make sure they have access to water at all times .Some large Breeds are fed with elevated Bowls I've never used them with bulldogs.

Note from the author;

 Responsibility when breeding , remember that you brought the puppies into this life and you should be caring always what happens to them , although this book is aimed at helping you solve problems you have to know when to call it as to what quality of life the future of your puppies will have, if you work hard to save a puppy and its not a healthy puppy , please keep it yourself , passing it on however good your intentions are or the adopters , things , lives and circumstances change .Rescues exist to help dogs but the truth is that your mistakes could cost £1,000s in vets fees so please think long and hard before rearing a puppy with problems .

Chapter 12

Serious conditions

Mastitis

Until recently having had no experience with this nasty condition in my own dogs I had not realised the devastating effects this can cause, you can see the photographs of the results of mastitis which are not for the squeamish ,I have had sent from a friend   for this book to make you aware of Mastitis.

Fig 34 horrible fast-moving problem can appear between feeds

What causes it?

Bacteria entering the milk gland which is a perfect incubation area allowing it to grow, it gains access by the nipple or by the maternal bloodstream, due to her lowered immune system it's possible to build up with quite devastating results. All nursing dogs have bacteria in the breast tissue but most of the time the dog copes with keeping the bacteria under control.

Symptoms to watch for

The swollen mammary gland that looks more red than the others, discoloured, more firm, lumpy texture, hot and painful to the touch, it may discharge pus or milk that looks deeper coloured.

If you take the bitches temperature, if its more than 103 f rectally its raised, poor appetite [*after been eating well*] pups dying suddenly unexplained, low energy after being normal after the birth.

Take your bitch to the vet as soon as possible if you suspect that mastitis is starting don't delay!

Various problems can develop along with the mastitis, dehydration, toxic shock, and sepsis, malfunction in the liver kidney and lymphatic system. The milk can become toxic and gangrene occurs.

It's recommended some blood work is done to check on other functions even if one can clearly see the inflammation in the teat. A Bacterial culture could be grown to ensure the correct spectrum of antibiotic is used

Probable Treatment

Antibiotics by injection and continuing a course orally, anti-inflammatory medication to reduce swelling, short acting steroid and some topical wound cleaners and soothing healing ointment.

If your bitch has become seriously ill you may have to put her on IV fluids, pain medicines and have her cared for at the veterinary hospital. Early treatment as soon as you suspect anything amiss will avoid this as it will be a disaster to feeding puppies and you will have to undertake hand rearing.

It's ok to manually drain and empty the affected teat, if the bitch can bear you touching it.

You may want to wean your puppies early, if they are over 2 weeks it should not be a problem as they will learn to lap quite quickly around 16 days. Starting them on solids after this age is quite easy.

Some Breeders cover the affected teat and allow the pups to feed on the good ones .Scrupulously clean bedding should be used, anti-bacterial hand scrub should be used before touching the bitches wound, supplementary feeding may be in order as if the bitch is feeling ill she will not make the required amount to meet the needs of her growing puppies even on her unaffected teats.

Sometimes if a bitch has an too much milk her teats will be hard and distended and feel a little hot this can be normal just circulate all the puppies and rotate the strong ones around so the milk gets drawn off as evenly as possible .On a teat that is hard I always put the greediest strongest puppy on it to completely empty it.

I use warm flannels to stimulate the flow of the milk and sometimes it will leak away. Watch carefully for reddened hot areas , which may be the first sign mastitis is starting, sometimes if you feed on that teat with a greedy puppy it will clear itself.

If you are feeding antibiotics to the mother you will be needing to use Bio organic yogurt to restore the flora in the puppies gut give about a teaspoonful from your finger twice a day, or get a Lactobacillus preparation from the veterinary surgeon

.

Fig 35

As you can see from the photographs, the affected area can burst and slough off or sometimes the vets will operate and try to close it, most people tell me that if the bitch doesn't lose the nipple that it will heal and be hardly scarred but you will see how terrible the results are if you don't check often and act quickly.

Any bitch who has suffered this condition must be very carefully monitored in future litters and it might be wise not to breed her again.

Dead tissue

Healing , amazing how fast it does !

Chapter 13

Orphan Puppies

Disaster may strike in any breed and you could find yourself left to try to hand rear a litter of puppies, if the puppies have been born around the correct date [63 days] you have a good chance of rearing them. Their internal organs should be properly mature, and they should have a sucking reflex that will enable them to go on the bottle.

Royal Canin have their first stage milk and inside the bucket you will find 3 teats of different sizes already with a hole in, so you do not have to start trying to create the perfect flow yourself, in the past I have had teats all around the kitchen as I tried desperately to create one that wouldn't drown the puppies, keeping them without the milk flooding down their nose and inhaled into the lungs is vitally important.

It will depend on how big your puppies are for you to make the choice however I do recommend you get in the substitute milk and bottles before you need them Royal Canin's kit is about £24 the vet can order it if you are not in their breeder club and it's a small price to pay to be prepared in case of disaster. You can use the milk for the bitch to drink or the puppies at weaning if you are not unlucky and need it in an emergency so it will not be wasted.

The vet can also supply a product called **Puppy Stim** it is a substitute for puppies who have not had colostrum, recently I had to use this and I felt it was worth buying as anything that gives the orphans a better start is worth a try, the manufacturer also recommends this for weak or failing puppies so as it has a good shelf life I think this would also be worth buying in advance.

Healthy puppies should feed quite well on a bottle if there is no mum, however the length of time in between feeds is quite short in the first instance and depending on the number of puppies and the help available to you it is important to decide if you can cope .I recently tried to hand rear 6 orphans on my own, as they had a strong suckling reflex I thought I could keep them on the bottle, it took me 20 minutes to feed and stimulate defecation on each one and they only took a small amount of milk by the time I had done the last one the first one was ready again! I managed alone for 5 days and then I realized I couldn't physically carry on that way if I had had help I might have been able to carry on with the bottle but I was so tired that I couldn't keep awake and was afraid they were going to inhale milk .

Tubes can be obtained from your vet who sometimes will be reluctant to supply they are long human feeding tubes but I did manage to source some especially made for puppies they are just the right length, they are obtainable from my web site but not always available [see appendix]once you have mastered tube feeding you should keep one in unused for emergencies , always discard the used one from previous litters as they are hard to ensure there are no bacteria in them and they do go hard and inflexible which could hurt the puppies throat .

My progress with this litter was I lost one puppy to pneumonia, I bit the bullet and decided to feed the two weakest ones by tube I am very experienced at this technique. I have the following directions which you should follow carefully feed every hour and half to 2 hours under feeding rather than over feeding but by 7 days they should be up to about 12 ozs there for I would feed 12mls [1ml per oz of body weight],gradually increasing so a 15 oz puppy will have 15mls every 2 and a half hours ,and a 30 oz puppy will get 30mls approx. 3 hourly.

 If the puppy develops diarrhoea it is being overfed, if diarrhoea is smelly and scours it may indicate a gastric infection always try to assess what type of diarrhoea the puppy has if it's not over feeding it needs veterinary attention urgently .

Puppy motions that look like seeds also indicate overfeeding. If the puppy cries it may have wind, Infcol can be given from a dropper and a warm tummy massage can help.

Always try to bottle feed if the pup is strong enough to suckle as the pup approaches the 2/3 week mark the gag reflex starts to apply and they fight the tube insertion and efforts to wean the pup should commence early, just before or around 2 and a half weeks.

Keep the tube spotlessly clean and sterilise it with baby bottle cleaner as heat will harden the tube. Flush it out very well after each feed as residue milk can stay in it. Do not keep the tube in sterilizer as this can kill off naturel good bacteria in the gut, just a quick soak and rinse and store out of liquid

I fed the weakest ones by tube and then tiredness overtook me so I tubed the remaining 3. I could feed all 5 in 40 minutes including toileting them .I continued this for about a week when they became so strong they fought me every time and as they were stronger I put them back on the bottle, they sucked well but it was still much slower than tubing however once they start to fight the tube insertion, it becomes very unsafe to persist feeding that way.

Early weaning is called for; as soon as the puppies can lap you are winning!

And finally, Good Luck if you succeed it is a very rewarding feeling, looking at your hand reared babies.

Fig 36

Note :

Expectations of how puppies grow that are hand reared must be taken into account ,the typical look is thin legs and a defined neck and quite a bulbous tummy this will slowly rectify when you are weaning but don't expect them

to look more than 2 weeks old at 4 weeks especially if like this litter of 8 who were orphaned at birth

Lily very slow to catch up also hand reared with no colostrum from her mum

THE PERFECT BULLDOG.

This Bulldog has no exaggeration one to aim for with your breeding

Chapter 14

Premature puppies

Definition of the circumstances of a premature puppy:

Puppies born before day 58 are at a disadvantage for survival, just like human babies their lung function is premature and the lining is not covered with surfactant, which protects the lungs from picking up infection, injecting with steroid is not done as it takes 48 hours for the drug to cross the placenta, and there is a high risk that it would accelerate premature labour if the bitch hasn't actually started to expel them.

For these reasons I never think it wise to pre book or elect a c section but to wait for your bitch to go into naturel labour if she does this early at least it's her body which has decided, and you do have a chance.

However too many puppies for bulldog bitches to carry safely are becoming a problem, if your bitch is cobby and short with not a long back, her room to carry a big litter is severely compromised, the puppies take up so much room she becomes unable to sleep because she cannot expand her lungs to take good breaths, she can't eat because her tummy has little or no room to hold food, she becomes quite stressed.

First of all a big duvet gathered up under her might give her a little respite so she can rest but as she approaches her delivery date each day this becomes critical ,if it is in the 6th week or 7th week that this situation is occurring seek veterinary advice because should this become critical you will have to make a decision to take out the puppies to save your bitch .Careful watch on her mouth membranes should give you the first clue she is struggling .Don't hesitate she will die if this goes on no sleep or food for even a couple of days .

This girl was a champion in the USA her belly was tight like a drum she was due on the Friday but died on the Monday night. Such a shame

MAKE NO Mistake if your girl is struggling don't risk her life , I cant express how important this is , Bitches die suddenly before during or just after delivery , you mated her you watch her keep her safe !

Case Study :

Fig 36 Mavis only 5 weeks in whelp

Recently my own bitch unexpectedly ,because she had missed before ,took and at 5 weeks she was an alarming size, she's quite a chunky girl anyway not small but is not long in back ,scan showed 8 plus and I started to worry , the days progressed ,she had only one mating so I knew within 48 hours when she had conceived ...Time passed and my worry increased she still had approx. 8 days to go and I found that each night, she stood up all night occasionally falling asleep standing up and then waking up as she hit the floor, I had been sleeping with her a few nights so I knew she had been awake and was getting exhausted. Suddenly when I checked her she was pale almost grey in her mouth and I felt no time must be wasted as those puppies needed to come out, I was not prepared to lose Mavis but was willing to abort the litter to save her.

Drove to the Veterinary Clinic and just as we pulled into the car park she groaned and gurgled and I realised it was not a minute too soon if I wanted her to live, I told him to do what he had to but save my girl .Mavis was opened up within 10 minutes of arriving and delivered 8 puppies and only 3 were alive and normal. Puppies were examined for defects and the three were ok but not at a stage where we thought they could be viable

Fig 37

I hired oxygen and already own an incubator [*I must say here that I totally disagree with using an incubator or special care unit unless there is a need for it i.e., prematurity, no normal healthy bulldog puppy needs to be raised in an incubator]* They had vitamin K, Steroid and Antibiotic injection.

We bought the puppies home and placed them in the
incubator with oxygen and temperature maintained between
90/ 95 degrees Fahrenheit, I fed them rehydration fluid and
put them on Mavis but they were very sleepy .Luckily for me
an old friend in the USA read that this and **told me to feed at
3 hourly intervals because they were using their energy to
feed and would start to fade** ,this did result in Mavis having
a very poor milk supply because she wasn't stimulated
enough so it was necessary to tube feed to top up on many
occasions .However I'm sure if I had done my normal routine
I would have lost them .

Fig 38

Because of their immature digestive system after the initial
meconium the poop they did was dark green the colour of
the discharge from birth, I fed rehydration fluid as well as
food because I thought the milk neat was probably the cause
of this, after a few days they started to poop normal colour.

I kept them in oxygen for 5 days; they never gave me a worry that they had breathing issues.

We gave oral antibiotics which I recommend if feeding by hand as it is so easy for pneumonia to set in we kept warmer until the day that they should have been born ,they were slow to open their eyes [day 20] ,and I would say that they did seem a week behind at the time of rearing at most stages Mavis milk dried up at 14 days so they were on syringes of puppy starter with milk added , it was no longer safe to tube feed due to the gag reflex but we soon got them licking off our fingers and a plate .When they could eat of a plate I relaxed a little I did make sure the food was really warm at all times whilst they were young .They were reared successfully and I have kept two of them and I'm watching to make sure there are no ill effects from such an early birth .

Ground breaking news

Whilst the vet removed Mavis's puppies I told him about a procedure done in the USA involving a bitch in stress , not eating unable to sleep and having trouble breathing the vet made a decision with the owner to save her from going into collapse he would remove two puppies from the large litter re stitch and try to buy time for her to carry the others to a viable date .It has been practiced there for the last few years. No one had managed this successfully here but my vet was interested in the procedure.

Due to circumstances beyond the vets control a heavily pregnant bitch was opened up too early and he found a very immature puppy 14 days early at least,

Fig 38

My vet called me, and we decided rather than remove all the puppies to certain death we could try the USA procedure. This done I had the job of overseeing the bitches care and we waited to see what would happen, we scanned for heartbeats after 2 days and were thrilled to see some strong ones, however on day 4 the bitch obviously started opening up as green fluid with a little brown blood was lost .Still early we prepared to lose them all however when opened up 9 puppies were removed 4 already dead but 5 were breathing they were shockingly small and they were a dreadful colour

fig 39

fig 40

fig 41

We had the incubator set up and oxygen and put them straight in there at the vets. They had vitamin K steroid and antibiotic plus vitamin K to inject at home on the second day in small dose 0.1ml.

These puppies were unable to suckle so no attempt was made to put on the bitch, they quickly lost heat whenever removed from the incubator and without oxygen. Two of the five died in the first 4 hours blood coming down their noses but 3 appeared strong if not tiny and not a nice colour, still purple ,one of these the very smallest died after 3 days which was sudden and went from eating normally to being dead in one feed time, no warning .

Fig 42

However we carried on, the next set back was the biggest one started urinating from his umbilical area, finding him wet underneath alerted us to this , it was one pup whose cord had come off really early and nothing was on the surface. It had partially scabbed up but still leaked. Consulting the vet, he said it shouldn't be a big issue and common sense told me that this was not a deformity but a failure of the tube to close off properly and I googled this and found a full explanation of it online. It was like this for a couple of days then it got less and less and completely closed up and sealed over.

We breathed again, we took them out of oxygen after 10 days, they continued to thrive being tube fed, they were we think at least 11 days early and if not for the oxygen /incubator I feel they would not be here. We fed really small amounts of the milk in the first days I strongly believe over feeding kills many weak puppies but gradually built up to 1ml per 1 oz of body weight by two weeks every 2 /3 hours. The puppies as I wrote this coming up to 9 weeks old and have thrived so far .

I feel that this procedure is worth trying with the aim to save the bitch and some of the litter, the timing should be such that it's felt if the bitch is likely to collapse through exhaustion or lack of food then to save your bitch, try it.

Careful removal of two puppies or three could buy the rest of the litter vital time in the womb after the procedure no drugs were given to the mother except antibiotics and a mild painkiller. She did not act as though she had been in labour, but if this had not happened so early she might have been confused but basically her hormones weren't altered .The saved puppies in this case were of course still way to early but if they were only a few days early it should have been possible to feed them on the mum as they would not have required oxygen and would not have lost heat so easily.

Since our experience I have heard of a vet in Liverpool who has tried this successfully also he took out 1 huge water puppy and re stitched then the bitch went another 8 days before going into labour and successfully gave birth to 8 puppies who have thrived .

The puppies removed then would probably have no chance of survival but as we hear of bitches just keeling over and dying with a big litter on board this procedure must be worth a try in an emergency situation, losing a bitch full of puppies is most heart-breaking and a big feeling of guilt doesn't help the breeder to cope with the loss.. Many bitches in 2018/2019 have been lost by this, so it's important we monitor big bitches.

Vets will act to save the bitch just make them realise that's what you want.

Do not take your bitches home if they are opening up early unless a self whelp is planned no value in waiting nature is telling you they are ready to be born .Many Losses have happened because of this

Chapter 15

Too many puppies

You have mated your bitch she is in whelp and now the burden of responsibility sits heavy on you. You choose to put her in whelp and now you need be observant to spot trouble before it happens!

This is now a time when you should keep careful watch on her mouth membranes; this is such an easy but informative method of telling you if she is suffering from any circulation problems.

The colour of her gums and inner lips should be a nice warm pink colour, if she is that and bright eyed one can assume things are progressing well. However, if she looks pale or bluish it's a very urgent trip to the vet to assess her ability to cope. If you press on the flesh it should refill back to pink in a few seconds if it doesn't this is a warning thing are not going to plan.

 It is worth mentioning here that the amount of eggs that are fertilized is huge but the number which can implant is smaller and influenced by natures ability and the size of the bitch and her resources, and previous litter scaring *[Hence the stud dog, as long as he's fertile really doesn't have an influence on the size of the litter as usual he is the scapegoat]but shouldn't be used by saying 'He throws big litters '*

Sometimes nature makes a mistake, the average number of Bulldog puppies born is 4 or 5 but there are large variations as to what is normal.

A situation can occur when a small bitch can conceive too many puppies for her system.

The first sign of which would be pale mouth acting uncomfortable and not resting or sleeping, refusing to eat or vomiting regularly. Rapid weight loss of the fat cells around her face and neck, legs etc. but a very large still expanding girth should alert you to a potential life-threatening situation. An X-ray or ultra sound could shed a bit of light on her quantity of puppies but sometimes you have to make a terrible decision to bring the puppies early.

Depending on how early it might not be possible for them to survive but if you wish to save your bitch at all costs, do not take chances if you are in this situation. I had a small bitch conceive and carry 13 all were born alive but hairless in places at 14 days before the due date, their mother collapsed and couldn't breathe we thought she had gone but as soon as the vet removed the uterus and the pressure on her vital organs she started breathing again. Unfortunately, all the puppies died within 3 days as they were much too immature to survive but the bitch lived on to be 10 years old at least but was never mated again.

My own experience of this is not unusual, several bitches I have known of have died for this very reason so keep a watchful eye on the very large bitch, and if you see her struggling consider the above and discuss with your vet .If it's only a few days early the bitch could have a steroid injection to help the puppies lungs. However because we do two mating's and fresh semen lives up to 5 days on average the date of the arrival of the puppies could vary considerably, most deliver on 63 days but many at 61 or even much late than 65.

Most of us want to save our bitches at all costs so hopefully if you are in this situation you can be forewarned and discuss at the earliest opportunity with your vet what to do.

USA Champion bitch lost due to too many puppies

Chapter 16

Which one to keep?

Bulldogs are really difficult to choose as a show prospect so much so I would definitely warn against selling any puppy as a show dog. You could venture to say promising but that's as far as any future statement you could really say, also at this point it's prudent to mention not to sell any puppy as breeding stock, if you do and the dog turns out to be infertile and the bitch never breeds you could find someone in our no win no fee society asks you for compensation somewhere down the road. While we're on the subject on selling your males make it quite clear that becoming a stud dog unless shown is unlikely so all my males are sold as pets and people understand that.

First of all if you are a beginner in the breed I would advise not to keep a dog puppy, if he doesn't turn out ,ok then you have a pet and eventually you will run out of space to keep your dog's safely and able to give them   enough attention .A bitch puppy can always be bred on if she doesn't turn out to be your ideal ,you have a choice of about 50 champion and show winning males at any time at stud in this country so you can try several different lines and mating's to see what works for the lines of your foundation bitch .

Looking at the puppy with a view to exhibiting there are a few pointers I can give you, assuming you have more than one puppy to choose from .Many breeders of experience chose a puppy still wet and never change their choice .However they know how their lines develop so it's safer to look at the points that are visible and the things that don't change .

Length of Back, in a male this should be quite short, bitches can be longer as this is allowable for the safe carriage of puppies in the future, there should be plenty of rib and depth of chest the front legs should be thickly boned and have straight strong pasterns [where it would be our ankle] in proportion the rear legs are longer elevating the rear slightly but in a very young puppy I do not like to see a roach too early.

The tail set really is important, that is where it starts it should be just down from the highest point and the tail should be directed downwards , ideally for health the tail should be mobile preferably straight but if kinky that's ok as long as it's not inverted inwards .Carrying a tail high above the top line on the move is a definite show fault, however some judges [*me included*] would favour a jutting tail to one tightly screwed inwards .Bulldogs should have a nice curve of stifle *[rear legs*], well let down at the hocks, if too straight and upright it will probably mean there will be some movement in the patella [*knee joint*] which can be seen on the move and is a common fault in bulldogs which we are trying to breed away from .Looking at the puppy it should give the impression it has a waist [*pear shape*] its rear end should be much lighter than the solid chunky front end which should have shoulders and look strong ,correctly proportioned it should look as though it could stand in a square .

Neck this is an important if overlooked characteristic, if the head looks as though it comes out of the shoulders, extremely short necked this is very likely to mean that the breathing could be compromised a nice balanced neck gives more room for the airways, fat gathers around the neck area as the puppy matures and what can look just a little short necked in a puppy can look 'stuffy' as a full grown dog

Head properties these are immature as a puppies, the head is the last thing to grow, again the placement of the ears should not be high up on top of the skull but positioned slightly over the side the ears play a huge role in how the puppies expression is evaluated and if the ear doesn't rose back this will be very much frowned upon .Nose rolls should not be large and overhanging the nose these look cute as a puppy but as an adult it's a horrid smelly sweaty area that gets infected easily and stained ,split nose rolls are my favourite usually have two slight creases back from the top of the nose ,it must remembered that if you only keep one from the litter you should think that the ones bound for pet homes should be easy to care for this makes for you to be aware of this in future breeding's. When mature the nostrils should be fully blacked out and looking at them face on they should have an area that you can put the tip of your little finger in , some puppies only have a line with hardly any opening[*stenosed*] this will make them noisy breathers and heavy snorers with low heat tolerance .Several head shapes I have seen in puppies , the standard asks for a brick head and my best puppies are the ones who when they are born are as wide at the foreface as they are across the ear area ,some puppies heads can only be described as triangular the front jaw being narrow although the head has still to grow it will not gain any further width on the jaw foreface in proportion as an adult

Teeth the puppies bite at 5/6 weeks should be level or almost level or slightly overshot ,if already very undershot you will find it will probably show its teeth and lower jaw will come too far forward as it grows it's supposed to sweep upwards giving a distinctive upside down u shape with the flews from front viewing .All puppy teeth seem to be quite perfect, in a straight line or just slightly spooned at around 6 to 9 weeks when you are deciding on your keeper but don't be surprised as when the little needles fall out the adult teeth often come through a bit higgledy piggledy, the main point should be that there is width in the bottom jaw if its narrow it will always be narrow

Eyes these will open at around 14 days give or take either way ,they are sort of navy cloudy blue at first which of course is not what we are looking for. It takes until around 5 or 6 weeks before we can see the true colour which should be very dark ,show little white when viewed from the front .The best way to see eye colour is at around 6 weeks take them to the window when the outside light is good and look carefully for any flashes of grey or blue, any thing other than really dark is another fault. Possibly in a very dark brindle the eyes are not so dark slightly amber but light eyes will get you knocked in the show ring.

Puppies should have the start if not completely around by five weeks of the eyeliner pigment , if little dots are there its highly likely that the eye rim will fill ,although this is not a requirement in the bulldog standard I know from experience that this lack of pigment gets them knocked , bulldogs can look 'piggy eyed ' when white and devoid of black eyeliner . After colour its prudent to see how the eye ball sits in the socket ,nice open eyes and not too much skin lose around the rims is good, as a tiny puppy the eyelids rarely show signs of turning in or out [*entropian or ectropion*]which is why you cannot guarantee to your buyers this condition may occur later .Loose baggy eyes besides giving a very sad expression also are prone to Cherry Eye[*Hadrian gland a tiny red bubble which can get large and infected ,doesn't hurt but looks like it should*]

There is a strong hereditary factor in cherry eye but also environmental conditions can cause it, overzealous cleaning with smelly products and also household bleach means puppies low to the ground can't avoid the fumes and eyes become irritated .Avoiding building work whilst you have a litter is also a good idea as I had a very bad experience with two litters and dust in my early days.

 Tear staining, a lot of puppies from early on have the start of tear stains, these are an exhibitors nightmare, for this reason if you have colour coat black around the eyes this saves a lot of work ,but mostly the face will have white on it and the best thing is to put some Vaseline or Sudocreme daily on the area to stop the start of any discoloured building up .

Coat should be short and close knit ,particular colours are not really favoured here unlike in the USA more the construction of the dog matters but some colour markings can be helpful for instance darker colouring around the eyes makes tear staining less obvious ,the even markings on front legs avoid an optical illusion that the movement is off, if ones white and the other dark .If you keep a white one it must be exceptional as it's probably the least favourite of the judges ,however the breed record of a top winner was called Ch. Kelloe White Glove tends to disprove that theory !

Try not to choose the most heavily wrinkled puppy as your keeper as very often these become overdone and are described as 'course' by breed specialist judges .It took me a long time to truly understand ' course' in the eyes of the general public the overdone dog is their most common favourite but if you want to win you are having to breed a dog **with little exaggeration** just strong breed qualities .

Feet nice tight feet with good knuckles are very desirable, long spread toes spoil many dogs chances if you regularly keep the puppy nails short from birth you should have good nails that wear down on walks on the pavement but if not you have nails which spread the toes in a very unattractive way. Care must be taken not to nip or catch the quick on a young puppy as they remember this pain and in the future nail cutting is a two man job and a fight at that, bulldogs have dew claws these are not removed but should be checked regularly as they grow around in a circle back into the pad if not cut.

Temperament excessively shy puppies do not like showing and if fear is obvious it might make the dog appear aggressive as fear shows itself that way .A puppy who approaches people and seems happy in the car will go a long way as a show dog .Try lots of socialising well before puppies leave you visitors noises car rides [of course no risks of infection by walking on public ground before vaccination time]Because of the bracheaphelic face when a puppy gets stressed or excited this is when a normally quiet breather starts to make a noise ,this is not good in the show ring it will get you glared at and people will think your dog is a bad breather .Try to take your show puppy out a lot while small and to ring craft as this excitement can ruin a good dogs chances and the new thoughts on the breed standards from the Kennel Club are judges must not award breathing noises .

Movement a bulldogs gait is like no other it's a funny driven at the front and kept up with from the rear sort of scuffing the ground . Young puppies are often extremely loose in the joints they can be fine one minute and be lame the next especially from 5 to 7 months where after which, everything seems to eventually come together.

I have found by experience that the best moving dogs I have are singletons….this is bizarre as one would think the rough and tumble of siblings play would be advantageous, but my own conclusion is that when I have just one puppy after it gets up on its legs I usually let it be more with its mother and as one poopy pup is easy to keep tabs on they have much more freedom to run around in the home than kept in a pen with five or six poop machines .I try to get my puppies out of doors as soon as the weather permits first for 30 minutes and in the summer they are usually out for several hours in small bursts at 5 to 6 weeks and by the time they leave its usual for mine to love the outdoors. Choosing the one to stay then needs observation of the puppies in an open area soundness is to be the main thing you as a breeder are looking for so only keep the sound most balanced little dog on the move.

Hernias what constitutes a hernia when does it need a repair and what are the reasons you can't show a dog with repaired hernia?

In Bulldogs hernias can be divided into proper needing repair hernias in which case showing and breeding should be out and an endorsement on that puppy to avoid being bred from to a tiny fleshy lump that really needs nothing doing to it at all and shouldn't interfere in any future exhibiting or breeding plans, sometimes the heavy vets clamp put on in moments after birth can cause problems as can the rough pulling of the bitch if self-whelping but in most cases the hernia has just popped out of a tiny hole in the midline which has failed to close during development .Hernias have an hereditary element which makes showing   a dog with a repair forbidden by the Kennel Club so it's not wise to keep the one with a real hernia .

Vicky with Champion Shack n Lo Leuger's Hot Fudge in Chicago USA , she co owns this dog

Chapter 17

When is the right time to Neuter or Spay a Bulldog ?

In the past it was not realised that the Bulldog along with many other breeds that are slow maturing need their testosterone to be around for about 18 months and possibly up to 3 years .Early castration in males leads to lack of masculine features and generally not developing the stature expected of the breed .There is no evidence that castrating will change either the sexual behaviour, humping etc. or aggressive behaviour. Some dogs need their testosterone to be *'comfortable in their own skin '* and removing this hormone can sometimes have an opposite effect, lack of male hormone leads to lack of confidence increasing his insecurities and possibly increasing aggressive tendencies due to fear .

Very often 'humping' is mistaken as sexual and it is more often a dominant behaviour due to stress.

Often retained testicles spotted at the first vaccination are also cited as an urgent need for surgery ,in actual fact the risk from anaesthetic in an under 1 year is far higher than the cancer risk but as the dog reaches 3 years old it should be removed preferably before 5 years when the risk is increased

.

Bitches should be allowed to mature but the myth all bitches should have a litter is best ignored in bulldogs because breeding your bitch could be risky also there is no evidence that breeding is necessary. There is a slightly increased risk the bitch may develop Pyometra [womb infection after her season] with this in mind after 18 months would be a good time to have your bitch done half way between her regular seasons. Only use a vet who is confident in operating on the breed.

Preston [Bonifacio Prestigious at Kezia] Vicky's once in a lifetime dog sire of 1 UK Ch and several RCC winners

Useful copies of simplified paper work it is really essential you provide the following for your own and your buyers peace of mind :

This is a sample of an endorsement lifting contract it is illegal to sell an endorsed puppy if the buyer is not made aware in writing of the said endorsement

Endorsement Contract

The Kennel Club provides breeders with a facility for 2 Endorsements

1 No Progeny can be registered

2 No Export Pedigree can be obtained

Both of these are able to be lifted only by the agreement of the Breeder.

..............................along with many reputable and Accredited Breeders have taken advantage of this facility to ensure their stock remains healthy and is not bred from before the appropriate age ,and to be able to know if any dogs we have bred leave the UK

We hearby contract that at the age of 1[One] year Males and 18 [Eighteen]months Bitches

Name of puppy ....

On Production of a Vets health Certificate stating the Health and Temperament are suitable to be bred from ,

.... will guarantee to lift the breeding Endorsement and give advice as to the future lines which the dog can be bred to.

For Export Pedigree application must be made BEFORE the dog leaves the UK

Signed ....Date ....

Puppy Breeder

I fully understand the terms and conditions of this contract which is being signed on purchase of the above dog

Signed ....Date ....

Dog Purchaser

Example of a simple Stud Agreement

Stud Dog Name ****************

Belonging to ....

Address ....

Owners Email ***************.co.uk

Phone --------------------- mobile -------------------------------------

Date of 1st mating 2007

Bitches KC name...

 Bitch owner ....

Address...

,,

Phone number...

Terms of Stud

Stud Fee £? Paid in Advance ?

If not paid in advance handlers fee to be paid by owner of bitch of ....

Registration Documents will be signed on receipt of stud fee in full

If paid in advance there will be free return stud with the same bitch .

Mating to take place at ....

Signed Stud Dog Owner ....

Signed Bitch Owner ....

If there are puppies one expects the bitches owner to abide by the Kennel Club code of ethics as outlined on the Registration Documents .No puppy to be sold before + weeks .

Advice and Help and support will be freely given to help raise healthy puppies and this will include an appraisal visit to see the puppies before sale .

Puppy Sales Agreement

Sales Contract Between Puppy Breeder ....
Address ....
....

Phone ....
Email ....

And Purchaser ....
Address ....
....

Phone ....
Email ....
Deposit already paid ....
For the sum of £ ....
For Purchase of ... Kennel Club Registered Pedigree Puppy ....
This puppy has been purchased as a   Pet Companion/ Breeding Stock / Show prospect [delete inapplicable /as both the later cannot be guaranteed I advise that Pet Companion be the purpose for most puppy sale , if the dog turns out as a show prospect or a breeding animal this must be considered a bonus No breeder however established can guarantee a 9 week old puppy will be a show winner or be fertile]
Sex ....   Date of Birth ....
KC Name ....
Pet Name ....
Colour and markings ....
Pet Plan Insurance in place ......Yes/No
Complete Statement of Veterinary visits this Puppy has had
First vaccine Date ....Next one Due ....
 The Breeders Vet performed a basic health check on ....It is recommended you take the puppy within 7 days to a Veterinarian of your own choice.
If any problem is found you may return in the same condition as when purchased ,and at your own expense the puppy to the Breeder for a full refund
All efforts have been made to breed a healthy puppy by using healthy parents however should any of the following hereditary diseases[undetectable at this age but] known in the breed develop the breeder cannot guarantee the puppy will not be free of
...................................[follow with a list of the most common diseases your breed is known for]
The Buyer understands by choosing this breed as in all living animals conditions can arise beyond the breeders control .
 PUPPY HAS BEEN MICROCHIPPED, number and date

....
Worming has taken place every 2 weeks since he was 3 weeks old with Drontal Suspension which we recommend as no reactions have been seen to this product
This is a true account of all treatment this puppy has received we have every reason to believe he is in good health from this record .
If this Puppy is Endorsed at the Kennel Club it has been fully explained to me what this means to a purchaser

Signed .... Puppy Breeder
Date ....
This implications of this agreement   have been explained to me
....Puppy Purchaser date ....
Whatever circumstances arise, please if this dog cannot stay with you return to me for resale or rehoming however long ahead this may be. Please keep intouch

Index of Terms

Information for you to look up as it changes all the time,added in 2019 .

I think the links to the current testing etc. are more useful as they will get updated and clarified over the coming years.

Since I started writing about breeding bulldog puppies, a lot has changed the way the breeders are tackling health issues means that your puppy buyers are aware of the various testing schemes , If you using the official schemes this illustrates you have taken every possible care to breed the healthiest puppies .

Never sell any puppy not vaccinated, Health checked ,and without a valid contract .

For Bulldogs the Breed Council one is still the best out there
https://www-bulldogbreedcouncil-co-uk-5c9b185bc3e00.checkout.weebly.com/#payment

For Information on the Bulldog Breed Councils Health Scheme please follow this link
http://www.bulldogbreedcouncil.co.uk/health-scheme-criteria.html

The Kennel Club have launched in conjunction with Cambridge University a Respiratory Function Grading Scheme , full details can be found on this link
https://www.thekennelclub.org.uk/rfgs

Web Links for New Dog Legislation

The Animal Welfare (Licensing of Activities
Involving Animals) (England) Regulations 2018
Guidance notes for conditions for breeding dogs
November 2018
http://www.cfsg.org.uk/The%20Animal%20Welfare%20Licensing%
20of%20Activities%20Involvi/d.%20Dog%20Breeding%20Guidance
%20Revised%2030.11.pdf
The Kennel Clubs guidance on the licencing laws October 2018
https://www.thekennelclub.org.uk/breeding/dog-breeding-
regulation/faqs-dog-breeding-regulations-in-england/

Changes to breeding regulations in England

As of October 2018 new breeding regulations are being introduced
in England by Defra and the Kennel Club is providing information to
its customers on how some of these changes will effect dog
breeders and some of those involved with dogs.

The main legislative changes being made are:

A breeding licence will be required for anyone breeding three or
more litters and selling at least one puppy in a 12 month period.
This is a reduction from the previous litter test of five or more
litters.
A licence is not required if documentary evidence can be provided
that none of the puppies or adult dogs have been sold.
Anyone in the business of selling dogs (even one or two litters in a
12 month period) may require a licence.